# Built to Win

# Sport and Culture Series

Toby Miller and M. Ann Hall, Editors

Volume 5    *Built to Win: The Female Athlete as Cultural Icon*
            Leslie Heywood and Shari L. Dworkin

Volume 4    *Taking the Field: Women, Men, and Sports*
            Michael A. Messner

Volume 3    *Imagined Olympians: Body Culture and Colonial
            Representation in Rwanda*
            John Bale

Volume 2    *To Show What an Indian Can Do: Sports at
            Native American Boarding Schools*
            John Bloom

Volume 1    *Pretty Good for a Girl: An Athlete's Story*
            Leslie Heywood

# Built to Win

## The Female Athlete as Cultural Icon

Leslie Heywood and Shari L. Dworkin

Foreword by Julie Foudy

*Sport and Culture Series, Volume 5*

*University of Minnesota Press*
*Minneapolis*
*London*

Published with assistance from the Margaret S. Harding Memorial Endowment
honoring the first director of the University of Minnesota Press.

An earlier version of chapter 2 originally appeared in *The Olympics at the
Millennium,* edited by Sidonie Smith and Kay Schaeffer (New Brunswick, N.J.:
Rutgers University Press, 2000), 99–116. Reprinted by permission of Rutgers
University Press.

"Resolution," by Nellie Wong, originally appeared in *Long Shot* 24 (2001): 89.
Copyright 2001 Nellie Wong. Reprinted by permission of Nellie Wong and
Long Shot Productions, Inc.

Published by the University of Minnesota Press
111 Third Avenue South, Suite 290
Minneapolis, MN 55401-2520
http://www.upress.umn.edu

Library of Congress Cataloging-in-Publication Data

Heywood, Leslie.
    Built to win : the female athlete as cultural icon / Leslie Heywood
and Shari L. Dworkin ; foreword by Julie Foudy.
        p.    cm. — (Sport and culture series ; v. 5)
    Includes bibliographical references and index.
    ISBN 0-8166-3623-0 (HC : alk. paper) — ISBN 0-8166-3624-9 (PB : alk.
paper)
    1. Sports for women—Social aspects—United States.   2. Women
athletes—United States.   3. Feminism and sports—United States.
4. Sex discrimination in sports—United States.   I. Dworkin, Shari L.
II. Title.   III. Series.
GV709.18.U6  H49  2003
796'.802—dc21                                                    2002156528

Printed in the United States of America on acid-free paper

The University of Minnesota is an equal-opportunity educator and employer.


12  11  10  09  08  07  06  05  04  03      10 9 8 7 6 5 4 3 2 1

# Contents

Foreword    vii
*Julie Foudy*

Acknowledgments    xi

Prologue: Women We Love Who Kick Butt    xv

ONE
Powered Up or Dreaming?    1

TWO
Sport as the Stealth Feminism of the Third Wave    25

THREE
A New Look at Female Athletes and Masculinity    55

FOUR
Bodies, Babes, and the WNBA    76

FIVE
Body Panic Parity    100

SIX
She Will Beat You Up, and Your Papa, Too    131

Epilogue: It's an Image    160

Appendix: Focus-Group Research on Youth Attitudes about
Female Athletes    167

Notes    177

Index    205

# Foreword

*Julie Foudy*

For me, sports have always been about expressing myself through competition, perseverance, laughter, and self-confidence. I started playing soccer, tackle football, and softball as soon as I could walk. As the youngest of four kids in a very active (most would say hyperactive) family, I had no other choice: sports were a way of life for the whole Foudy household. Our vacations centered on ski trips, hiking trips, and sport outings. Mom never told me I couldn't play tackle football because it "wasn't feminine." Dad never told me that skateboarding was for guys. I just followed my passions—and being outside, playing anything, was the first one I can remember.

Those opportunities shaped my life. I have traveled to more countries than most would consider sane. I have forged lifelong friendships with teammates who redefine character and selflessness. I have learned the value of faith in teammates and faith in dreams. I thank my mom and dad daily not only for giving me the opportunity to embrace sports but, equally important, for making sports gender-free.

I used to play tackle football with the boys after elementary school. If new guys joined our game, my guy friends would work the system and say, "Ohhhhh, okay, okay, I guess we will take the girl." Then we would promptly kick the new guys' butts. Before they knew what hit them, we were celebrating our victory. I gained confidence from these experiences. I gained respect. I learned to love competition. Winning was not just okay, it was preferred. I was a young girl who loved sports and the boys thought I was cool. What else could you want at eleven years old? I look back on my mindset at this age with wonder. When most girls were facing confidence issues and crises, I was self-assured and happy. I had bouts of waning confidence, but I'm grateful I got through those turbulent teenage years with my self-esteem intact. My explanation for this is sports.

When I finally discovered that I probably could not be the next wide receiver for the Rams, or even the center for the Lakers at 5-foot-5, I had no female role model to watch or emulate in team sports. I couldn't be Kareem Abdul Jabbar, so who could I be?

How times have changed. Now young girls can dream of being Mia Hamm, Lisa Leslie, or Lisa Fernandez. They have whole teams to watch and emulate. These girls don't have just national teams to watch—they have professional leagues such as the WUSA, the WNBA, the LPGA, and on and on. I can only imagine what a twelve-year-old girl felt sitting in the Rose Bowl at the Women's World Cup Final in 1999, watching women do great feats in front of 94,000 people: empowerment at its finest. Girls' dreams have now advanced from "Well, I hope that someday I can play in a World Cup or an Olympics" to "Someday I will play in a World Cup or an Olympics"—from hopeful to tangible. There is a big difference between a hope, a dream, and a prayer. For girls today, this dream has now become a reality because those before them have done it. That cultural shift was not lost on our World Cup team; we understood that this World Cup was about more than soccer. In fact, before that game was played, we were often criticized by the hard-core male soccer reporters who said that our insistence that the World Cup was in some fundamental way about women's rights was taking away from the focus of soccer. We would respond with a smile, "Yes, exactly. This event is much more than just soccer. You will see." Indeed it was.

But even as we gained unprecedented attention for women's sports, with our *Newsweek, Time,* and *People* magazine covers, some critics claimed we were just getting all this attention because we were an attractive-looking group. Some people said the emphasis was on our looks, not our athletic achievements. Since the World Cup, that question has come up frequently in reference to women's sports—valuing female athletes for their bodies and looks, not for what they have accomplished.

This is the controversy that *Built to Win: The Female Athlete as Cultural Icon* begins to explain. The authors are athletes of the same post–Title IX generation as my World Cup team; they have had similar experiences in sport and they know what sport can mean, the confidence that it can give, and the effect that huge numbers of women participating in sport after Title IX can have on traditional gender roles. Clearly, the world is not the same anymore. No one in our generation assumes that only men can achieve things, or that women are only valuable for their looks. Unlike earlier generations of women in sport, Leslie Heywood and Shari Dworkin know how things have been different for us, how we have come to be taken more seriously as athletes, and why images of femininity can be used ironically, as parody and camp, as our World Cup team did on the *Late Show with David Letterman.* We glammed it up for Letterman and we posed just off the practice field covered in mud for Annie Leibovitz. Both looks define us, both show parts of who we are. *Built to Win* understands that.

Our World Cup team was refreshing, goofy, and tightknit. We loved to compete, we loved to laugh, and we did both very well. We thought that David Letterman's calling us his "babes" was humorous, not degrading like some feminists claimed. We were all Letterman fans to begin with, and we loved his style of humor, so we played it up and sent him a team picture. We posed wearing just his *Late Night with David Letterman* shirt and soccer cleats. We hiked our shorts up high and posed Rockette-style to be even more absurd. And I think this irreverence to traditional feminine poses attracted fans and young kids. Being feminine was not a goal or a showcase. If people found us attractive, great, but more important we were natural, we were down to earth, we were just like every girl in the stands watching. We did not go through special routes to make it to this level. We did not put on extra makeup because it was game time. We were just ourselves. We simply worked hard, persisted, and believed. We came in all shapes and sizes, from 5-foot-0 Tiffeny Milbrett to 6-foot-0 Michelle Akers. We were proud of our accomplishments and our muscles, and people were drawn to that.

Plus we kept winning. Our culture loves winners, and we were not naïve enough to miss that detail. Our standard response to reporters when asked the "babe" question was, "So, you are telling me that 94,000 people would have come to the Rose Bowl if we were playing for fifth place, just to watch hot women run around sweaty? I don't think so." Had we performed poorly in this World Cup, I am most certain people would be asking, "What Women's World Cup?" Fans love winners. Athletics is about winning. Had we failed to perform, this historical tournament would have a whole different visceral complexion, no question. Brandi Chastain did not rip off her jersey after scoring the winning penalty kick just to show off her abs—she ripped off her jersey in a moment of emotion, ecstasy, and pure celebration. Yes, to some extent we may have fit into a mainstream definition of attractive (in other words, as society—read: the media—defines an attractive image), but, more important, we were athletes competing at the highest level. That is what young girls and boys saw. That is what keeps them coming back to watch our national team, our league, our sport. Being competitive, sweaty, confident (and laughing through it all) was not only acceptable on our team, it was our key to success. Call us babes, call us feminine, call us whatever, but this I assure you: people will never forget that we are World Cup champions first and foremost.

*Built to Win* helps explain the contemporary view of what was once considered an oxymoron, the female athlete. Heywood and Dworkin show what the world is like now for female athletes, how gender roles are different, the ways athletes have helped change perceptions and will, I hope, continue to change attitudes so that whether you're a girl or a boy really makes no difference.

We live in a new gender world—a world where I have always been able to express myself through competition, through my involvement in sport. That world still has a long way to go, but it has made my life and my teammates' lives very different from the generations that came before us. We have had the opportunity to play in front of 94,000 screaming fans. We have our own professional leagues. Men in our generation don't assume they are going to be the achievers and we are just going to be their cheerleaders. *Built to Win* shows the difference this makes—about how far we have come and how far we have left to go, the goods and bads and everything in between.

*Built to Win: The Female Athlete as Cultural Icon* speaks to me because it's about my world. It puts that world on center stage in all those classrooms that talk about gender and image and social roles. I like to think that, as this book says, my teammates and I and all my other fellow female athletes have contributed to a world where I can express myself through competition and no one tells me not to be aggressive or tough, a world where no one thinks athletic women are unnatural or "unfeminine"... a world where we are heroes instead.

# Acknowledgments

In terms of inspiration, I would like to thank Susan Bordo, whose philosophically complicated yet accessible and enlivening readings of images and understandings of cultural currents made *Built to Win* possible. Susan, you are truly my mentor and my friend. I also thank Ann Hall, series editor of Sport and Culture for the University of Minnesota Press, for her painstaking review of the manuscript draft and for her tremendous support and inspiration generally, and Toby Miller, also a Sport and Culture series editor, in whose work I have found the excitement and validation of a rare complementary vision.

To my "Cultural Studies of Sport" classes at Binghamton University from the fall of 1998 through the spring of 2000, thanks for the resistant readings to traditional feminism and for insight into how images play for particular demographics in contemporary culture. To Donna Lopiano, indefatigable leader of the Women's Sports Foundation, thanks for an uncompromising vision of how to turn academic insight into public activism, and for welcoming me into the foundation's fold. To Julie Foudy, one of the first new women's sports icons as a soccer player extraordinaire and president of the Women's Sports Foundation, my heartfelt thanks for her words and thoughts in the foreword to this book and for the unparalleled example of her athletic career. To Don Sabo, friend and mentor, thanks for talks and dreams and support for this book and my "third wave" conceptualizations more generally.

To Kari Fasting and her wonderful Norwegian crew, thanks for your sustaining spirits and the chance to first present material that appears in chapters 4 and 5. To Susan White, feminist film critic at my alma mater, the University of Arizona, thanks for organizing the film conference "Tough Guys" and giving me the chance to do the work on *Fight Club* that forms the core of chapter 5. To Sid Smith, thanks for the chance to contribute an essay to *The Olympics at the Millennium,* which became part of chapter 2, and thanks to Rutgers University Press for permission to reprint it here.

To Michael Messner, who first pulled me into the world of sports sociology, thanks for an education in the vagaries of a whole social science world beyond the textualist base of the humanities approaches in which I was intellectually trained. To Allen Guttmann, thanks for your work, *The Erotic in Sports,* which gave me a way to think through some of the paradigms I had taken for granted that definitely needed to change.

Thanks also to my athletic training partner Bill Townsend, who for the past seven years has made my dream of continued sports competition a reality and who has always respected me even if I am a girl who can bench only 250 pounds to his 500. To LuAnne Blaauboer, who from our earliest years taught me the importance of physicality and solidarity in the fight for gender equality. To my husband, Barry Baldridge, fellow gender rebel and companion in all of my life.

And finally, thanks to my dear coauthor, Shari Dworkin, who not only taught me to fall in love with data but is down there in the trenches with me crafting a vision outside of the box, keeping me alive with her humor, generosity, and sheer power of brains. Thank you, Shari, for everything we have been able to produce.

Leslie Heywood


I am grateful to Pitzer College and the Haynes Social Science Fellowship. This summer support helped pay for travel and technology, and offered solid momentum on focus group data collection, analysis, and writing.

I appreciate all of the institutional and personal aid in gathering access and consent to numerous schools for our research. To the warm and generous teachers who offered their time, guidance, and open classrooms, thank you. To the students who gave us energy and engagement and their visions of societal trends, you certainly deserve honorary Ph.D.s. To Lindsey Dawson, a research assistant who put in extra time and energy with great commitment: you are owed powerbars. Thank you, Isabel

Howe, for your time as a research assistant and your careful, diligent edits and copyright help.

Thank you, Faye Wachs and Cheryl Cooky, for offering cites, valuable discussions, and support. There cannot be enough thanks to extend to long-time close friends and colleagues. Michael Messner deserves special thanks for his continual and unrelenting professional, intellectual, and social support. I offer extra special thanks for Darcy Buerkle, for her critical reads of this work, for her endless discussions and support, for her unyielding patience and wisdom.

I reserve my final thanks to Leslie Heywood for bringing me on board to join her in this work, for being who she is, for the way all of her runs wildly and brilliantly with the wind, and for pulling me deeper into theory while being open to that data taming. Thank you, Leslie-Lester, for this chance to stretch and push one another, for how you always clear and create something new on the trails, and for what this might do for all who are touched by it.

Shari L. Dworkin

# PROLOGUE

## Women We Love Who Kick Butt

In the October 1995 issue of *Outside* magazine, the cover story, "The Ubergirl Cometh," proclaimed a new archetype for women:

> The age of Gabrielle Reece is upon us. She's big, she's strong, and with thousands more like her out there, she's replicating fast. . . . Reece leads a pack of women who are currently redefining our image of the female athlete, inspiring a generation of young girls to take control of their bodies and pride in their strength. . . . Can you deal with that?[1]

In January 2001, the cover of *Vogue* magazine was set in resplendent tones of reds and blues and proclaimed "The New American Hero." The hero's chin was lifted high, and she gazed directly at the viewer, broad shoulders sloping into a red sequined gown that fit her not like a strange disjunction between power and glam but as its very incarnation. V-back and S-curve, latissimus muscles sloping easily down to solid, sequined mermaid hips, thighs that explode into Marion Jones, the one who rules fierce winds. We know her well, telescoped with images from Olympics, power shoulders, thighs that blur the world so much faster than anyone else. Thighs like tree trunks, lightning, Marion's wings. Dreams of solidity, dreams of wings: an athlete on the cover of *Vogue,* contradiction upon contradiction, a figure for the new millennium. Feet strongly rooted in contraposta, she was a statue, she was living flesh, she was quite possibly the most beautiful woman in the world.

From the novelty it seemed in 1995 to its utterly mainstream status by 2001, this image of female athlete is new. Mass-market appeal to the female athlete is new. Offering up athletics as a solution to social problems

Femininity toughens up: Gabrielle Reece in an ad for Nike in *Women's Sports and Fitness* (August 1997).

most often suffered by women is new. A large and growing demographic of women who participate in organized sports is new. The assumption that enough women live in the athlete's world—defined by bravery, competence, and strength—to make up a substantial, viable market is new. Female athletes were once oddities, goddesses, or monsters, exceptions to every social rule. Now the female athlete is an institution.

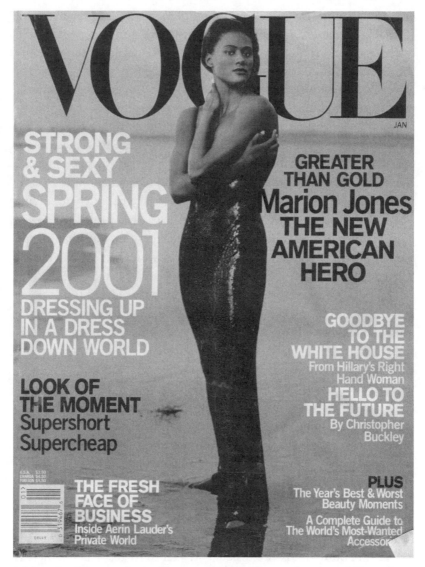

Athletes from the margins to the center: Marion Jones on the cover of *Vogue*, January 2001. Photograph by Annie Leibovitz. Courtesy of *Vogue*, Condé Nast Publications, Inc.

At least a century in the making, she's the product of politics and cultural shifts: the growth of a consumer, information-based economy that meant more women in high-paying jobs, the expansion of the entertainment industry and therefore sports, a culture marked by progress, backlash, change—race rights, gay and lesbian rights, women's rights, a culture taking notice of girls and the different women they become.[2] Chief among these was the passage of Title IX, the Education Act of 1972, which was used to fight for equal funding and facilities for women's sports in any institution getting money from the Fed.[3] This one piece of legislation, brought about through the collective struggles of the women's movement, would make millions of women into athletes, changing the shape of the ideal female body in seemingly exciting new ways. That Title IX is currently under attack marks both the widespread acceptance of female athletes and a conservative reaction against that acceptance.[4] The female athlete, set against old Victorian ideas of feminine incompetence, physical weakness, the woman's place is in the kitchen, serving up grub for her family, centered on everyone else but herself.

Ideas about gender roles and ideal body shapes shift and change, and the rise of the female athlete as cultural icon wasn't just about Title IX. What particular shape of the female body "plays in Peoria" follows cyclical trends that are determined to some extent by racial, political, sexual, and economic codes. There was, for instance, some acceptance of a more muscular female body in the gender-progressive flapper era of the Roaring Twenties, an acceptance that followed gains made by the suffragettes who successfully canvassed for a woman's right to vote. But this acceptance decreased with the more conservative gender relations that developed out of the 1930s Depression, an occurrence perhaps parallel to where we seem to be moving in the post-Enron, post-9/11 world of the early twenty-first century. These kinds of historical shifts were literally embodied by one of the greatest female athletes of all time, Babe Didriksen. Babe was muscular and androgynous in the 1920s, but became increasingly "feminine"—in the sense of growing her hair and wearing dresses—in the '30s and '40s in response to constant media criticism of her "masculinity," criticism that was a mask for fears about her sexuality.[5] From Louise Brooks to Rosie the Riveter to Angela Bassett, there is more public acceptance of a muscular ideal for women in or immediately following periods of prosperity like the '20s, '60s, and '90s, when definitions of traditional womanhood are being challenged. One can only hope that the economic downturn in the early twenty-first century won't be followed by a similar historical shift back to traditional femininity and all its implications of limitation for women.

The shift toward a limited kind of muscular athleticism in the 1990s seemed more widespread than in earlier periods (though it is possible that the current reality of images everywhere makes it seem so), and can be linked to both the gains made by the women's movement in the '70s and the booming American economy of the '90s. But the rise of the female athlete as icon was also partially the result of a shift in attention to the status and condition of girls in America and their cultivation as a consumer market. Mid-1990s media attention to the athletic women who were, in the words of the *Outside* magazine article quoted at the beginning of the chapter, "currently redefining our image of the female athlete, inspiring a generation of young girls to take control of their bodies and pride in their strength," tended to invoke the issue of girls' self-esteem. Such focus on this issue, and the attention to female athletes as a new body image and participation in athletics as a solution, were to some extent responses to the famous 1991 study of the American Association of University Women, "Shortchanging Girls, Shortchanging America." This was the first extensive national survey on gender and self-esteem, which reconfirmed earlier work like that of Carol Gilligan. The AAUW study showed that for girls, adolescence with its imposition of traditional gender roles brought a loss of confidence in their abilities to succeed, bitterly critical feelings about their bodies, and a growing sense that they aren't valued by the world around them with a resulting sense of personal inadequacy.[6]

Since the AAUW study, the question of girls and self-image has been raised as a public-health issue of some importance. There is a growing understanding that self-esteem is a problem for girls since they are devalued by the larger culture. This understanding has led to social initiatives like the "Take Your Daughter to Work Day," a national program where parents are encouraged to do just that so their daughters can see themselves as having opportunities and a sense of possibility for their lives. Along with these initiatives, one of the most frequently advanced solutions for the esteem problem is sports. Recently the National Girls and Women in Sports Day, a day designated for the recognition of female athletes, was coupled with a "Take a Girl to the Game" program, which was in turn modeled on "Take Your Daughter to Work." Such events showed a growing consensus that a lifestyle for girls and women that includes sports or regular physical activity of some kind would, as the *Outside* article put it, "inspire a generation of young girls to take control of their bodies and pride in their strength."[7]

The emergence of the female athlete as the new ideal image matched these social initiatives to value girls. As an article in the *New York Times Magazine* pointed out, the athletic, muscular woman as an image with mass appeal had little historical precedent and that, while slow in catching on, spread like California brushfires in the mid-'90s.[8] Around the time of the 1996 Olympics, Holly Brubach celebrated the new "Athletic Esthetic," a "new ideal emerging whose sex appeal is based on strength." Looking at female athletes and the explosion of ads that showed athletic women, Brubach wrote:

> These women exude competence; they can carry their own suitcases. Their muscles, like the fashion models' slenderness, are hard-earned, but here the means is not abstinence but exertion. Though their bodies have been meticulously cultivated, their bodies aren't the point: the point is their ability to perform. What is most striking, given that it's the other two ideals that are calculated to please—to win the admiration of women or the affection of men—is the fact that these athletes seem content in a way that the other women don't.[9]

The kind of personal integrity Brubach alluded to in the athletic image is not a new idea. In the past, female athletes and their achievements were much adored, though the level of acceptance may not have been as widespread as it is now. The biggest change can be seen in the way athleticism for women now seems normal, part of girls' and women's everyday lives rather than the lives of the exceptional few. During the "Golden Era of Women's Sports" in the 1920s, women's golf, tennis, and swimming received a great deal of national attention, and the athletes were dubbed "America's sweethearts." For instance, Helen Wills was a celebrated tennis player in the 1920s, Sybil Bauer broke the men's world record in the backstroke in 1924, and Gertrude Ederle swam the English Channel and broke the men's world record by more than two hours in 1926. Like the admiration of the slim, boyish flapper as an ideal body image, the public celebration of their feats was linked to the rise of middle-class leisure activities and increasing tolerance for new freedoms and pleasure for women, including sexual freedoms. Yet, given that female athletes also provided powerful challenges to assumptions of female inferiority and male physical superiority, they also motivated some criticism by the media. Willis, who was initially admired for her graceful strokes on the tennis court, was, after a particularly long winning streak, depicted as "heartless and lacking in warmth"—rhetoric somewhat reminiscent of that used to describe competitive female superstars like Martina Navratilova or Venus Williams in our own era. Female athletes, it seems, are idolized only if they don't succeed "too much." To some extent old stereotypes remain: for a male competitor to be "heartless" and win all the time is a mark of determination and success; for a woman it is a mark of aberrance that holds her up for censure.

Media attention tends to follow cycles that first embrace and then show ambivalence toward female athleticism. Advocates of women's sports, from educators to participants, however, have been talking consistently about the benefits of athletic participation since the late nineteenth century. It wasn't until very recently that the arguments about benefits gained mainstream cultural currency. What happened to make arguments that once fell on deaf ears register so powerfully on the national radar in the 1990s? What made public perceptions of the female athlete shift so radically from female athletes who were quickly stigmatized by the "mannish lesbian" stereotype to the glorified "women we love who kick ass" of the present moment?[10] What happened to facilitate the formation of women's professional leagues in basketball, softball, soccer, and even football?[11]

The result of long historical struggles, and economic, political, and social cycles, part of this current cultural shift in attitudes about athletes has a demographic explanation. At the time of Title IX, one in nine women participated in organized sports, while now the statistics are one in 2.5. More bodies, more interest. But what lies behind increased interest and participation? By the early 1990s, from growing numbers of girls and women participating in sports to a public focus on girls' self-esteem as a public health issue, many vital elements were in place to support a widespread acceptance of women's sports and the deconstruction of some old stigmas. Yet greater mainstreaming of the female athlete—the shift from grudging mainstream acceptance to adulation, full iconic status—did not take place until 1996, "The Year of the Women" at the Olympics. What kickstarted public consciousness? What precipitated the move from the female athlete's near invisibility in the mass media to a more ubiquitous presence in American commercial culture, selling everything from Motrin to chewing gum?

One-third of all college women participate in competitive sports. If intramural and recreational sports are included, the percentage is much higher. There are millions of female athletes and athletes to come who are eating, growing, laughing even as we speak. Maybe these new athletes won't have quite so rough a ride. There's been some grass cut, a trail

Boy-toys: Calvin Klein ad in *Vogue* (February 2002).

blazed, some brush cleared out of the way. But in their place spring new hurdles: a growing cultural conservatism that pushes for traditional models of gender, a lack of consistent Title IX enforcement and a challenge to its conceptualization, diminishing support for policies and laws that institutionalized women's sports in the first place, a growing cult of beauty that relies on cosmetic surgery (and technology itself) to achieve its images,

Buff as we wanna be: K-Swiss ad, *Sports Illustrated for Women* (May/June 2000).

popular rhetoric that blames women's sport for cutting men's sports, and a media industry that continually glamorizes the pain and sacrifice associated with competition. This glamorization—evident in the sensation created by 1996 Olympic gymnast Kerrie Strug who completed her last vault badly injured, but anchored a gold for the team—creates momentary stars who pay with their long-term health and are quickly replaced.[12]

In our commitment to look at sport and media images in all of their complexities, we will examine the cultural production of images of female athletes and how these images might shape the perceptions of youth, from a muscular female body advertising sportswear to "The Year of the Women" at the 1996 Olympics to the controversial phenomenon of athletes posing naked for men's magazines. At the same time, we explore how the recent development of a male beauty culture and the marketing of the male body, and the reactionary politics forwarded in response to this trend such as those seen in the movie *Fight Club* (reactions that mark the commodification of the male body as an established trend), might work in conjunction with the mainstreaming of the female athlete to question traditional gender distinctions. Our questions are defined in the contemporary context of hyped-up consumerism, media culture, late global capitalism, and its effects on the recent development of elite-level women's sports and fitness practices in the United States and the popular images they have generated. We draw on textual analysis, focus group interviews, content analysis, critical theory, and gender theory to develop the arguments contained here, which we use to enter debates surrounding the cultural constructions of both male and female bodies, gender norms, the representation of women in sports, and how younger audiences read and interpret these representations in their own lives.

Because they attempt to speak to readers both within the academy and outside, some chapters may be of more interest to particular groups rather than others. Chapters 2, 3, 4, 5, and 6 potentially speak to both audiences. Chapter 1, which focuses mainly on theoretical and methodological debates, may be of interest primarily to academics. Chapter 2, "Sport as the Stealth Feminism of the Third Wave," discusses the mainstream emergence of women's sports in America at the time of the 1996 Olympics, arguing that the representations of female athletes that emerged did so in conjunction with corporate America capitalizing on and cultivating women as a mass market. We show how these representations were part of a larger trend. Chapter 3, "A New Look at Female Athletes and Masculinity," asserts the importance of "masculinity"—defined as competence, competitiveness, and strength—for the female athlete and women in general and addresses some arguments against it. Chapter 4, "Bodies, Babes, and the WNBA," argues that changed demographics and economic indicators, along with the phenomenon of female athletes posing

Gender flip: Avon ad, *Vanity Fair* (May 1997).

in highly sexual ways for men's magazines, is a symptom of both the way sport can function to create the illusion of a strong, individual, modern self and the way traditional gender stereotypes are diluted in postmodern culture, fostering a sense of invulnerability from such stereotypes in the athletes. This phenomenon dovetails with that explored in chapter 5, "Body Panic Parity," which examines how gender, in conjunction with the diversification of markets, is made increasingly fluid in mass-media representations that sexualize (and feminize) the male body and perpetuate a male beauty culture. This fluidity demonstrates a need, we argue, for a mode of analysis that revises the standard second wave feminist objectification thesis—the idea that only the female body is objectified, and that in the mass media mainstream images present only women in objectified ways. Attempting to begin to see what effect, if any, such gender fluidity is having on youth culture, chapter 6, "She Will Beat You Up, and Your Papa, Too," presents a diverse collection of data based on focus group research with youth located in the southwestern United States. It explores how they—as the most targeted consumer demographic—are reading images of the female athletic body and how those images have impacted their constructions, interpretations, and views of gender in contemporary America.

Female athletes as the girl next door: ad for Citizen watches in *Condé Nast Sports and Fitness for Women* (May/June 1999).

There is a need for this focus on the negative and positive aspects of contemporary consumer culture and its images of female athletes simultaneously. Since the 1996 Olympics, interest in female athletes as subjects for trade press books, among other things, has exploded. Encyclopedias such as Anne Janette Johnson's *Great Women in Sports* and Markell, Waggoner, and Smith's *The Women's Sports Encyclopedia* provide short biographies of a wide range of female athletes.[13] Motivational

Dissolving borders: multiracial women take over an old male standard, Reebok ad,
*Women's Sport and Fitness* (May 2000).

sports autobiographies like Gabrielle Reece's *Big Girl in the Middle* and
Jackie Joyner-Kersee's *A Kind of Grace* head the personality hit-parade
list, which includes autobiographies of Sheryl Swoopes, Monica Seles,
Rebecca Lobo, Dominique Moceanu, and many others. Madeleine Blais
wrote a best-selling chronicle of a high school women's basketball team,
called *In These Girls, Hope Is a Muscle*. Two bobsledding champion sisters

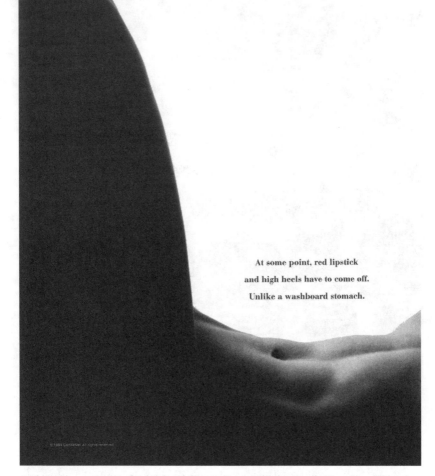

Nothing at a beauty counter could make you as confident as the body you can give yourself. And our groundbreaking tools and expert information are the only resource of their kind.

**PHYS.com**
Fitness from the outside in

At some point, red lipstick and high heels have to come off. Unlike a washboard stomach.

Girls just want to get abs: ad for online training advice, *Condé Nast Sports for Women* (May 1997).

interviewed a number of female athletes for their narrative account of female athletes, *The Quiet Storm: A Celebration of Women in Sports.*[14]

As these titles suggest, the tone of these mass-market books has been affirmative, celebratory in the high Nike key. With the exception of Joan Ryan's *Little Girls in Pretty Boxes,* which is an exposé of the sports of gymnastics and figure skating, and Mariah Burton Nelson's *The Stronger*

*Women Get, the More Men Love Football,* there is little discussion of a more complex and critical analysis of women in sport within trade books.[15] Though many articles have been written, no book has explored the proliferation and meaning of the most recent mass-media images of women in sport, which now sell everything from Mountain Dew to Rolex watches. Female athletes—and their imagery—are new institutions that are doing important cultural work. While numerous feminist researchers on sport have examined images critically in important, article-length studies, no books have explored what meanings youth culture gives to various images of women in sport, what meanings and idea systems they engage with and use to make sense of these new images.[16] This is the gap that we hope to address.

The athletic female body: a body for herself, for her own strength and breath, her own use. A new multicultural, multiracial, perhaps even multisexual image, a new ideal for the millennium. The demographic possibilities for this ideal emerged sometime in the late 1970s, when an increasingly racially diverse population met Title IX, and a large number of women were able to make competitive athletics part of their lives, an image many had been struggling to craft back when Nike was still a gym shoe, when large numbers of female athletes hit the weight room, practice fields, and mountain roads for the first time. But are images of female athletes actually interpreted like this by girls and young women? Which images? Which girls and young women, and what role do the images play in their lives? Are these images really "redefining femininity" and contributing to the inclusion of all women in sport as the rhetoric claims, or are they offering false promises? Do these images inspire young boys to respect and admire female athletes, and will this make a difference in the ways gender and power are constructed and perceived? And, perhaps most important, does the female athlete as a new ideal for women help bridge what Ellen Samuels calls "the splits between consciousness and desire and self-awareness and self-image that so many of us live with today"?[17] In other words, does the female athlete work as a progressive new ideal for women, an image a woman can aspire to without feeling like—as in the case of waify Calvin Klein or silicon-enhanced Victoria's Secret models—she is blindly following a cultural script that demeans her? The answer, as this ad for PHYS.com shows, is quite complicated.

# CHAPTER ONE

## Powered Up or Dreaming?

In the early 1990s, the near invisibility of female athletes in popular culture began to undergo a startling reversal. Although there was still a marked absence of women's televised games, meets, and races, or reports about their athletic feats in the papers, corporations such as Nike began to make female athletes highly visible in their ads.

Invoking all the benefits of sport for women's health and self-esteem, these corporations started to capitalize on the largely unheard public-health arguments that had long been put forth by physical fitness educators, coaches, and athletes. For good and ill this capitalization—and the public response to it—helped catapult the female athlete into her current iconic status. Reebok was the first to appeal to the women's market in the early 1990s, followed quickly by Nike, which began to base its campaigns on championing women's rights inside and outside sport.[1] The "Empathy Campaign" seemed to negotiate perfectly the dreams and fears of a continually growing and mostly untapped demographic of women for whom athletic participation became central in the late seventies and after. As post–Title IXers who had competed in sports all our lives, before the mid-1990s we found that although we had the chance to play the men got all the mainstream attention. The mass media had few images of female athletes with whom we could identify, and nothing to let us feel our athletic experiences were validated and valued by the culture around us.[2] The male athlete was glorified from every corner, but the public silence about female athletes was marked. *Sports Illustrated*, for instance, had only four covers featuring female athletes in

twenty years.[3] In the early 1990s, given pressures to diversify and conquer the "women's market," corporate America stepped in to fill that
void, giving us extremely positive, even heroic images of women in ads
for everything imaginable, and a way to publicly proclaim our identity
as athletes—athleticism as fashion. Of course, because they *had* validated some of us, those who were most likely to enjoy the possibility of
being touched by their message and afford their products were much
more likely to buy them.

The first ad campaign we can remember that addressed issues crucial
to athletic female identity appeared in 1992. In what now seems a historical (in the sense of being part of the past) moment, we opened *Vogue*
magazine and there it was, our innermost thoughts rising up in black
and white: *"Did you ever wish you were a boy?"* Nike hailed us, in itali-
cized white letters surrounded by a black block. "Yes—just this morning!" was our immediate, nonreflective response, and more than a little
avidly we read on: "Did you? Did you for one moment or one breath or
one heartbeat beating over all the years of your life, wish, even a little,
that you could spend it as a boy? Honest. Really. Even if you got over it."
Yes, of course, every day, all the time. They're the ones who get the column
space in the paper, their games talked about, televised, as if they're the
only athletes around. Entitlement buoying them up like pillars, it's in
the way they walk, the tones in their voices . . . they're the ones everyone
is sure are stronger and smarter because they're not girls. . . . How did
you know?

Well, we didn't have to feel that way anymore, the ad promised—it
said, now we're telling you you're okay. You're not less. Give yourself a
break: "you wake up . . . you learn to stop beating yourself over the head
for things that weren't wrong in the first place." Nike, publicly—right
there in *Vogue* magazine with its millions of readers—had pinpointed
years of conflict and psychological struggle. They were naming it: there's
nothing wrong with being a girl. Despite all the messages within media
and elsewhere, you're not less, and I'm telling you now, in black and
white, on this very sheet of paper: "And one day when you're out in the
world running, feet flying dogs barking smiles grinning, you'll hear those
immortal words calling, calling inside your head *Oh you run like a girl*
and you will say shout scream whisper call back '*Yes. What exactly did
you think I was?*'"

There it was—in good poetic meter no less—an affirmation against our deepest fears, insecurities, tearing senses of what we were valued for and what we weren't. Like many other women in the post–Title IX demographic, we loved that ad. Some of us cried when we read it, and posted it on our walls, and bought nothing but Nike for the next five years, despite rumors of sweatshop conditions in their factories offshore. Millions of women boosted Nike profits by billions in those years. That ad, and others like it, made some of us feel that finally, after years of the self-doubt that comes with invisibility, we were valued by the culture that had previously ignored us. The ads touched those most likely to feel that women could have more power in the world, that endless hours of athletic labor were worth something to someone somewhere, and, perhaps most important, to ourselves. Or if we were not athletes already, those ads gave us the hope that in an anonymous world indifferent to most people's existences, we *could* do something that would gain us recognition and value. That ad copy couldn't have played young professional, upwardly mobile women any better.[4] We were a demographic waiting to be tapped, and that tapping involved the creation of a new ideal image for women that relied on a clever mixture of liberal feminist and American individualist ideals: the trained, determined, self-reliant female athlete, the chick who can "do it for herself," who gets beyond all the old gender stereotypes and limitations and does whatever she pleases.

Like all iconic images, the female athlete as a new cultural ideal has generated much controversy and discussion. That discussion is sharply divided depending on where it takes place. On the one hand, academics and cultural critics who write on women in sport tend to view all forms of mass media and its representations critically, seeing them as part of the devastating globalization of late capitalism, which only serves to bring about, in the words of feminist sociologist Melisse R. Lafrance, illusory

> feelings of choice (through consumption) and postfeminist empowerment . . . our liberal nostalgia and corresponding delusional notions of freedom and choice. . . . Nike is seductive precisely because it allows us to disavow our material realities in favor of a cozier truth wherein structural relations of domination and subordination can be overcome by equipping oneself with a great looking pair of shoes.[5]

In this view, the marketing of women's empowerment through sport fosters regressive illusions that obscure real, structural inequalities inherent

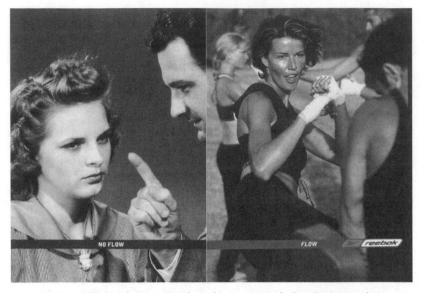

That was then, this is now: sport and gender norms Reebok style, *Women's Sports and Fitness* (June 2000).

to a market system and the sports world that is intrinsically part of it, a world that serves to empower only a very few individual women and (at best) ignores all the rest.[6]

Consuming, identifying with, and/or imitating the image of the female athlete from this point of view would be taking part in a form of what sport studies professor David Andrews calls a "superficial affective euphoria." In his work Andrews wants to disrupt such euphoria in response to contemporary images and, through his critical readings of them, offer "resistance against the creeping superficiality and meaninglessness of contemporary promotional culture."[7] Though we agree with Lafrance's and Andrews's compelling stance, we also think there is another, more potentially positive side to "promotional culture."

Starkly opposed to the positions articulated in academic work is the position expressed in advertising rhetoric, women's sport advocacy groups, mass-media reporting, many public-health journals, and sub-urban neighborhood grocery-store conversations, all of which wildly embrace the image of the female athlete and tend to make girls' and women's participation in sport, which they connect to the image and its recent omnipresence, into a panacea for all social evils. According to the Women's Sports Foundation, for instance, some of the benefits of sport participation include:

a more positive body image than that held by girls and women who
   don't participate;
higher self-esteem;
reduction in the symptoms of stress and depression among girls;
learning how to take risks and be aggressive;
learning goal-setting, strategic thinking, and the pursuit of excellence in
   performance and other achievement-oriented behaviors, which are
   critical skills necessary for success in the workplace;
development of leadership skills as well as the ability to work as a team;
academic success and higher graduation rates than those who do not
   play sports;[8]
prevention of osteoporosis and breast cancer;
having lower levels of blood sugar, cholesterol, and triglycerides, and
   lower blood pressure;
more energy and a greater sense of well-being; and
greater confidence in their physical and social selves.

Advocates, especially those coming from a "liberal," "equal opportunity" perspective, use this research to make the argument for the development of women's sports participation on all levels.[9]

We recognize that there is a difference between sports participation and the image of the female athlete. In addition to its benefits sports participation can lead to problems like overtraining, playing with pain, or developing an eating disorder. We suggest, however, that just as the benefits associated with sport participation can have a darker side, the image of the female athlete (which has been enabled by a consumer economy interested in the cultivation of every possible market), can function in positive ways. Yet academics, who tend to take the first position, and sport advocates, who tend to take the second, don't have much conversation. The academic critique is located in the academic infrastructure of conferences, journals, and university press publications, while the gung-ho, "let's go" rhetoric of mass-media advocacy takes place on the larger cultural stage. Both arguments have credence, but can be incomplete, for each tends to emphasize one part of the larger picture. While mainstream images of the female athlete can function in multiple ways, both positive and negative, some academic discourse tends to negate the positive role that cultural images can play in daily life. Yet neither do these images herald a completely new era in which all problems are solved by the greater social acceptance and representation of girls' and women's sport participation.[10]

While pioneering women's sports sociologists, historians, and cultural studies scholars like Susan Birrell, Susan Cahn, C. L. Cole, Margaret Carlisle Duncan, Kari Fasting, M. Ann Hall, Jennifer Hargreaves, Mary Jo Kane, Carol Oglesby, Nancy Theberge, Patricia Vertinsky, and many others have been fundamental to the development of the academic conversation around women's sports since the '70s and '80s, and Michael Messner, Don Sabo, Jim McKay, and other scholars have pioneered conversations around masculinity and sport, wider public discourse on the subject has lagged. Since 1996, however, women's sports have emerged as a public-health issue of national importance. The President's Council on Physical Fitness and Sports Report, "Physical Activity and Sport in the Life of Young Girls: Physical and Mental Health Dimensions from an Interdisciplinary Approach" (to which some of the above scholars contributed) cites a "comprehensive awareness that exercise and sport are not just about physical movement but personal development, identity, and values as well." Scholars have begun to research the impact of athletic participation on the lives of girls and women and have found a significant correlation between sports participation, high grade-point average, and sense of self-esteem and achievement later in life. The President's Report further emphasizes that "research studies must utilize an interdisciplinary perspective," and the development of "research teams that enhance partnerships between scholars and practitioners."[11]

But the touted benefits of sport are sometimes analyzed critically within academia, especially since women have long been kept out of sport, and the benefits have not been similarly enjoyed across groups of different women. In this perspective, sport is viewed as an institution that doesn't challenge some of its potentially damaging core assumptions—assumptions that are often associated with masculinity—that women are increasingly adopting today. These assumptions include the classic sport story in which the athlete is "heroic" if he or she sacrifices all for the win, physically dominates opponents, is alienated from his/her own body so as to perform like a machine, and sees his/her own value as a human being only in terms of athletic performance. One suggestion that these critiques of sport offer is that women's participation may be much more beneficial in the sense of public health and wellness if that participation is performed within a setting that adopts an alternative approach to sport from this individualistic, competitive, male-oriented ethos that characterizes most sport institutions today. As Jennifer Hargreaves writes,

> gendered heroism is being constantly challenged by women who are appropriating the narratives of maleness and transforming themselves from victims into superstars. According to many feminists, to claim an identity that used to be exclusively male in a macho, sexist culture is symbolically heroic. However, what is often forgotten is that the fierce concern for equality props up the violence, corruption, and commercialization and exploitation that plague men's sports.[12]

Hargreaves's perspective—that individualism, competitiveness, superstardom, commodification, and violence are part of male sport culture and are decidedly not heroic and cannot be a wholly progressive or positive identification for women until sport fundamentally changes—marks one of the most influential feminist interpretations of sport today. Historically, these ideas come out of a radical feminist stance that defines itself in opposition to liberal feminism.[13] Though these terms, *radical* and *liberal* feminism enjoyed a more widespread currency in the conversations surrounding feminism in the seventies and eighties (for reasons articulated in chapter 2), they still underlie many of the debates within popular culture and feminism, and seem particularly applicable to some of the underlying assumptions in conversations about female athletes.

Much maligned within the academy, *liberal feminism* is usually defined as, in the words of feminist sociologist Caroline Ramazanoglu, "a long tradition of campaigning for improved rights and opportunities for women without seriously questioning the existing organization of society." The liberal tradition has had the most mainstream and perhaps activist impact in reference to women in sport. As M. Ann Hall writes, "feminist activism around sport has been almost exclusively liberal in philosophy and strategy. Attempts to push the agenda to a more 'radical' feminist approach have not met with much success. However, the scholarship about gender (and sport) is becoming increasingly more radical in its critique." For Hall and many others, liberal feminism and its attempts at reform are inadequate within the sport context because "they do not always see as problematic the fundamental nature of male-defined sport with its emphasis on hierarchy, competitiveness, and aggression."[14] Liberal feminist ideals are also critiqued for their obvious overreliance on principles of "equal access under the law" which clearly do not always work as successfully as intended, are difficult to enforce, work to privilege certain groups of women over others, and do not account for the backlashes that can occur during times of progress, such as a loss of hiring female coaches and athletic directors for decades after Title IX passed.[15]

To some extent, the divide that Hall highlights between liberal approaches, which have fought for women's equal access to the "male" sport network, and radical approaches, which seek to transform the nature of sport itself, echoes the argument that female physical educators had with "male sports" in the first half of the twentieth century. The argument was centered around, in the words of Susan K. Cahn, a pitch for a separate, "'feminine' brand of athletics designed to maximize female participation . . . [female sport educators] scorned 'masculine' aggressiveness and competitiveness" and believed that "commercial, highly competitive sport was inherently undemocratic . . . privileg[ing] the talented minority over the neglected majority."[16] The "participatory" model of sport, associated by female educators with women and "female nature," emphasized the right of all girls to participate and have fun in sport and deemphasized winning and achievement ("A Sport for Every Girl and Every Girl for a Sport" was a popular motto). This alternative sport model was constructed in opposition to the competitive, individualist model of sport that was associated with men and "male nature"—the model with which we are much more familiar today.

## Historical Influences on Third Wave Feminist Sport Perspectives

Ironically, at least partially because of its pro-individualist, competitive stance, what we will try to articulate here as a "third wave feminist" position on sport refers directly to these debates and has more in common with the early radical feminism of the 1960s than it does with the cultural feminism that began in the mid-'70s and came to be known as "radical."[17] Precultural feminism, first known as "radical feminism" according to historian Alice Echols, was much more like what is now called "third wave feminism" (specifically the strain that emphasizes similarities between women and men and the artificiality of gender constructions) because the early radical feminists "in defying the cultural injunction against female self-assertion and subjectivity 'dared to be bad.'"[18] The continued presence of the later strain of cultural feminism in discussions of sport shows itself in suggestions that when women participate in the institution, they will face what the men face—for example, injury and commercialization. In general terms this perspective, which is often called "radical," criticizes "male sport" for its inherent violence and argues that women's sports should remain a kinder, gentler version (because women are more "team-oriented" and "cooperative").[19]

In general, our third wave position is directed more against the kind of cultural feminism that would argue for "a female counterculture . . . where 'male' values would be exorcized and 'female' values nurtured" than it is against the earlier forms of radical feminism. From the third wave feminist perspective, binaries like male/female, active/passive, strong/weak, violent/peaceful, and competitive/cooperative belong to essentialist constructions of male and female "natures" that have long been contested. Echols notes how in the contemporary lexicon cultural feminism with its alternative and separatist "feminine" values has become conflated with radical feminism, which, though it had separatist strains, "generally repudiated the idea that men and women are essentially different and advocated the degendering of society."[20]

In this particular critique of essentialism, contemporary third wave feminism has more in common with the '6os radical feminism than it does with the later cultural feminism that took over its name, as do the contemporary elite female athletes whose achievements question the idea of essential gender difference and contribute to the very "degendering of society" that early radical feminism sought.[21] Mary Jo Kane's formulation of the gender continuum in sport is foundational here. Kane argues that because individual athletes are encouraged to participate in "gender appropriate" sports such as figure skating for women and football for men, because the media largely remains silent about women's participation in "male" sports like rugby, football, and hockey, and because women who excel at these sports are constructed as being "like men," sport "works to suppress evidence of a [gender] continuum" in which women can be shown to possess "masculine" characteristics and men to possess "feminine" characteristics in greater and lesser proportions, with different individuals located on different points of the spectrum.[22]

Far from extolling a "gentler" model of sport for women that is advocated by some strains of contemporary radical feminism, the gender continuum model of sport demonstrates why women's participation in traditionally violent "male" sports like football, hockey, and boxing, and men's participation in traditionally "female" sports like synchronized swimming or figure skating is so necessary to destabilizing traditional notions about gender that limit girls' and women's (as well as boys' and men's) possibilities. Similarly, contemporary consumer culture provides cultural imagery that makes male bodies into objects—as all bodies are objects within consumer culture.[23] Simultaneously, popular media representations present a range of athletic female bodies as heroic and self-determining, and that function within a number of sign systems, including gay male and lesbian cultures. As Toby Miller puts it,

> the present moment of change is a radical one—and I guardedly welcome it. Sportsex is both intensely discriminating in its identification of commodities and consumers and increasingly attuned to difference . . . the urgent drive toward the creation of markets to deal with overproduction has turned the Sportsex body to the forefront of contemporary capitalism. It is both a sign and source of social change.[24]

Given this change in popular imagery and the gender expectations to which it is linked, and the way it has influenced female athletes within what might be deemed the post–Title IX generation, it is clear that we need new critical frameworks to accommodate that change. A third wave feminist perspective provides one way to do this. As Leslie Heywood and Jennifer Drake define it, the third wave, among other things, assumes that

> the second and third waves of feminism are neither incompatible or opposed . . . [the third wave] embrac[es] second wave critique as a central definitional thread while emphasizing ways that desires and pleasures subject to critique can be used to rethink and enliven activist work. . . . [I]n the current historical moment, third wave feminists often take cultural production and sexual politics as key sites of struggle, seeking to use desire and pleasure to motivate struggles for justice.[25]

This definition, based as it is on the concepts of contradiction and hybridity, helps to explain the approach taken to female athletes and images in *Built to Win*.

Sarah Gamble writes, "the primary difference between third wave and second wave feminism is that third wave feminists feel at ease with contradiction. Because they have been brought up with competing feminist structures, they accept pluralism as a given." Heywood and Drake identify some of the third wave's origins in "critiques of the white women's movement that were initiated by women of color, as well as from the many instances of coalition work undertaken by U.S. postcolonial feminists," arguing that these different views helped to fundamentally shape the necessarily multiple and often contradictory standpoints of what has come to be called the third wave.[26] Those standpoints can tolerate the tension between critique and appreciation, the idea that images can do negative and affirmative cultural work simultaneously, and that both masculine and feminine, competitive and participatory models of sport offer a range of possibilities for women and men.

Our critique, then, is similar to and different from the radical critique—it espouses strands of early radical feminist ideals of "degendering society," an ideal picked up later by postmodern feminists like Judith Butler with the idea of the gender performative—gender as a set of traits we perform rather than possess innately. Unlike the early radical feminists, however, and in line with strains endemic to cultural studies, we acknowledge that market conditions can be oppressive to some, empowering to others, and offer the potential to do progressive and regressive cultural work, sometimes simultaneously. The complexity of the current historical moment is highlighted by factors previously mentioned, which helped lead to market conditions that could begin to sell a strong female athlete icon to a more financially powerful female demographic. As Miller writes, "sports' gender politics at the elite level today are far from a functionalist world of total domination by straight, orthodox masculinity because of the niche targets that these commodified signs are directed toward (such as straight women and gay men) . . . the beneficial aspect to cataloguing sports is its challenges to gender convention."[27]

## The Economic Basis of Need for New Interpretive Paradigms

We take these contemporary market conditions as a point of departure from which to examine how, and in what contexts, the new mainstreaming of the female athlete images does its cultural work. This is not to imply that there is not structural inequality on many levels, or that the contemporary world of images erases this. It is of significant importance, however, that the terms of that inequality have shifted in the United States so that in the generations born after 1960, inequalities are less gender-based: "families have been affected by the decline in earnings for men and the increase in women's labor force participation," and in the younger age groups, the "gap between young men's and young women's incomes narrowed to 5 percent in 1994."[28] For both young men and women, however, debt-to-income ratio is prohibitive, so that the real struggle becomes just paying the bills. These demographic characteristics are important for our purposes here because the second wave feminist analysis of representation is based on economic considerations that characterize an older demographic in which men typically held the "good," permanent, high-paying jobs. Such jobs have now largely vanished for both men and women, replaced by part-time, service-industry jobs without benefits. For the audience most likely to be interested in images of the female athlete, the structural conditions of their lives are such that male power is only a fantasy that cannot, in any substantive way, be interpreted as real. No one has economic "power" except for the multinationals, and this affects how the images are interpreted and received by young women and men. However, on the level of institutional infrastructures in sport, men's sports are still much more consistently funded and at greater levels, creating a discrepancy of infrastructures in which consumers of or audiences for the images come from a position of shared struggle—young men and women both struggling to pay their Citibank bills—while the athletes who are the source of the images themselves suffer in their own particular situations from inequities that still have a gender basis. As we will argue in chapter 4, especially in the case of the controversial, sexualized images of female athletes, these demographic characteristics are crucial for an analysis of how the images are created—why female athletes pose for them in the first place—and understood. For a demographic in which there is more structural equality, the images read differently, and for a demographic that has experienced the commodification of bodies, male and female, on every level, and even the normalization of porn as part of the context in which they grew up, the images read differently than they do for older age groups not accustomed to that normalization. Such structural discrepancies in demographic characteristics suggest that we need a much more flexible paradigm for interpretation than the objectification thesis.

Our work differs from earlier traditions in the field of cultural studies, such as those associated with Richard Hoggart, who "deplored the growing commercial penetration of culture which was affecting the communities, families, language and sensibilities of working class people."[29] The irony is that the very homogenization of commercial culture that Hoggart wrote about in 1957, a homogenization that only grew exponentially worse in terms of its pervasiveness in America in the '90s, was also characterized by a splintering of markets. This splintering legitimized the public emergence of "others" as a multiplicity of consumer demographics to which advertisements appealed, making their alternative images and cultures visible. Therefore we guardedly analyze the image of the female athlete as a marketing ploy that has some positive dimensions. In order to make sense of these paradoxes, we need to draw from interdisciplinary methodologies. According to Lawrence Grossberg, Cary Nelson, and Paula Treichler, who have long been prominent in the field,

> cultural studies is not merely interdisciplinary; it is often . . . actively and aggressively anti-disciplinary—a characteristic that more or less ensures a permanently uncomfortable relationship to academic disciplines. . . . Its choice of practice, that is, is pragmatic, strategic, and self-reflective.[30]

Our study takes a place along the spectrum of the documented turn within cultural studies from an "economic Marxist model of culture as the reflection of 'ruling class' interests and 'mass culture' as the sedative pap designed to be consumed by the workers" to an emphasis on "the agency of ordinary people in contesting and producing cultural meaning."[31] A third wave feminist analytic as we practice it here includes both poles, emphasizes the difficulty of a single reading or determinate interpretation of any image, and acknowledges the importance of (multiple) subject positions toward any interpretation.

From advocacy to critical theory to more artistic narratives that "resonate with emotion and lived experience, marry[ing] life events and inner musings, inner sense-making . . . thick description at its thickest," there are as many rhetorical strategies used to discuss sport as there are Olympic sports.[32] Methodologically, we include several strategies here. Our focus is on the linguistic, representational dimension, for, as Henry Giroux writes, "developing a new attentiveness to how culture mobilizes power, many proponents of cultural studies have expanded textuality as a medium of analysis to the broader study of structures, institutions, and relations of power."[33] We also make use of a sociological perspective that increasingly embraces qualitative methods, postmodern ethnographies, and focus group methods.[34] *Built to Win* comes out of a cultural studies methodology that bridges the linguistic, the empirical (and more): cultural imagery, which is, in Giroux's words, "pluralistic, shifting, and hybrid," and the real meaning that people make and create out of that imagery given their differential positioning in social structures—"diasporic in its constant struggle for narrative space, culture becomes the site where youth make sense of themselves and others."[35] Various intertwinings of agency and constraint within disciplines and subjects have produced new possibilities, as does the attempted bridge between academia, advocates, the larger public conversation, and broader research forums.

## Poststructuralism and the Question of "the Real"

The bridges between the linguistic and the empirical are crucial, because while each is limited in its own way, each has served to question and open up the other. Paula M. L. Moya expresses the linguistic position when she writes:

> Poststructuralist critics inspired by deconstruction have tended to analogize and thus understand social relations with reference to linguistic structures. The deconstructionist thesis about the indeterminacy of linguistic reference led many U.S. literary theorists and cultural critics to understand concepts like experience and identity (which are fundamentally about social relations) as similarly indeterminate and hence epistemically unreliable.... Because meaning exists only in a shifting and unstable relation to the webs of signification through which it comes into being and because humans have no access to anything meaningful outside these sometimes disparate webs, there can be no "objective" truth. The desire for "truth" or "objective" knowledge is therefore seen as resting on a naively representational theory of language that relies on the following mistaken assumptions: first, that there is a one-to-one correspondence between signs and their extralinguistic real-world referents; and second, that some kind of intrinsic meaning dwells in those real-world referents, independent of human thought or action. Knowledge, insofar as it is mediated by language, cannot be said to be objective.[36]

While this linguistic conception of "reality" can be exciting in its revisionary tenets at first (and did to some extent help sociology to break out of the kind of "categoric" research, often quantitative but not necessarily so, that desperately needed concepts of intersecting social locations and "real" narratives), a purely textual focus causes a quandary for academic activists interested in the "real" conditions of human "experience." Similarly, while quantitative methods could provide "hard" data, it rarely questioned the status of its own foundational and limiting assumptions.[37]

A good example of a kind of pluralistic methodology that considers both is Susan Birrell and Mary McDonald's "Reading Sport Critically," where they write that their "goal is to join the interdisciplinary and political commitments of cultural studies and critical theories with recent developments within qualitative methodology, especially the poststructuralist-inspired 'linguistic turn.'" They note that this "linguistic turn" in the social sciences that enables their call for a critical sport studies occurred at roughly the same time that it was "becoming fashionable for scholars in literary criticism to focus on nonliterary texts as serious objects of study." The application of postmodern theory to sport, however, can share similar limitations to those confronted by those working on any subject from a textualist base. Recently, many have been making the "linguistic turn" part of a relational and pluralistic methodology.[38]

Similar tensions between textual and empirical research have invigorated what Marjorie Garber, Beatrice Hanssen, and Rebecca Walkowitz call "the turn to ethics." "There was a time," they write,

> not so many years ago, when "ethics" was regarded in the realm of literary study as a "master discourse" that presumed a universal humanism and an ideal, autonomous, and sovereign subject . . . the critique of humanism was an exposé of ethics. Things have changed. Ethics is back in literary studies, as it is in philosophy and critical theory, and indeed the very critiques of universal man and the autonomous human subject that had initially produced a resistance to ethics have now generated a crossover among these various disciplines that sees and does ethics "otherwise." The decentering of the subject has brought about a recentering of the ethical.[39]

The tension between theories of a decentered subject and ethical struggles for social justice play a key role in debates, conversations, and factionalizations within that divergent group of scholars whose work focuses on sport, as well as between those working as women's sport advocates outside the academy. Like the "turn to ethics" within literary and philosophical studies, sociology, with its link to public policy, emphasis on grants, and distributive justice research, is an important component of research agendas that are simultaneously sensitive to assumptions about the more fractured nature of identity that characterizes the linguistic approach. The method we use here, then, could be seen as part of the turn from the structural to the linguistic to the ethical, a hybrid that makes use of all three "turns."

"We are fortunate," sociologist Laurel Richardson writes, "to be working in a poststructuralist climate, a time when a multitude of approaches to knowing and telling exist side by side." New approaches expand the range of knowledge, while "in social sciences—including sport social sciences—the unexamined, fact-oriented, plain prose-style, linear narrative expectation (past theory, literature review, present hypothesis, methods of test, findings, future research) limit what can be known and what can be told."[40] But it is not the case of doing one form of writing or another, either exclusively theoretical writing, or narrative writing, or the "fact-oriented" kind of writing that Richardson describes here. While narrative may serve as an inspirational and highly concrete example of the meanings and importance of sport, a form of writing that is only in the literary mode may not be considered "real research" by policymakers, and its larger meanings and connection to the world outside the characters in the story might be missed by some readers.[41]

So are we, or are we not, these stories and cultural images all around us, what yearnings do our engagements with them mark, and how do we talk about them? This is a tension in the critical paradigms utilized throughout this work. Answering this question involves confronting tensions within the larger fields of critical theory and within sport studies itself, which tends to be divided, as Ann Hall points out, between "categoric research" (empirical/positivist research that "studies sex or race differences in athletic participation, performance, and abilities, and attempts to explain their existence in terms of biological factors and socialization"); "distributive research" ("which examines the distribution of resources . . . and focuses on inequality in opportunities, access, and financial resources"); and "relational analyses" ("which begin with the assumption that sporting practices are historically produced, socially constructed, and culturally defined to serve the interests and needs of powerful groups in society"). In order to account for the rise of the female athlete as icon and to begin to examine the multidimensionality of that icon and some of the cultural work that she does, we had to employ an even more mixed-breed, hybrid creature than all of these. If photographer and curator Jane Gottesman has recently asked (and answered) the question "What does a female athlete look like?" in her stunning photography monograph and traveling exhibition *Game Face: What Does*

How good does
a female athlete
have to be before
we just call her
an athlete?

*Game Face: What Does A Female Athlete Look Like?* A traveling photography
exhibition organized by Game Face Productions at Olpin Union, University of Utah,
Salt Lake City. Hosted by the Women's Resource Center from January 29 through
March 29, 2002. For visitor information, go to gamefaceonline.org. Proudly
sponsored by MassMutual Financial Group, including OppenheimerFunds, Inc.
The Game Face book is published by Random House.

MassMutual
FINANCIAL GROUP          OppenheimerFunds

What does a female athlete look like? Gwen Torrance in an ad for *Game Face*
in *Sports Illustrated for Women* (February 2002).

*a Female Athlete Look Like?*, answering this question about the female
athlete as cultural icon requires an articulation of what a third wave
feminist rubric might look like.[42]

What it looks like from the perspective of traditional, positivistic,
and humanistic disciplines in the academy is a kind of mongrel. Its
subject matter or content—cultural images—and its form—narrative

analytics—might look to some like a sphinx or satyr, some mythologi-
cal creature of discordant parts that can never quite functionally exist.
Like the hybrid, sometimes contradictory analytics of third wave feminism, our perspective here has made use of multiple methodological
strategies that mix the theoretical and textual with the empirical and
structural, as well as making use of multiple rhetorical strategies that
mix narrative and critical, creative and expository writing.[43] It combines strategies devised from training in the humanities, social sciences,
and the fine arts. It is difficult, and beautiful, and some might think it is
sometimes rough. It is what Jim Denison and Robert Rinehart identify
as "combined theory/narrative pieces...grounded in everyday, concrete, and specific events and research protocols, using fictional strategies to make their conclusions more explicit...a storied research account must contribute to our understanding of social life while also
being artistically shaped and satisfying" in their argument for the valid-
ity of "sociological narrative." "This is a tough task," they note, "and requires a high level of skill and dedication both to the craft of writing
and to the analytical skills of a scholar."[44]

This description should help to explain what might be seen as our
Frankenstein's monster, the methodological patchwork that gracefully
lumbers through this book, sometimes roaring, sometimes eloquent,
sometimes incomplete given its tending to too much at once, always striving for the human dimensions that never seem quite possible in purely
analytical academic work. Many voices appear in this book, voices that
represent our attempt to provide, in Henry Giroux's words, "a discourse
of opposition and hope," but an opposition that fully recognizes its own
complicities and the difficulty of positing oppositional spaces.[45]

With this work, we join the rapidly developing cultural conversation
about sport and media images, and the impact these central cultural institutions have or don't have on the perceptions of early twenty-first-
century youth cultures. The President's Council on Physical Fitness and
Sports Report, "Physical Activity and Sport in the Life of Young Girls:
Physical and Mental Health Dimensions from an Interdisciplinary Approach," emphasized that future research should "include participants
from racially, ethnically, economically and ability-diverse backgrounds
because gender interacts with these diversities in complex ways."[46] By
choosing schools with diverse racial and socioeconomic demographics,
and by talking to both boys and girls to do our focus groups, we have

attempted to provide a broad range of reactions to media images. Feminist theory has long argued that gender needs to be studied in relation to these different variables, but sometimes media analysis exclusively involves the perceptions of the scholar reading media texts him/herself, or a statistical analysis of how often women appear in sports coverage or some related question rather than analyzing the perceptions of the audience. As Laurel R. Davis points out,

> in the past many scholars focused on the power of media texts to affect the audience; now they focus on the ability of the audience to interpret media texts in a wide variety of manners. . . . The meanings of any particular media text are influenced by the meanings producers intend to convey, features of the media text itself that encourage and discourage particular interpretations, the perspectives of audience members, and elements of the wider sociocultural environment that influence the production process and perspectives of both the producers and audience members.[47]

We found that in reading images of the female athlete, fifth through tenth graders expressed a lively, contentious, skeptical, cautious, entertaining, enraged, celebratory range of views that indicate that women's sport helps to both reinforce and challenge traditional gender ideals—and more. For instance, in a fifth-grade classroom nestled within a poor neighborhood situated in the dry desert of the Southwest, a Hispanic boy indicated that he liked the picture of Marion Jones, standing in muscular glamour on the beach, "the best." When asked why, he shyly declared that "she could protect me." While challenging the old discourse of white male protectionism of white (wealthy, frail) women, he may have also been reinvigorating ideologies about black womanhood, which have long included ideas about strength and autonomy given historical inequities. But now that the spectacular physical feats of the Florence Griffith-Joyners and Marion Joneses of track and field have become part of popular cultural imagery, perhaps it is now more possible for young boys to fantasize about the potential physical protection of women. Perhaps they can expect women to fight back by day on the school grounds, at frat parties, and by night at the dinner table someday.

Another example of the range of views images can inspire comes from the image of Jeanette Lee, Women's Professional Billiards Association (WPBA) champion, in a publicity still. Dressed in a tight black dress,

Marion in charge: the fastest woman in the world, Nike ad, *Condé Nast Sports and Fitness for Women* (May 1998).

standing behind a pool table, long sleek hair immaculately in place, she stares at the viewer with an expression that seems to incarnate her nickname, "The Black Widow": she is a femme fatale with a pool stick, ready to strike you dead, whether through her gaze or the devastating click of ball on stick. "No way, we have a women's pro billiards association?" asked one white female high schooler. "We have a men's?" a biracial male added as a retort. Engaging with the image in a wholly postmodern feminist fashion, fifth-grade girls had quite a bit to add: "That's too girly," called out one girl, age ten. "It makes me feel that just because I'm a girl doesn't mean that I am weak" added a second, age eleven. In another classroom, out of a rather annoyed small body came a fiery question: "How come she dresses so fancy just to play pool?" Another young girl showed her understanding of a binary gender order quite simply: "I think some men might like that she doesn't have big muscles." One tiny female voice added in a rather sophisticated manner, "I think she brings more interest to spectators." Third wave indeed. We invite you to consider the cultural work that the image—and their voices—perform.

As the chapters that follow will argue, signifiers are multiple and contestable, products are subject to interpretation and can have unintended effects. While it is true that the most economically privileged have the most access to the cultural mythologies (such as self-determination and cultural value) that the new images of the powerful female athlete create, and that these mythologies can serve to mask structural inequalities, it is also the case that images of female athletes are no longer solely confined to the demeaning prescriptions of limited gender roles. There are now a wide range of images available, from the most retro forms of sexualization—Martina Hingis in a full-page ad for American Express in the *New York Times* sport section the day after the 2001 U.S. Open, posed facing the camera, lips pursed, tennis racket suggestively grasped between her thighs, skirt hiked almost to her hips, the ad's text reading "Femme Fatale since 99"—to the most unambiguously powerful—Marion Jones in a "Got Milk?" ad dressed in her track singlet, biceps gracefully flexed looking ready to race, serious game face in place, text reading, "Wanna race? Milk has nine essential nutrients active bodies need. It can't be beat. And neither can I." Like the wide range of available images, viewers bring a range of perspectives to the images, and a host of imaginative interpretations that they make use of in various ways—some hegemonic, some oppositional, some in-between.

Even so, the rise of the female athlete as cultural icon can be and is criticized on the basis of its individualist orientation. Jennifer Hargreaves writes,

> remarkably few of our "media heroines" of sport connect their roles as stars with politics and ethics. Most of them have been "selfish heroines" who seek individual glory and financial gain; most of them have failed to speak out openly to oppose the damaging features of modern-day sport. The main thrust of women in sport has been to follow men.... Because popular heroic narratives are so concerned with the creation and representation of the individual, collective struggles and achievements are underplayed and often ignored.... There is a strong argument for returning to the 1970s anti-individualistic feminist principles that commodified heroines/stars should be replaced by "real" women.[48]

Hargreaves points to the irony that, though it was collective struggle that brought female athletes the forms of (still limited) opportunity they now enjoy in the first place, they often are unaware of this indebtedness, or of their responsibility to "give back" to the women's activist community that enabled them.

We make a sustained argument for both individual development and collective action, for the cultivation of traditionally masculine characteristics as well as traditionally feminine ones, for women's and men's

Beautiful? Handsome? Both? Marion Jones and new gender and beauty ideals, *Sports Illustrated for Women* (February 2002).

participation in the aggressive "male sport" model and the more partici-patory "female" version, for engagement with and critique of the media as well as recognition of its more affirmative potentialities. As Hargreaves's *Heroines of Sport* so clearly shows, worldwide there is a desperate need for collective struggle for the advancement of women's athletic partici-pation and the need for the recognition of multiple models of sport.

Celebrities for the larger good: ad for the debut of women's professional soccer, *Sports Illustrated for Women* (March 2001).

But rather than marking the negation of such efforts, iconic female athletes can contribute to such efforts in unique ways. Many forms of engagement are valuable—it needn't be one pole or the other, a "return to 1970s anti-individualistic feminist principles that commodified heroines/stars should be replaced by 'real' women," or the individual athlete media icon. Why not both icons and "real women"?

For better and worse, media culture is a big part of our world, and, as in earlier cultural forms such as novels, cultural mythologies of the individual heroic occupy a seemingly intransigent place within it. Hero(in)es occupy the powerfully motivational space of desire that can be mobilized toward larger aims of many kinds. "Real women" simply do not have the same kind of signifying effects or provide the same forms of motivation or identification. Iconic female athletes, through "following men" in that heroic tradition, offer more than individualistic concerns and a way to mask and devalue collective struggles for justice. They also offer a sense of possibility and belonging to a world where women aren't always on the sidelines cheering somebody else, where they are active agents in the world and people are cheering them, as in the case of women's soccer and their collective struggle—assisted by the star power of Hamm and Chastain—for better pay and benefits for the whole USA team, individual hero(in)es can contribute to collective struggles. As both cultural critics and women's sports advocates, we can work with them. Though with problems and limitations, iconic female athletes in contemporary media culture can function as one resource in the ongoing struggles for social justice.

# CHAPTER TWO

## Sport as the Stealth Feminism of the Third Wave

In the years since the 1996 Olympic games, the American cultural landscape has changed for the better, at least for the female athlete. 1996 was the "year of the woman" at the Olympics. The year the cover of the preview issue of *Sports Illustrated* featured women, specifically five African-American members of the women's basketball team, and their coach, Tara Van Derveer. The year hurdler Kim Batten was featured on one page, Michael Johnson the next. The year women athletes showed up in ads for every product you can imagine, ads attesting to female power and self-assertion, like the State Farm ad for the basketball team featuring a woman driving toward the basket that read, "These days little girls don't live down the lane—they drive down it."[1] The year the women's gymnastics team and swimmer Amy Van Dyken appeared on Wheaties boxes. The year there was emphasis on women's achievements, not their looks, like the *Sports Illustrated* feature on sculler Ruth Davidon, which headlined her status as medical student and doctoral candidate, not her hair.[2]

Structurally, however, it wasn't as clear as the media made it seem that "we'd come a long way." Despite the fact that 36 percent of the athletes in this Olympics were women, up from 30 percent in 1992, 36 percent still leaves 64 percent of the competitors men. Even worse, there were only seven women among the 106 members of the International Olympic Committee. Of the 271 athletic events, 165 were for men only as compared to 95 for women only; only 11 events were mixed.[3] Like the full implementation of Title IX, it was clear that we still have a long way to go in the achievement of full equality for women athletes.

Still, in this Olympics, unlike any of the Olympics that had preceded the Atlanta games, the focus on female athletes was part of a much larger national focus on women in sports. It was the first Olympics in which the legacy of Title IX of the Education Act of 1972 was fully visible: "the first generation of women who've had a lifetime of opportunity to play," noted Donna Lopiano, executive director of the Women's Sports Foundation. For the first time, "what you see is the female athlete as a rule, not the exception." That "rule" had profound consequences for the representation of athletes. Unlike the "genderized" coverage of, for instance, the 1984 and 1988 Olympics analyzed by Margaret Carlisle Duncan— coverage that emphasized female competitors as women first, athletes second, ignoring their skills and focusing on their looks while male athletes were described as "powerful" or "great"—in 1996 the emphasis was primarily on women's skill and achievements. According to Val Ackerman, president of the WNBA, "the Atlanta Olympics elevated women's sports to a new high" because of the changes in media coverage, facilitating, among other things, the development of professional leagues.[4]

In an interview with the Feminist Majority before the 1996 games, Olympics expert Carol Oglesby was asked whether she thought coverage of female athletes would improve from what it had been in earlier Olympics. Oglesby answered, "The media have been put on notice about their coverage of women—the amount of coverage and the characterization of that coverage. We can watch to see whether commentators refer to women athletes by their first names, while calling men Mr. so-and-so. How will women be portrayed in the commentaries and profiles on athletes?"[5]

If the media had been "put on notice," clearly there was more sensitivity in 1996 to stereotypic coverage. That male athletes were fathers was discussed almost as often as the female athletes who were mothers (and starting a new tradition, many male track athletes as well as women did their victory laps carrying their sons or daughters).[6] In fact, commentators insisted, the women made for the most interesting stories in 1996. "The 1996 Games will be remembered, no doubt," writes Jere Longman, "as the year women took over the Olympics—setting the stage, perhaps, for an assault on the largely male preserve of professional sports. For it is women who are expected to provide many of the memorable accomplishments, the media focus, and even the controversy of the centennial Games."[7]

While the Atlanta Olympics coverage featured some of the usual sex-ist clichés, such as the alleged "catfight" between sprinters Gail Devers and Gwen Torrance, emphasized the women who were mothers as well as athletes, and dwelled unnecessarily on the heroic sacrifice of Kerrie Strug (making it seem as if female athletes did not in fact sacrifice them-selves every day), on the whole it was an improvement. Yes, the gym-nasts, long seen as more "traditionally feminine," still received a dispro-portionate amount of coverage in relation to other female athletes. But women's track, once seen as so "masculine" and taxing that there was a movement to ban it as an Olympic sport for women after the 1928 games when a woman collapsed at the finish of the eight-hundred-meter race, was at the center of national consciousness that summer. After the 1996 Olympics, Jackie Joyner-Kersee, a heptathlete who, despite the fact that her quest for defending her gold medal was lost due to a torn ham-string, was uniformly cited by children and others as the female athlete they admired most. Devers and Torrance became household names.

In a world where women athletes are almost never featured on the same par with the men, the *Newsweek* and *New York Times Magazine* covers featuring women Olympians were a marked improvement, as were the *Time* profiles of women's teams and individual athletes in their summer 1996 special edition. Photographers, perhaps for the first time, used the same kinds of shots and lighting techniques when photograph-ing male and female athletes. Whereas previously the conventions fea-tured athletic action shots of men and sexualizing beauty shots of women, the July 1996 issue of *Life* magazine featured portraits that combined both athleticism and beauty, in men and women. There were naked por-traits of powerlifter Mark Henry, the torso of sprinter Michael Johnson, long jumper and sprinter Carl Lewis, diver Russ Bertram, and the U.S. men's water-polo team, all shot with the same conventions—the human body as an art form—as those used in the naked portraits of female fencer Sharon Monplaisir, diver Mary Ellen Clark, sprinters Gwen Tor-rance and Gail Devers, heptathlete Jackie Joyner-Kersee, volleyball player Holly McPeak, and Margo Thien and Nathalie Schneyder from synchro-nized swimming. The photographs, by Joe McNally, were gorgeous studies of erotic beauty, athleticism, and artistic form: macho men and porno princesses these weren't. Equal-opportunity sexploitation?[8] Here the in-terrelated cultural threads of the corporatization of sport and a greater fluidity within mainstream gender roles combined with the acceleration of visual images and a new body aesthetic to produce a new hybrid: an athletic image that challenged some of the old codes of male active/ female passive, white mind/black body, male subject/female object, and heterosexualization.[9] These bodies were both radically their own and simultaneously presented for *anyone's* enjoyment: in their gender-fluid coding and their insistence on form, they solicited much more than the white male gaze.

Even more explicitly, in terms of improving on sex stereotypes in the representation of athletes, many national newspapers and magazines made the connection between the prominence of women in this Olympics and the women's movement's fight for equality in other arenas, including athletics. According to *New York Times* sportswriter and author Jere Longman, "women make for better stories . . . because women have struggled so long and resolutely to overcome cultural, racial, and religious obstacles, their accomplishments carry a resonance particularly associated with the Olympics: sacrifice, struggle, elusive victory gained at great odds." Female athletes, sportswriters suddenly seemed to think, were the true Olympians, unlike the spoiled male athletes who were all sponsored by multimillion-dollar contracts and who seemed to have their eyes on nothing except the bottom line.[10]

For the first time, much attention was given to the fact that twenty-seven countries did not send women to the Olympics because of Islamic dress codes, and there was a good deal of focus on women whose performances have helped the political cause of women in their respective countries.[11] Rather than being ridiculed or ignored, female athletes were being used to make a mainstream argument for women's political activism. And this was not, as some might have it, merely a case of "activism lite," the superficial recognition of a few elite women that masked the continuing struggles of the majority and diverted our attention from them. Instead, 1996 marked a point where athletes, through their visibility, rearranged mass-media iconography and commonplace ideas about gendered bodies and athletic performances to such an extent that five years later, in 2001, a young Hispanic boy from a poor part of Southern California declared to us during focus group interviews that he liked Marion Jones the best, because she looked like she "could protect" him. At the same time, a fifth-grade African-American boy from a working-class neighborhood in Southern California would tell us that Jeanette Lee could "kick his ass in a game of pool," and numerous young males from a more well-off school told us that they "admired" Chastain's "athleticism" and "confidence." The times, they are a-changin'. But how much? And in what contexts? And at what price, to whom?

The 1996 Olympics marked a positive turning point for a number of activist struggles. The American women came through in part because of more industry support and the greater allocation of resources for which feminists have long argued and won gold medals in basketball, soccer, softball, synchronized swimming, and gymnastics, serving as the catalyst for, in the first three cases, the later development of women's professional sport leagues. The women's 4×100-meter relay team won gold in track, while Amy Van Dyken won four medals in swimming. But just as significant as the winning of gold medals was the national interest in the stories of Mary Decker Slaney,[12] diver Mary Ellen Clark (a platform diver who suffers from a fear of heights), and Jackie Joyner-Kersee even though these women didn't win gold, giving credence to the long alternative sports tradition primarily promulgated by women's physical educators that argues that winning isn't everything.[13] The stage was set like never before for women's sports to be implemented as a vehicle for some women's advancement. It came to serve, as will be argued later, as a necessary if somewhat disguised vehicle for a feminist agenda that had been widely discredited in the mainstream press by this time. Sport became an unlikely form of stealth feminism.

But why women, why 1996? What social forces were responsible for this change? Who put the media "on notice"? Why did it respond? Why, after decades of being ignored and/or ridiculed, were female athletes suddenly the focus of national adoration? What was responsible for the sudden interest in and support of athletic women?

## Just Sell It: The Times, They Are A-Changin'

It started with just a whisper at first, a few hints. As always, on the level of mass public consciousness, we heard it from Nike first, in the spring of 1996: "If you let me play / I will like myself more / I will have more self-confidence / I will suffer less depression / I will be 60 percent less likely to get breast cancer / I will be more likely to leave a man who beats me / I will be less likely to get pregnant before I want to / I will learn what it means to be strong / If you let me play sports." Nike's "if you let me play" advertising campaign was the first nationwide, mass-media spot to call attention to what female athletes, and those who did

Got milk? Nikki McKray, Lisa Leslie, and Sheryl Swoopes show their celebrity status, *Condé Nast Sports and Fitness for Women* (May/June 1999).

research on them, had known for more than a century. Sports helps with self-confidence. Playing sports is good for your health.[14] No kidding.

By the early '90s, corporations like Nike had begun to capitalize on discourses of individual choice, determination, upward mobility if one works hard enough, and the largely unheard arguments made by physical-fitness educators, coaches, and athletes themselves for years about the benefits of sports for women. In 1994 the dollar sales of women's athletic footwear topped men's for the first time, and in 1995 women spent $6 billion compared to men's $5.6.[15] Advertisers responded in kind, taking up the cause of female athletes and the empowerment rhetoric that they imagined would extend sales to their target demographic even further. As Jere Longman noted, "as women have moved out of the home and into the workplace, their purchasing power has grown, and with it the fortune of female athletes."[16] This capitalization on a newly dollared demographic—increased awareness of Title IX and the public response to these advertising campaigns—helped catapult the female athlete into her current iconic status.

Facing a stagnant market in men's sports equipment and apparel, the sports industry found a new frontier, a largely untapped domestic consumer market in women, and that market needed a new image to consolidate it. Women, who had been athletes for a long time but largely ignored as such, could both easily supply that image and respond to it with consumer dollars.[17] Indeed, as Donna Lopiano noted in an article discussing Olympics coverage of women, until 1996 the sports press dedicated only 10 percent of television hours to women's sports. More column inches were devoted to horses than women. But since the early '90s "major corporations like State Farm, General Motors, Visa, and Kodak are using female athletes in large-scale advertising and promotional campaigns."[18] Corporate support, Lopiano argued, would lead to more affirmative coverage of women in the 1996 Games, which would have larger social consequences:

> through the coverage of female athletes in the 1996 Games, we'll see
> a more balanced picture of women in sports—our achievements,
> our failures, our joys, and our fears. We'll see great women athletes
> blow away the mist of prejudice and stereotype with their spirit, skill,
> persistence, and courage. We'll see the true story of women in sports.[19]

For the most part, Lopiano was right. Although it is characteristic of writers in academic circles to uniformly criticize corporations and corporate capitalism in all situations at all times, in this case it was corporate America that seemed to have the most positive influence on opportunity for and social acceptance of female athletes. The visibility given to female athletes and to other groups previously marginalized by race, for instance, was dependent upon the need to cultivate new markets and had the effect of bringing the previously marginalized into the cultural center in terms of our day-to-day iconography, what people see.[20] This has the effect of normalization: the "margins" became a part of everyday American life.[21]

Due in part to this corporate embrace, by the time of the 1996 Olympics, audiences had already been primed to see female athletes in roughly the same terms as males and to extend the positive qualities of female athletes to women in general. In fact, while once female athletes were dismissed as "not serious," "too masculine," or were assumed to be "dykes,"[22] the summer of 1999 found a nation captivated by a women's soccer team—so captivated that the covers of *Sports Illustrated, Newsweek, People,* and *Time* were simultaneously graced by stunning images of the athletes—a few of them sweaty and not in "babe" mode—from their Women's World Cup victory. The Saturday afternoon of the match garnered major network coverage and Nielsen ratings higher than those for NBA finals. Those of us unfortunate enough to be watching from home saw the unprecedented spectacle of a sold-out Rose Bowl and a rowdily mixed crowd of all ages, genders, and races, 94,000 strong, giving it up for America's new heroes, screaming their lungs out in support of not football or basketball players but female athletes, women.

It was a sight we never thought we'd see in our lifetimes. And maybe it was this sense of wonder and vindication that explained our tears that afternoon when Briana Scurry's save and Brandi Chastain's final kick changed the history of women's sports—and we believe women's lives in general—for a long time. Maybe that explained the tears of a a sixty-year-old retiree who erupted in jubilation a few minutes after the game, saying, "Did you see that? Did you see all those people? Cheering for women? Women?! The world will not be able to forget this!"[23]

In the days following the match, news commentators debated the question of whether the support for the Women's World Cup was an anomaly, a one-time success based on clever marketing, or whether it indicated real change in public respect and support for female athletes. In the media hub-bub, this debate was part of the radio call-in shows on which we were asked to speak about the implications of the World Cup for the future of women's sports. Some detractors argued that our nation will never (despite the success of the WNBA) support a women's professional league, that women just aren't as interesting players, and that when the American consumer shells out their hard-earned dollars

We rule: ad for Women's World Cup, *Sports Illustrated for Women* (June 1999).

for sports entertainment, it will never be for girls. We argued otherwise, and the amazingly affirmative calls that followed those of the naysayers indicated that our cultural landscape has in some ways shifted for good.

The attitudes of these radio-show callers marked such a radical departure from similar shows even two years earlier that we were almost convinced that our time as female athletes has finally arrived. The callers were still all men, but rather than the standard "men are stronger than women" and "women athletes will never be on the same level as men" that characterized the conversations two years earlier, this time the callers chimed a different tune: a soccer dad called in to testify how wonderful soccer was for his daughters, how it taught them competitiveness, teamwork, and a strong sense of themselves. A diehard sports fan from Georgia commented that the women's teams at the University of Georgia were uniformly better and more exciting to watch than the men's.[24] A schoolteacher called in to say how he'd seen sports change and empower his female students' lives, transforming them from shy, withdrawn girls hesitant to take part in group conversations and activities to self-confident speakers who asserted themselves in every context.

Despite a media thread that focused on Chastain's victory gesture of stripping off her team jersey in the manner of men's soccer teams—which, because women are "different," exposed her Nike sports bra and "we can't have that" (this thread conveniently ignored the fact that many of us wear our exposed sports bras to the grocery store all the time)—most of the cultural conversations following the World Cup seemed to reflect nothing short of a real love for women's soccer. Such adoration is usually reserved for the baseball or football team with whom one is on the most intimate terms, whose every action dominates one's heart, mind, and imagination, like Nick Hornby's beloved Arsenal in *Fever Pitch*. The astonishing *Newsweek* cover that featured Chastain in all of her muscular glory, on her knees in joy, fists raised in victory, biceps and shoulders as chiseled as her face, full of exhaustion and triumph and amazed relief, seemed to give license to all women's sports fans: this was it, this was serious, this was sport in all of its emotion and soaring. Women's sports were now iconic: Wheaties boxes were quickly produced featuring each of the World Cup starters, the first time soccer players of any gender have been featured; Gatorade featured a competition between Mia Hamm and Michael Jordan in various sports, set to the tune of "Anything You Can Do, I Can Do Better," that showed Mia getting the best of Michael at practically every turn. Girls and women aren't weak little things anymore, get it? Women's sports aren't on the margins anymore. The "women we love who kick ass" had seemingly arrived.

For those of us who had been athletes for a long time, it was a bit like what feminist rocker/actress Courtney Love said of her sudden spate of magazine cover appearances in the late '90s: that after years of invisibility or vilification, "it's like being popular all of a sudden. You know?"[25]

After years of women being told that they are too muscular or too big, too aggressive and domineering, our bodies and the attitudes that go with them have become more accepted and even at times glorified, offered in the mass media as models of strength, possibility, and personal integrity for young women, an example of our growing power in the world. How could the situation be any better? Powerful body = cultural power, the equation goes. We're hooked.[26]

## Looking Too Good, Maybe

So, yea sports! Yea the cultural acceptance of strong women! Yea improved self-esteem for girls, the opportunity to learn competitive skills that might be transferable to the business world, sports showing us there's no limit to what we can do. Things are looking pretty good for girls, it seems. Now we can have it both ways. According to Gabrielle Reece, the poster girl for the new version of athletic femininity, "I get out of bed, throw on the Lycra, pull my hair back, lace up my shoes and oh-so-deliberately apply my lashes. Then I go out and spike the ball into my opponent's face. This open display of schizophrenia is fun. Men aren't so lucky. They generally aren't allowed to wear lipstick with their work suits."[27] We have it all! Things are looking very good. Too good.

Throughout the mass media, sports and the body image that goes with it have taken a turn beyond validating women's athletic participation. Recently sports and working out have been offered as a cure-all for systematic equalities of all kinds. Mass media focused on sports presents a world in which systematic inequalities don't exist. It's a level playing field and we're all out there doing our best. Sports are the great equalizer, the inclusive haven that now gives us all a leg up, the thinking goes, an equal chance to strut our stuff. Whatever race, whatever gender, we all can play and reap the benefits.

"I can do anything I want to do," a young Hispanic girl tells the viewer forcefully in a late-'90s Nike television spot, which, with striking, inclusive images of mixed races, genders, and ages, presents athletics as an arena in which all personal pains, fears, and inadequacies are overcome. But what these images neglect to analyze is the very real lack of opportunity that a young Hispanic woman born in the inner cities of America might likely face—a poor school district, low graduation rates, and poor access to health care, solid wages, and affordable, safe housing. What might she feel about herself and her life chances—no matter how great her legs are from playing sports while she can? All social problems cannot be solved by simply lacing up the latest Nike shoe named after a woman, such as the Air Skeek named for skier Picabo Street, and getting your body out to the slopes or the soccer field or the track.[28]

There is a logical leap from the premise that participation in sports provides positive experiences that will build character and opportunity to the conclusion that having a strong body will automatically get a girl (or a boy, for that matter) a significant place in the culture. All this yea-saying, which presents itself as a solution for political problems like structural inequality, has an unmarked, profoundly political dimension. It makes some of us feel good. It makes some of us feel great. That's how it works. Whoo-hoo! You, go, girl! But it's a double-edged sword, a pill that might kill, and a recent turn in athletic advertising makes these darker political implications explicit. Lately athletic female participation has been joined to the political discourse of women's rights, suggesting that to further our position and power as women in this culture, all we need to do is work out. Forget political activism of the type that got us Title IX in the first place—girls just wanna get pecs. Leslie has made the argument elsewhere that physical activity such as women's bodybuilding can function as a form of political activism, a way of developing self and consciousness that can lead to larger, structural changes, and heal past abuses, but she was careful to emphasize that these individual forms of development could not take the place of organized, concrete activisms of the kind that led to the implementation of Title IX, which was a major factor behind the fact that so many women today do have the possibility to work out and play sports.[29] Contemporary advertisements—as well as magazine articles, books, sports videos, and other forms of mass media—make the argument that working out is the only form of activism we need.

A Reebok insert that appeared in the February 1998 issue of *Condé Nast Sports for Women* is a striking example in this trend. The insert is a booklet of fourteen pages and comes with a women's training CD for the PC. The first image on the insert is a female hand, white against a black background, fingers raised as if to take an oath. The text, in red, is spread across her knuckles: "please repeat after me." Inside, a woman in an orange Reebok bra top lifts weights, and on the facing page the words, "I take me, to have and to hold, from this day forward, for better or worse, for richer, for poorer, in sickness and in health, to love and to cherish, till death do us part, so help me, God. I do."

This woman-affirming parody of the conventional wedding vows is followed by political discourse that borrows from both the Declaration of Independence and the liberalism found in that milestone treatise of first wave feminism, the Declaration of Sentiments: "WE HOLD THESE TRUTHS TO BE SELF-EVIDENT: that all women are created equal and independent, that from that equal creation they derive rights inherent and inalienable, among which are the preservation of life, liberty, and the pursuit of happiness." Clearly, according to the ad, those rights and the pursuit of happiness are bound up not with race, class, gender, or sexuality inequality, but with the liberation of working out, for the following page, interspersed with more images of women running and walking, says, "on my honor I will try to make my health a priority, make it to the gym, vote women into office, balance work, kids, relationships, and all my other roles without losing my mind and to live by the MAKE-MYSELF-HAPPY LAW."

What looks like a kind of politics, voting women into office, is undercut by the insistence that making oneself happy means going to the gym in addition to balancing traditional roles. Happiness, self-fulfillment, and progressive politics come from working out—get it? More shiny images, more cleverly appropriated political texts, and then the caveat, a woman kickboxing to the text of "I have the right not to remain silent, to put myself first, be sexy, intelligent, and tough all at the same time. To be rich and happy. Anything I desire may not be held against me. Do you understand these rights?"

Well, yes, actually we think we do: the concept of rights has become a matter of isolated self-fulfillment for those who are most privileged to attain it, which keeps some women working on themselves (becoming the icons who "have it all") rather than working together to really change anything (everything's great, what do we need to change?). Never mind attacks on welfare mothers and their children, a lack of resources in inner-city schools, a lack of safe and affordable housing, racist attacks on immigrant women of color, attacks on affirmative action and abortion legislation, and the fact that many inner-city women will never get to see a university where fights over Title IX will be played out. Some of us get to have muscles now. Those some of us—often white, middle-class women—get to be tough chicks, tough and sexy at the same time. We've got it all. We understand that the desires the ad seems to applaud—the expansion and development of the individual woman—is undercut by the all-too-familiar, not very individual script haunting the ad's surface: a happiness that is dependent upon privilege, wealth, and following the gender script of the '90s, femininity Nike/Reebok/Gabby style "women we love who kick ass." So are all women really getting the chance to kick ass? And when they do, are they really getting embraced equally within the public eye? We wish we could be as reassured as most of the other female athletes and their fans around us seem to be and that we could rest easy that our cultural moment has come.

But we can't. Despite its triumphant, inspirational rhetoric, the affirmative model Nike and others offer is no magic pill that does away with the reality of inequitable conditions in a single stroke, particularly since these images are circulating in a material reality in which many inner-city students of color might face dilapidated schools or death more easily than gaining access to sport.[30] And, for those who will go on to secondary schools, 90 percent of secondary and postsecondary institutions are still not in accordance with Title IX. Sports do help women develop competitive and cooperative skills that may serve them well in the business world later—if they make it there. And even when they do, a different return on their investment still might occur given race, class, and gender inequalities.[31] The level playing field is still a-ways away. But that's not evident from the pumped-up rhetoric of the advertisements.

Nike, of course, is an easy target. A 1999 ad campaign plays to what third wave hip-hop feminist Joan Morgan addresses as a central concern for young women today in her book *When the Chickenheads Come Home to Roost: My Life as a Hip-Hop Feminist:* our negotiations with beauty culture and the difficulty of balancing feminist ideals with structural realities and personal relationships that are not always amenable to those ideals.[32] An ad placed in *Seventeen* and other young women's magazines shows a little girl in a baseball cap, hand enveloped in a heavy leather baseball glove, and asks, "Will she look at magazines and think she has to be as thin as the models she sees? Think that independence makes her less desirable?" Nike posits sport as the answer to these issues, asserting that "if she plays sports, if she's strong and healthy and self-assured . . . these issues won't bother her at all."

Really? Won't they? Issues like the tyranny of ideal bodies don't just vanish when you start to play sports. Indeed, many women argue that the "babe factor" in sports, the controversy surrounding the marketing of female athletes according to their physical appearance rather than their performance, just reinforces traditional roles and creates yet another oppressive body ideal for girls to follow. Some feminists, for instance, criticize Brandi Chastain's nude posed-with-a-soccer-ball-for-cover shot in a recent men's magazine and are critical of the way "the babe factor" (the fact that most of the players were attractive in conventionally feminine ways) contributed to the success of the Women's World Cup. Female athletes, they argue, still have to rely on their looks rather than their skills to get attention or, alternatively, only certain "appropriately" feminine female athletes seem to draw the commercialized benefits of that attention. Some see the sexualization of women's sports as a betrayal of the benefits sport has to offer girls and women. Joanna Cagan writes that for her, "in a lifetime of fluctuating self-esteem and crippling body image, sports has facilitated the few times when I am too happy and preoccupied to run my normal painful analysis of my body and how it rates on the old sexy-meter that drives Hollywood and New York City. . . . If I pick up a glove, a bat, a basketball, I am judged on what I do with them—not, for once, on how I look using them." Cagan sees the media hype related to the 1999 Women's Soccer World Cup as a betrayal of that appearance-exempt space and writes that "in the end, I was forced to witness one of the painful lessons of high school come true on the world stage: the pretty girls always win."[33] This debate will be taken up in some detail in chapter 4.

The athletes themselves, such as soccer player Brandi Chastain and volleyball player Gabrielle Reece, tend to see physical appearance as a marketing asset that is not necessarily gender-specific, pointing to ways the male body has itself become sexualized and commodified in recent media culture, and the ways male athletes are increasingly valued for aesthetic reasons as well as for their athletic successes. When Leslie asked Women's Professional Billiard Association champion "Black Widow" Jeanette Lee how she would respond to the argument that individual female athletes who use sex appeal as a promotional strategy hurt female athletes as a whole by reinforcing the cultural assumption that women are of interest primarily as sex objects, not athletes, she said,

I've heard this quite a bit. . . . I've always felt proud to be a woman athlete and felt that my being myself is sometimes construed as intentionally using sex to sell myself. . . . I believe sexiness come from your self. . . . I'm being me, and if that's sexy, well fine, but I'm not going to try to be extremely conservative when it's not who I am. . . . We all come from different places that make us who we are. . . . I think women should be themselves and respected for that whether they are sexy or not and people shouldn't automatically assume that our sexiness is a promotional strategy. . . . I know that when I dress sexy, I don't do it thinking, "Oh, I'll wear this dress because it's going to help me with promotion.". . . I wear it because I love the outfit and I feel attractive in it and it's fun to feel good about yourself. . . . If other people chose not to believe that, I feel sad that they are so closeminded that they feel they can't believe a person's honest opinion.[34]

Lee articulates an opinion on the question that is repeated again and again by athletes of her generation. To explain why that opinion is much more than simple naivete or lack of the proper feminist consciousness, we need to explore, in a more complicated fashion, what it means to be a woman asking feminist questions in the twenty-first century. We need to take into account not just the feminist conversations and assumptions that characterize academic circles, but also the contradictory demographic context in which these athletes find themselves. In this cultural moment when corporate outsourcing and downsizing have lessened the overall wage gap for young women and men, and everyone is enjoined to "sell themselves" on the market to "make it," and in a sports world where resources are still skewed toward men, both factors have a powerful effect on female athletes and their views about self-promotion.

## The Third Wave: Negotiating the "F" Word in a Postfeminist Context

To fully answer Cagan's objections and Lee's defense of the sexualization in women's sports, it is necessary to give a brief account of what we mean by "third wave" feminism in this historical moment. While feminism has always fought to establish itself in a hostile context, some historical periods, like that following the civil rights movements in the nineteenth century and the late 1960s, seem more amenable to movements seeking to accomplish social change. What are normally referred to as the "first" and "second" waves of feminism in this country came to being in just such periods, while the feminism of a younger generation sometimes referred to as the "third wave" struggles to articulate itself in a quite different context. We say "sometimes" because it is often not clear that there exists any unified or even fragmentary movement for feminist social change among young women today, a period in which feminism is routinely referred to as the "f" word and seen as a dated concept. Feminists of the second wave find that the very young women they would seek to teach roll their eyes at the mention of words like *patriarchy* or *oppression* and take the ambivalent posture that has come to be characterized as "I'm not a feminist, but . . ."

The '90s was a rough decade for feminism, marked by what Susan Faludi named "backlash" and characterized by a demographic and generational shift that highlighted the sometimes stark differences between feminist women of the baby boom and their Generation X and Y daughters.[35] These generations, the first to reap the benefits of their mothers' activism, have often taken feminist ideas and struggles for granted, but, as Joan Morgan writes, "ironically, reaping the benefits of our foremothers' struggle is precisely what makes their brand of feminism so hard to embrace."[36]

A black feminist whose birthdate places her on the cusp of Generation X and the boomers, Morgan identifies herself as "a child of the post–Civil Rights, post-feminist, post-soul hip hop generation" (21). This generation, Morgan writes, is sometimes complacent: "it's up to our elders, we figure, to create a bandwagon fly enough for us to jump on" (22). That maybe second wave feminism doesn't seem "fly enough," that it is, Morgan writes, "a bad-ass bolt of cloth [that we've got to] fashion . . . to our own liking," means that we've got something to fashion in the first place because of the rights second wave feminism gave us. We are, writes Morgan, "the daughters of feminist privilege. . . . We walk through the world with a sense of entitlement that women of our mothers' generation could not begin to fathom. . . . Sexism may be a very real part of my life but so is the unwavering belief that there is no dream I can't pursue and achieve simply because 'I'm a woman'" (59).

Third wave feminism is a product of that contradiction between the continuation of sexism and an increasingly realizable feminist dream that today many women do have more opportunity.[37] This changed social context calls for a feminism that, in Morgan's words, "fucks with the grays" because those grays mark the ambivalent, slippery social conditions third wave feminism has to negotiate. In order to be effective, third wave feminism must be like the hip-hop music Morgan loves, full of breaks and samples from earlier vibes, layered with many voices, with backbeats and counterpunches and flows and grooves that don't always move in a straight line, full of contradiction and melodic duels. "I discovered," Morgan writes, "that mine was not a feminism that existed comfortably in the black and white of things," because she found that her experience left her with truths that didn't fit easily into her mother's feminist models. For instance, "I got my start as a writer," she says, "because I captured the sexual attention of a man who could make me one. It was not the first time my externals would bestow me with such favors. It would certainly not be the last" (56).

Her mother's feminism, Morgan thinks, doesn't allow for the complication of men who do real, concrete things to facilitate women's careers, but do so because of a sexual relationship with or attraction to that woman. While such an exchange would be an anathema to some second wave models, the third wave might find it a provocative contradiction that can be mined. While Morgan sees (somewhat problematically) the second wave of feminism as reducible to "the 'victim' (read women)/ 'oppressor' (read men) model," which she says "denies the very essence of who we are" because we live with a privilege our mothers fought for, she also points to the contemporary need for "a feminism brave enough to fuck with the grays" (59). She and other young women characteristically call for a feminism that can answer "decidedly un-P.C. but very real questions" such as

> can you be a good feminist and admit out loud that there are things
> you kinda dig about patriarchy? Am I no longer down with the cause
> if I admit that while total gender equality is an interesting intellectual
> concept, it doesn't do a damn thing for me erotically? Are we no longer
> good feminists, not to mention nineties supersistas, if the a.m.'s wee
> hours sometimes leave us tearful and frightened that achieving all our
> mothers wanted us to—great educations, careers, financial and emo-
> tional independence—has made us wholly undesirable to the men
> who are supposed to be our counterparts?[38]

While Morgan's model presupposes heterosexuality, she is coming from a black feminist perspective that is reluctant to "take sides" against the black men she sees as brothers who are also severely oppressed because of race. Her subject position and questions make visible some of the fault-lines we most need to negotiate as feminists living in the new millennium.

Part of the social context we negotiate today is a context in which the predominant popular and some academic paradigms about gender based in the "hard" sciences are swinging away from the social constructivism that characterized the 1970s, '80s, and much of the '90s back toward genetics and biological determinism.[39] Differences between the sexes are once again routinely asserted as innate ("Men are from Mars, women are from Venus," remember?), and this assumption marks many current theories about gender and its impact on social problems. Three recent, influential, and reactionary books on women and feminism offer a glimpse of a cultural trend that feminists of all generations need to consider: a return and a seriousness granted to arguments that rely on biological determinism and that advocate reactionary ways of life. Wendy Shalit's *A Return to Modesty,* for instance, advocates a desexualization and return to traditional courtship roles in response to what she sees as her generation's most pressing problems, correctly identified by feminists:

> I had heard of those who claimed that being a woman was not all fun and games, but those people were called feminists, and as every budding conservative knows, feminists exaggerate . . . but the feminists were right . . . all round me, at the gym and in my classes, I saw stick-thin women suffering from anorexia. . . . I began hearing stories of women raped, stories filled with too much detail and sadness to be invented. . . . A lot of young women are trying to tell us that they are very unhappy: unhappy with their bodies, with their sexual encounters, with the way men treat them on the street—unhappy with their lives.[40]

Shalit wants "conservatives to take the claims of feminists seriously," and she wants feminists to "consider whether the cause of all this unhappiness might be something other than patriarchy," because this unhappiness is the case even on the most nonsexist of college campuses. She writes, "now that we have wiped our society clean of all traces of patriarchal rules and codes of conduct, we are finding that the hatred of women may be all the more in evidence" (14). By "patriarchal" Shalit seems to mean "traditional," for she advocates a return to romance and traditional courtship between the sexes to address this hatred, which necessitates, she thinks, a return to "modesty" for women and to the sex-only-within-heterosexual-marriage model of sexuality. Views such as Shalit's—which generate much media buzz—are part of the hostile, antifeminist social context that feminism has to negotiate today. It cannot be assumed that her assumptions—which seem absurd from any kind of feminist perspective—have disappeared from American culture.

Similarly to the reactionism of Shalit, F. Carolyn Graglia attributes most cultural problems and unhappinesses in women's lives to the feminism that expanded the workplace. In *Domestic Tranquility: A Brief Against Feminism,* she argues that what feminism wanted to do was destroy the nuclear family by getting women into the workforce, and that forcing women to work undermines their "natural propensity for nurturing." Feminism wanted women to be the same as men by getting them to work and thereby deprived women of their greatest "propensities and gifts." Feminism, not the larger culture, denigrated the role of the traditional homemaker. Graglia baldly advocates a blind return to conventional gender roles (as defined by white middle-class norms) as the solution to violence against women and women's exhaustion and unhappiness.[41]

Another "women's issue" that is being taken up by writers from a reactionary perspective is girls' and women's unhealthy focus on body image and appearance, and this issue has been well documented. On October 20, 1998, in New York City, two major corporations, Nike and Procter and Gamble (Secret antiperspirant), and an organization, the Partnership for Women's Health at Columbia University, announced a social initiative, "Helping Girls Become Strong Women," in response to an on-line survey conducted by *Seventeen* magazine and *Ladies Home Journal.* The survey stated that 50 percent of 1,100 girls polled reported feeling depressed once a week or more often; 29 percent felt somewhat or very uncomfortable with their body image; and close to 50 percent were unhappy with their appearance. But the usual feminist critique—that young women are uncomfortable because of unrealistic images of beauty in the mass media—is being challenged in an influential new book whose emphasis on biology is a corollary to the arguments advanced by Graglia and Shalit.

In *Survival of the Prettiest: The Science of Beauty,* Harvard psychologist Nancy Etcoff suggests that a preference for beauty (defined as the media images present it) is universal and is hard-wired into the human brain: "the idea that beauty is unimportant or a cultural construct is the real beauty myth." She argues that beauty has a survival value, and that positive response to beauty is a biological adaptation shaped by natural selection. The prettier are treated better, end of story. Echoing some of Joan Morgan's concerns, in her review of *Survival of the Prettiest* in *Spin,* rock journalist Kim France asks, "Am I the only right-thinking, Camille Paglia–hating, modern feminist chick who has long suspected [the feminist critique that the emphasis on beauty as a cultural, corporate construct] just wasn't so? . . . It's far more troubling to consider that beauty may be a more valuable asset than a Ph.D in comparative studies." These questions, this ideological climate, and our own relationships to cultural images and biological arguments is precisely what third wave feminists have to negotiate today. Due to their popularity we can't just laugh and dismiss these arguments as irrelevant, for they inform the contexts of our lives. Most crucial to our purposes here, the newly iconic image of the female athlete is one of the few sites of resistance against this trend. The image is one of the few spaces where, unlike elsewhere in the media, female masculinity (the "gender continuum" perspective in which women are from Mars, Venus, and everywhere in between, as are men) is validated rather than ignored or repressed with a too-easy insistence on essential sexual difference (this point is developed further in chapter 3).[42]

Athleticism can be an activist tool for third wave feminists and can have important social consequences. Today, women nationwide are participating in classes like kickboxing, spinning, rock-climbing, and boxing, relegating to the cultural dustbin mythologies of the "weaker" sex and assumptions of female incompetence.[43] Any day you can walk into your local gym and see the women sweating alongside the men and walking in the same proud way, owning their bodies like never before. Since the 1996 Olympics and national interest in women's sports, the WNBA is enjoying limited mainstream success, and national attention has turned toward women's college basketball. Several women's sports magazines were launched to immediate acclaim. In the excitement and media hype that followed the World Cup, it was easy to become convinced that women's negative experiences in the world of sport were now historical, a part of earlier attitudes and times. It is much more exciting, empowering, much more comforting to believe that everything has changed unequivocally for the best, that the problems had vanished in the wave of rapt faces gathered to cheer the U.S. Women's Soccer team that hot afternoon in July 1999. It is much more comforting, but . . .

## Contradictions for Third Wave Feminists in Sport

From the rapt faces of girls (and boys) adoring their new sport heroes to the booty call on MTV to the WNBA's insistence on the traditional married lives of its players, the third wave is about negotiating a whole lot of contradictory things. Despite the hope and joy generated by this latest turn in the history of women's sports, another story was being forgotten in the glow of the television cameras and pro-girl Gatorade ads and *Newsweek* magazine covers. This was a dangerous forgetting, one that threatens to make all the positive chatter about women's sports into that—just chatter. While sports are indisputably a positive source of strength and self-development for girls, they can accomplish this only if the environment in which female athletes throw their javelins, kick their soccer balls, and swim their fast and furious laps is an environment that respects girls and takes them seriously as athletes.

Here's where the contradictions begin, and worlds and conversations and social discourse collide. As theorists, we are trained to ask questions about social institutions, our social practices, the ways we live our lives. But we are encouraged to write about these questions in abstract terms only the specialist can understand so that the discussion takes place only in a very limited context, working from a set of assumptions that is highly critical. From this point of view, the evolution of women's sports is often suspect, seen as a cultural form that encourages girls to adopt the self-destructive, instrumental, win-at-all-costs model of men's sports. Women who go to gyms are slaves to the new beauty ideal, that of the athletic body. We're just creating another impossible standard against which girls will measure themselves and find themselves wanting.

Unlike some of our academic feminist colleagues not in the sport field, however, we are also athletes, and have been so all our lives. This means we have a problem with abstract arguments about women's sports, because we've spent our lives doing them, not just talking about them. It's harder to make generalizations about the destructiveness of the sport beauty ideal when we know that our gym time, time running the trails, or time spent coaching and competing in powerlifting meets are some of the most meaningful moments of our lives. This means we can't be critical in the same distanced ways. But neither can we simply sing the praises of sport, as if all we need to do is get girls out there kicking the soccer ball or doing the slopes or softball fields and all of our problems will be solved. Both sides of the argument, the world of the academic critique and the world of the Nike ad, are dangerously incomplete. And we mean danger in the most literal sense.

The story of Danielle, a college senior at Loyola Marymount College in Southern California, most clearly shows what we mean.[44] The oldest daughter in an African-American family with four children, Danielle started running at the age of eight. Both her parents were athletes, and they encouraged her. At first sports were fun for Danielle and often served as an escape from pressures and conflicts associated with family and school. Her initial sports years, which involved daily running workouts and training with weights, invigorated her, made her feel "like I could kick some ass, you know, strong, like I was part of the world and had a place in it." But as the years wore on, due to questionable coaching practices and cultural and internal pressures to maintain an ideal body image, her sport training and competing made her feel debilitated and weak, on both literal and metaphorical levels.

A cross-country runner and 400-meter sprinter in track, Danielle described year-round practices both of sprint and distance types, sometimes extending to four hours each day. She and her fellow athletes were often referred to as "horses" by their coaches, she said, and their training reflected this same dehumanizing spirit. By the time she was sixteen, her body was wracked. She described coaches' pressures to train and compete even when she was in excruciating pain, coaches who would make arguments about needing points to win even when faced with an athlete who was clearly breaking down, whose well-being seemed almost irrelevant to them in the overriding focus on the win. Danielle described being "bruised from the inside out," where the tissue of her hip would not heal, developing arthritis in all of her joints, and being diagnosed with ulcerative colitis at the age of sixteen. The latter condition still plagues her badly enough at her current age of twenty-two that she faces either colon removal or intensive drug and steroid treatments within the next year. The chronic exhaustion she developed as a secondary symptom of the colitis has made her feel anything but strong.

In addition to an emphasis on overtraining, Danielle told the all-too-familiar story of coaches who felt authorized to invade the boundaries of her private life. She recounted one practice in which her coach publicly chastised her for dating an Asian boy, yelling derogatory slurs about her body and boyfriend out loud in front of the track and football teams.

She reported coaches frequently calling or dropping by her house to monitor her activities, and a near-constant focus on her body, sexuality, and weight. Basic human activities such as eating or dating were rigorously policed, making her feel dirty, guilty, self-conscious, and uncertain of her own opinions or rights.

While sports, as a recent Nike ad promises, "can make us happy to be exactly who we are," such self-acceptance is possible only under safe conditions that do not characterize many sport (or societal) environments today. When asked if she was singled out for such treatment, Danielle reported that while the coaches did not treat all athletes in the same way, it did happen to a large group of them, largely those seen as having the most athletic potential. She finished her high school years as an athlete feeling mentally, emotionally, and physically drained, a ghost of her earlier confident, more fun-loving self. It is a story we have heard far too many times to believe that hers is an exceptional case, and it's a story we've lived to some extent ourselves.

While research has shown that sport can function as a bolster for low self-esteem, an aspect of treatment for depression, and as a form of recovery from disease and even domestic violence and abuse, what has not yet been made clear is that it is precisely this group of athletes—those from abuse backgrounds, and those who suffer from low self-esteem and/or depression—who are perhaps most at risk for overtraining and psychological manipulation from coaches. Similarly, sport is potentially affirmative for those who are underprivileged by race and class and also for many young athletes who are lesbian or gay and are searching for a safe place away from parental and peer rejection. Sport is a possible arena for affirmative feedback and valuation based on the athletes' athletic performance, excellence that can sometimes work to mitigate against the other forms of devaluation. This makes athletes suffering from forms of devaluation—abuse, poverty, racism, homophobia—even more invested than others in their performances. Like the eating disorders that are sometimes an occupational hazard of appearance-based sports like figure skating, gymnastics, long-distance running, or even swimming, sport training itself can bring an illusory sense of control to the athlete, who uses the regimented nature of her training to compensate for the unpredictable violence around her. Those who are most devalued by the world around them may be most likely to orchestrate their athletic participation in such a way that it becomes obsessive and subject to exploitation by coaches. In a world where you are "only as good as your last race," athletes with such backgrounds are likely to overinvest in sport as the sole site of their identity.[45] This tendency combined with coaching philosophies that often emphasize training through pain, disassociating from the body and treating it as a machine, and winning at any cost are a virtual prescription for disaster, for it is precisely those athletes who do not know their own boundaries or limitations who are at most risk for long-term health consequences associated with overtraining.

Danielle's story is not unique. In fact, the main themes of her story—sport as a space that was initially empowering but became increasingly destructive and dangerous to her physical and psychological well-being—resonate in the stories of many athletes. A consistent pattern exists where the sports culture and environment they competed within tore them down instead of building them up. Over and over, women (and men, increasingly) say that a world in which an athlete is only as good as his or her latest win, a world where coaches invade personal boundaries, and where eating and sexuality are constantly monitored is destructive to self-esteem. "He stole our joy," one Kentucky athlete said of her Division I collegiate coach. "He took what had been our life and joy, and made it into dread." Another athlete reported how her 125-pound, 5-foot-5 body was continually an object of public ridicule from coaches and male athletes on her team. She was forced to do extra time on the exercise bike after practice and called "Jackie Snax" whenever a coach or team member saw her put any food in her mouth.[46] Reports of this kind of fixation with their bodies and eating habits, which served to make their experiences in sport much less the affirmative space recent rhetoric claims, were nearly universal among the women I've talked to. In sport as it is practiced nationwide, today, its positive potentials are simply not being fulfilled.

Sport, like any social practice, can be rethought and reconstructed. Social theorists discuss what they call "incorporating practices," actions that become part of bodily memory through repeated performance until they become habitual. Sport, as women's sports marketing now promises, can be practiced in such a way that strength becomes habitual for female athletes, in turn strengthening their sense of achievement and self-esteem.[47] But all too often, the stories we hear about actual athletic practice suggest that sport can also be an unsafe space where destructive incorporating practices become actually enmeshed in our flesh. If athletes train to respond as a machine, disassociating from pain, the consequences are psychological as well as physical, for they learn to respond to external cues to the exclusion of internal, and learn to disregard feelings (or blame themselves for the feelings). Their boundaries violated, their sense of personal rights compromised, athletes will often continue to abuse themselves long after their competing days are done. Here "second wave" feminist concerns about violence and the destructive potentialities of sport practiced in the individualist, competitive model must occupy center stage.

## Women's Athletics as "Stealth Feminism"

Clearly sports are an arena where feminist questions emerge, but it has not always been defined or considered as such. Athletes do not necessarily consider themselves feminists, and many feminists would not consider themselves athletes.[48] Though the female physical educators who largely oversaw women's athletics until the 1980s were reluctant to embrace feminism through the mid-seventies, the cause of women's sports most dear to them was given its biggest boost by the passage of Title IX. The feminist movement was largely responsible for its passage. Female athletes unquestionably needed feminism then. According to sports historian Mary Jo Festle, "passage of Title IX reflected the feminist tenor of the early 1970's . . . the women's liberation movement had begun encouraging women to demand more opportunities, break free of stereotypes, reclaim their bodies, and exercise their strength."[49] In academia, as M. Ann Hall writes,

> In the early days, my colleagues in sport and physical education—both male and female—were almost entirely resistant to feminism. Now, despite pockets of intransigence, there is a small but critical mass of feminist and pro-feminist scholars around the world whose focus is the sociological study of gender and sport . . . [but] my nonsporting feminist colleagues are mostly bemused by my continuing fascination with sport. For them, the highly competitive, sometimes violent, overly commercialized sports world represents distinctly nonfeminist values and is a world they generally ignore. . . . I have seen my task as advocating the inclusion of sport on the feminist agenda and ensuring that feminism is very much part of a sport agenda.[50]

Hall wrote this in 1996. It is arguable that her task has been fairly widely accomplished on the popular level today, though perhaps not in as overt terms as she discusses here. For if female athletes needed feminism in the '70s to get them the resources they needed to play, today—in the context of what happened to feminism in the '90s—the situation is reversed. Now feminism—second wave, third wave, liberal, radical—needs female athletes.

As we have discussed, feminism in the '90s suffered from as much (perhaps even more) bad public relations and media representation as ever, with pundits claiming that younger women disassociate themselves from the term in record numbers. Feminism is that thing you just don't want to be. From the faux feminist posturings of Katie Roiphe and Camille Paglia and the Independent Women's Forum, to the antisex/prosex, antibeauty/probeauty, victim-feminist/power-feminist debates, for many young women, "the word feminist conjures up a very different image from the powerful, exhilarating one it once did."[51] Accusations of feminists as man-haters became louder than ever in the mass media of the mid-'90s, often spoken by women who claimed to be part of a "new feminism" (what "real" feminists like Anna Quindlen called "babe feminism" and Susan Faludi called "pod feminism"). Within the academy, ever more acrimoniously divided by the arguments between feminists who fall under the label of postmodernism or cultural studies feminism and those who follow some form of cultural feminism or identity politics, and by splits along the lines of race, sexuality, class, and even generational lines, there is little sense of unifying cause, direction, or collective movement. Since the 1996 Olympics, female athletes are giving feminism a platform that cuts across the divisions of race, class, and sexual orientation that continue to fracture the movement. As the editors of *Teen People* wrote in October 1998, "few people would argue against school sport."[52] There are increasingly productive alliances of feminist organizations around issues related to women's sports, as well as significant feminist ideology in organizations like the Women's Sports Foundation.[53] Through their work on women's sports issues, every day feminists are advancing their causes in a kind of stealth feminism that draws attention to key feminist issues and goals without provoking the knee-jerk social stigmas attached to the word *feminist,* which has been so maligned and discredited in the popular imagination. At this historical moment, feminists need athletes to help advance agendas such as equal access to institutions, self-esteem for all women and girls, and an expanded possibility and fluidity within gender roles that embraces difference.

Surely, when we visited hundreds of students at schools and found little boys who whipped the WUSA soccer schedule out of their pockets, obsessing about the latest player statistics and whose sport heroes are now Mia Hamm and Julie Foudy, we found boys who have a different view of women than boys in the generation before them (one colleague told me a story about his sons, who were fighting in the backyard over which one of them got to be Brandi Chastain when they were playing soccer). This fact, coupled with the public critique of men's sports as too caught up with money and violence, suggests a drive, at least in some quarters, to embrace women's sports and/or scale back the machismo quotient for male athletes.

It's a reciprocal relationship. Athletes need feminism because some disquieting realities persist between the pro-women's sports rhetoric and the hype, and disparities in resources certainly exist between boys' and girls' sports teams all over America. While many parents and the community at large seem to assume that sports is a golden world unto itself, exempt from the problems that people face elsewhere in their daily lives, the same issues of racism, sexism, heterosexism, and class bias inform what happens in sports, albeit in new or increasingly subtler forms. For women, that means negotiating not only the above, but a set of gender-specific issues first brought to attention by feminists: issues like access, differential resources, devaluing girls and women when compared to boys and men, dealing with being called a lesbian if you get too strong, sexual harassment, and sexual abuse; and women's health issues like the female athlete triad, a syndrome associated with overtraining that is characterized by disordered eating, amenorrhea (cessation of menstruation), and osteoporosis (bone loss).

The 1996 Olympics were a focal point for a growing trend in support of athletic women, a trend that has since grown into successful women's professional leagues, mainstream women's sports magazines, images of athletic women throughout the media, a new athletic body ideal, and a growing industry in literature about women's sports. National attention has turned to women's sports, and sports for women are being offered as the contemporary cure-all of all social problems affecting women. Yet some of the same social problems that affect women in the world at large affect women in sports. We are poised at a time when the phenomenon of women's sports could go either way: it could prove to be a fickle advertising trend, a Band-Aid that directs attention away from the real kinds of activism necessary for social change, or it could build on the activism of women's organizations that have embraced the cause of sports, inaugurating the kinds of change that are claimed for sports in much public health discourse.

In some ways we are hoping for the latter and hope that this means new opportunities for all girls and women, not just a select few. We longed for such a world when we were competing in the '80s and had to use men's cleats and uniforms when asked to suit up for a race. The benefits of sport we experienced—increased self-esteem and well-being, goal-directed achievement, and increased assertiveness—are now well documented and accepted. The reasons why sport has always been a fundamental part of our lives—the ways it makes us feel powerful, part of something larger than ourselves, and that, as "girls, we have the right to be aggressive, not be so ingratiating or quiet, and take up more space"— is now part of public lore. Yet the less publicly discussed and less affirmative aspects of sport made clear by sport sociologists are still part of many women's experiences. There needs to be more to the sport experience than media hype. If it is truly to be a refuge and place of character-building for our daughters, friends, lovers, heroines, acquaintances, and the generations that come after them, we need to move beyond the "sport is great for girls" model and confront some of the darker realities of racism, homophobia, and more, that are part of the sports world. We need to face them with bravery and conviction.

Still, one place that gives us a sense of bravery is the gym, and it was one of the only places that taught us to be strong, to speak out, to push our presence onto the world with a little more assurance than being "nice" allowed. It's one of the places where we feel most safe. It makes other places, like the streets, the academic conference room, feel more safe than they would otherwise. It might be naive to suggest that somewhere among the chin-up and dip bars, the thousands of pounds of iron plates, we found a way to talk back and stand up straight. That amidst the rhythmic clank of metal, mixed with human voices, shouts, grunts, cheers, the churn of elliptical trainers, we found a way to maneuver and think. A world filled with guys and more girls over time, with raucous laughter and certainly sweat, a world where we do worry about our body images and work both to achieve and to mess with socially dictated aesthetic ideals. More than ideals, real violence: bodies are trespassed upon every day. Spit on, beaten up, hit. Raped, cut up, maimed. Starved, built, changed. Female athleticism gives us one story of bodies that fought back. This is one story of what let them survive, about how women's athletics can reconfigure lives. For all its limitations, the gym and spaces like it are places where each day we see women walk in and extend themselves further each time, walk out a bit taller each time. We get stronger and stronger along the way, have the endurance to stay a little longer, and bring that endurance to a struggle for change beyond laptops, ivory towers, bench presses, purely physical strength. We look at the world from a different height, with a different intensity of the blood. Welcome to this world, and a dollhouse it isn't. Sports are great for women. Sports can contribute to social problems. Sports are better for some women than others at this very moment. All sides of the argument are true.

# CHAPTER THREE

## A New Look at Female Athletes and Masculinity

> I do not believe that we are moving steadily toward a genderless society or even that this is a utopia to be desired, but I do believe that a major step toward gender parity, and one that has been grossly overlooked, is the cultivation of female masculinity.
> —Judith Halberstam, *Female Masculinity*

### The Importance of Being "Lester"

Benchplay. Arcs of muscle swung through space. Steel frame on which the bar rests, waiting for weight plates. Thick discs of iron, 45, 35, 25 pounds. Black rubber floor for dug-in feet. Human backs like bridges, the weight of the world between. Humidity, liniment, sweat, grind in the joint, exhalation of shadows more than double in size. With your broad back and hard waist you are under it, raw, a breathing monster slowly lowered to your chest. It weighs much more than you do. Your back is arched, thighs tight. You draw breath until your chest fills. You feel the bar sitting there, waiting, and when it touches your breastplate your breath rushes from your lungs and up weight flies, just wind. This is your home. You are magnificent, every movement smooth. You pad through the gym, shoulders relaxed and tight. You take wide strides; this space is filled with you. This is the one place where you are not seething in smallness, bright hair and smiles, ferocious in your cage.

They watch you go. They shift a little, dart a quick look at their biceps and then back at yours. They step back. When they watch you do pullups, you can see them in the mirror, shaking their heads. Your back is strong, stronger than theirs. They approach you once in a while: "You've got the best arms here." They tell you and let you go. They do not expect you to talk to them, except maybe to tell them what they might do for their triceps. They might ask you to spot them. You are part of an invisible circle where guys trade tips about the development of strength and assist each other there. You are part of the work that's being done there.

I (Leslie) am a powerlifter, classic mesomorph, compact limbs and shoulders as broad as a beam. I train four days a week with a male powerlifter, lifting literally thousands of pounds in a given session. I have a constant low-grade ache in my back and chest. I've been lifting since I was thirteen, but I didn't take it seriously—didn't test my own strength—until seven years ago, when another training partner, Terrance, watched me bench-pressing 135 and scoffed, saying that there was no question I could do much more. Because I am female, I'd always thought that was "a lot of weight for a girl" and never really tried to push beyond it. Terrance didn't see me as male or female, just someone who trained hard. He was right. In a single year, I went from a 135 bench to 185. When Terrance left, I started training with some other guys, Billy and Chris, and it was then that "Lester" made his public debut.

It took me twenty years to become Lester. He'd always been there, from the time I followed my father through house and woods and mountain streams, wanting to do everything he did, so much that my mother got me a toy chainsaw for Christmas to match his. From the time I armwrestled the strongest sixth-grade boy at an assembly in front of the whole school and won. Since I tore out my ponytails and took off my dresses, hiding them at the bottom of my locker while pulling on my best friend's brother's beat-up boy clothes. But Lester was officially named much later, the day I broke the 200-pound barrier on the bench, 200 and then 225. Two hundred is one of those turning points that clearly separate one class of lifter from the next, the men from the boys and certainly the women from the men. It was the day I went from being "strong for a girl" to just plain strong, seen no differently from "them." Not knowing what was coming but willing to try, I sat myself down on the bench that day, flat on my back, pulling myself under the bar with a clean heave. I'd always faltered on this weight, getting it only an inch or so off my chest, like some biological limitation I'd never transgress. But today was different, I could feel it going down. I could feel the bar, the weight on it, but there was the sensation of not feeling it, too. This time, there was no sticking. This time, the weight flew up like it wasn't there, and as I racked it at the top, Billy and Chris roared with joy, jumping up in the air shouting, "Lester! Lester! She's with the big dogs now!" Everyone around us was staring, and I felt years of frustration drop away.

It was a small thing, the shift from Leslie to Lester. A single bench press in a single gym, lost in the backwoods of an upstate New York town. It didn't change the world. It surprised a few people, maybe. It certainly added nothing to any institutional political cause (though it certainly was a kind of body project, like the ones discussed in chapter 4). But I felt inside something, part of something. An acceptance I've never felt in any other place. *This* is who I was, at least partly, that invisible part people didn't usually see, a part that now they had seen and proclaimed it with great joy at high volume. The part of myself I'd always been encouraged to smother, feel ashamed of, tamp down as something monstrous at all costs, brought into the legitimacy of public space.

Intellectually, though, I knew my elation wasn't matched by some thinkers, that what I was feeling would, from that perspective, be a clear indication of backward thinking. A critic who clearly sums up this position is Varda Burstyn in *The Rites of Men: Manhood, Politics, and the Culture of Sport:*

> U.S. culture, influenced by men's culture, is marked by an intense denigration of the "feminine" and its associated qualities of softness, receptivity, cooperation, and compassion. Today's erotic athletic flesh is hard, muscled, tense, and mean. The unquestioning emulation of hypermasculinity by women does not constitute "androgyny" or "gender neutrality," but rather the triumph of hypermasculinism.[1]

Although she agrees that "there is great value for girls and women in learning to be active and instrumental, in reclaiming the active 'masculine' parts of themselves that their historical exclusion from sport was meant to suppress," in her unease with the hypermasculinity of the contemporary "sport nexus," Burstyn misses out on Lester's complicated and contradictory joys. Since Lester is interpretable as an instance of exactly this triumph of hypermasculinity she outlines, or of a woman's misguided identification with "male" values, Burstyn would perhaps critique his production and purpose, and would think my pride in my "hard, muscled, mean" flesh is a tangible sign of a blind internalization of dominant masculine norms and the success of those norms in colonizing women's imaginations. She sees the recent success of women's competitive sports as fatally marred by masculine values, and Lester is linked to them. Burstyn argues that "sport has acted as a political reservoir of anti-democratic and elitist values that coexist with, and have often overwhelmed egalitarian, cooperative, and democratic values." Though she is pro-activity and pro-strength for women, she still somehow associates the former qualities with masculinity and men and the latter qualities with femininity and women, as if it is women's responsibility—since they are somehow "different" than those "naturally" elitist men—to transform rather than fit into the antidemocratic institution of sport. Since, through his acceptance of "masculine" sport values Lester falls in the first category but names a body that is biologically female, h/she can't be accounted for by this position except as evidence (in Burstyn's view) of the way women blindly internalize "male" thinking.[2]

Perhaps our differences in thinking could be to some extent generational, or at least theoretical, for Lester isn't alone. In *Punch: Why Women Participate in Violent Sports*, Tae Kwon Do martial artist Jennifer Lawler writes,

> As an academic feminist, I was aware that the majority of feminists
> would not approve of my enjoyment of aggression. While I grieved
> over my excommunication from cultural feminism—the idea that
> men and women are naturally different and that women must somehow
> remain morally pure, nonviolent, and uncorrupted by a male-dominated
> society—I felt in my heart that I was a truer feminist than many of the
> scholars who disapproved of me and women like me, because I knew
> something they did not: I knew that women had masculine traits they
> could embrace instead of scorn. I knew that by finding and examining
> these traits and accepting them as part of who I was, I could be a fuller,
> more complete *person*—not a woman-victim, not a man wanna-be.[3]

But the form of completeness that Lawler articulates here is not something that cultural sport feminists like Burstyn would endorse, for, by the assumptions of what seems to be the model she relies upon, masculine traits are overly valued by the culture and dangerous, while feminine traits are undervalued and humane.

Fine with me if she disses the system that produces and valorizes guys and their sometimes ridiculous guy culture like that seen on *The Man Show* or in *Maxim* magazine, but here she's also messing with my world. Burstyn addresses the unconscious dimensions of cultural engagement with sport—my engagement with sport—when she argues that contemporary global culture has been constitutively formed by what she calls the "hypermasculine sport nexus." She defines "sport nexus" as "that web of associated and interlocking organizations that includes sports, media, industry, government, public education, and recreation." In her analysis, contemporary sport is "a school for masculinity" that articulates the "relationship between masculinism and capitalism" and shows "how masculine dominance is constructed, embodied, and promoted in the associations, economies, and culture of the sport nexus." Her analysis further shows "how sport . . . generates the ideology of hypermasculinity, an exaggerated ideal of manhood linked mythically and practically to the role of the warrior."[4] But Lester is nothing if not a warrior. The battles he fights are against assumptions of limitation, that I have to be small and self-limiting, self-contained. Though Burstyn doesn't seem to want individual women to be small, she, like the cultural feminists Lawler critiques, requires a "higher" morality from women, arguing that it is women's responsibility (because of their innate difference and "better" natures?) to not embrace the male sport world too fully. But why, by this logic, does she fail to request the same duty from men?

Throughout *The Rites of Men* Burstyn is careful to stress the importance of women's sport participation and need for physical activity to counteract old stereotypes of feminine weakness, but she is critical of competitive athletics in all forms. She sees the recently successful developments in competitive women's sports as fatally imbued with masculine values. As much as I agree with her analysis of the sport nexus and its debilitating effects on all athletes, men and women (indeed, my memoir *Pretty Good for a Girl* is the narrative chronicle of just such effects), at the same time I am a passionate advocate of the sometimes controversial idea that it is a positive cultural development for women to have access to and participate in the kind of "anti-democratic and elitist" formations that the vastly influential sport nexus develops and sustains.[5] Burstyn writes:

> There are indications that the sport-media complex is responding to women athletes and women audiences as a potentially profitable market. This can be seen in the inauguration of two women's professional basketball leagues and the planned launch of a sport magazine for women to be published by *Sports Illustrated*. If such ventures succeed, we must ask to what extent does accepting the values and behaviors of hypermasculine men's culture, embodied in the core men's sports,

strengthen or weaken women and society? There will be no social gain if, through learning the mind set and morality of hypermasculinity, women in effect lend their efforts to its broader perpetuation in the name of gender-neutrality or gender equality. . . . While asserting their right to be physically active and strong and socially instrumental and influential, *women should, nevertheless, be transforming physical culture into one that validates the expressive and cooperative dimensions of existence.* Women need to continue to value those qualities in themselves and in cultural life, rather than abandon them to the hierarchism and violent instrumentality of the dominant sport culture. Perhaps women can contribute to a new definition of instrumentality, one not based on violence or coercion, but on give and take and mutual creation.[6]

Burstyn's writing marks a set of assumptions characteristic of some critiques of sport as well as some popular media discourse today—the idea that it is the female athlete who is (or should be) innately more "cooperative" than her male counterpart, and that the recent high-profile status of elite female athletes contributes to an idealized cultural image of masculinity that should not be emulated by women since that is a form of "selling out" or contributing to a way of being and thinking these critics want changed. It is the female athlete's responsibility, in this view, to provide a counterpoint to the violence of male sport culture. Regardless of whether this is the explicit intention, such arguments lead back to a naturalization of sexual difference and the projection of the traditional feminine on female athletes whose diversities along the spectrum of gender are negated. Lester is criticized, perhaps even disallowed as a blind replication of destructive masculinity. Ironically, and a little tragically, the masculine female athlete, previously the object of persecution in the mass media, is just as likely to be presented as an ideal today. A shot of softball player Crystyl Bustos in the August 2000 *Teen People*, for instance, shows the idealization of a Hispanic, "masculine" woman, who is presented as part of a photo spread on Olympic hopefuls. Because the shot is in black-and-white, it is coded as something to be taken seriously, as a form of art, and this, combined with the lighting, cues the viewer to see her as beautiful. The shot is of her torso and head, and her hair is tied back in a long braid. She's in a tank top and is shot from the side, arm raised so that her softball glove rests on her forehead, bringing the focus to her muscular shoulder and its tattoo, and her well-developed bicep. She looks like she has just paused in the middle of a game, for there are drops of sweat on her shoulder and tricep. She looks straight at the viewer as if she was sizing up the competition, and the play of shadow and light makes her look solid, substantial, both like a statue and vibrantly alive, ready to spring into action. You wouldn't mess with her, but that kind of determination, traditionally coded masculine, isn't presented as aberrant. It is presented as heroic, an ideal, something girls can identify with. That a venue as mainstream as *Teen People* could present an ideal image of a woman like this, while within some feminist arguments a masculine woman like this is criticized, seems to point to limitations in those arguments.

Such dichotomization in thinking about gender has been thoroughly questioned in feminist theory, at least since the mid-1980s, in the work of those thinkers associated with the poststructuralist turn that goes by the name of "gender studies" and is unlike the cultural feminism that often informs "women's studies" and relies on an assumption of sexual difference. Theorists such as Teresa de Lauretis have formulated gender as a concept that is "not so bound up with sexual difference." For those working in this wing of the field, "the notion of gender as sexual difference and its derivative notions—women's culture, mothering, feminine writing, femininity, etc.—have now become a limitation, something of a liability to feminist thought."[7] The late '80s and early '90s marked an opening space for the discussion of gender in which sexual difference and the feminist theories based on it fell under question, as in the opening sentences to Judith Butler's widely read treatise *Gender Trouble:* "contemporary feminist debates over the meanings of gender lead time and again to a certain sense of trouble, as if the indeterminacy of gender might eventually culminate in the failure of feminism. Perhaps trouble need not carry such a negative valence."[8] At that time, on the popular level, Madonna was "troubling" gender with her Blonde Ambition tour, and movie stars like Linda Hamilton and Angela Bassett were starting to sport biceps and kick ass. Thelma and Louise dropped the feminine guise and started shooting, and Jodie Foster in *The Silence of the Lambs* cemented her "masculine persona" through scenes like the opening sequence where she "colonizes the traditional territory of men by demonstrating her superior physical fitness on a trail that many men would find impossible to finish."[9] Female masculinity had begun to surface both in the academy and on the mass-media screen.[10]

But while many gender thinkers in the academy continue to practice in a vein that questions sexual difference, by the mid-'90s tensions within

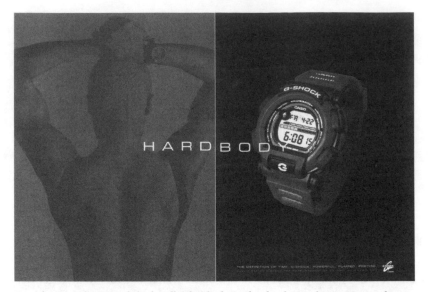

Female masculinity and the hardbody ideal: G-Shock ad, *Condé Nast Sports for Women* (October 1997).

feminist theory and more generalized questionings of theories based on poststructuralism led to a questioning of gender studies' basis in social constructivism—the idea that even our biology is shaped by the cultural discourses that give it meaning. And while the female athlete, as we argued in chapter 2, began to emerge as a gender-troubling icon in the mid-'90s, the reverse was also happening in popular culture. The mid-'90s saw the reemergence of fully essentialist tracts such as *Men Are from Mars, Women Are from Venus,* tracts that helped to reinstitute fundamental sexual difference as unquestionable. These tracts also claimed to be the answer to all cultural woes and gender wars that ostensibly resulted when women and men stepped outside of the "proper" bounds of femininity and masculinity and claimed to be something they "weren't." If we just understand how men and women really "are," the argument ran, all the conflicts between men and women would be magically resolved. There were progressive potentialities that considered the sexual difference model a liability since that model always carried a similar baggage to the "separate but equal" model of white/black race relations that began in 1896 and was not "officially" halted until 1954. The idea that men and women are "different but equal" is a pretense that covers over the fact that ideas of difference preserve the old hierarchy of men over women and therefore is not a basis on which to base gender-progressive platforms. But these progressive potentialities were neutralized as the old notion of innate gender difference crept back in.

If only sexual difference was still asserted as a "liability" today in mass culture and some forms of feminism rather than as a given truth. Burstyn's position, which is characteristic of some feminist thinking in its essentialist bias, marks a debate at least a century old between supporters of masculine competitive sport, the "elitist" model that Burstyn outlines above, and supporters of feminine "participatory" sport, which advocates mass participation and deemphasizes winning. According to sports historian Susan Cahn, "several generations of professionals sought to protect the reputation and health of female athletes by devising separate, less physically taxing versions of women's sport. In effect educators created a respectable 'feminine' brand of athletics." Yet such positions were not the only positions forwarded in the first half of the twentieth century. There is a historical precedent for Lester and the gender studies that would explain her/him. Cahn writes that "over the course of the century, advocates of women's sport developed numerous and often competing strategies to cope with the dissonance between masculine sport and competitive womanhood. The boldest among them accepted the charge of masculinization but claimed its positive value. They contended that women's athleticism would indeed endow women with masculine attributes, but that these qualities would benefit women as well as men, contributing to female emancipation and eliminating needless sexual distinctions."[11] As evidence that women can be part of a talented minority associated with competitive sport, Lester disproves stereotypes of female incompetence and weakness, and, more important, shows that men and women and the qualities associated with them can be broken into something other than polarized categories. The critical tradition Burstyn's writing seems to sometimes be located within—the tradition that is associated with essentialist cultural feminist categories that de Lauretis cites, such as women's culture, mothering, feminine writing, and femininity—distrusts "eliminating needless sexual distinctions" because, in Burstyn's terms, such an elimination would mean the celebration of traditionally masculine qualities like domination and strength over traditionally feminine qualities like cooperation.

That's probably why some of my feminist friends were horrified by the advent of Lester. "Shouldn't you tell them [my training partners]," one said, "that calling you 'Lester' instead of 'Leslie' because you can bench a lot of weight implies that women are weak? Shouldn't you tell them that you can be strong and be a woman, too?" Well . . . yes, but . . . But admit it or not (and a lot of the time, for strategic reasons, we don't admit it), there is now a whole demographic of us post–Title IX babies who have played sports our entire lives and have grown up suckling competitive individualism (a feminist bogeyman) like mother's milk, and it has nourished us. We want to be like Lester, to have his size and stature. Many writers on female athletes play down the competitiveness that makes us want to do sports in the first place, emphasizing how female athletes are more motivated by "teamwork" and their relationships with each other. It's necessary PR in a culture that until very recently has seen the female athlete as a contradiction in terms, a freak of the natural gender order and necessarily suspect in sexual terms. Teamwork's great. So is kicking ass. Why can we have one and not the other? How about both? As Mariah Burton Nelson writes, "call it the Champion's way. The Champion competes openly, aggressively, joyously, with respect for her opponents, and without apology for her own desire for excellence. She competes honestly and ethically. She refuses to conquer anyone, but she also refuses to accept the second-class status of the Cheerleader."[12]

The Cheerleader model of self-effacement—supporting others' efforts while deemphasizing your own—is exactly what essentialist definitions of female athletes prescribe. My training is in many ways more successful because of its male communal aspect—training with the guys, as one of the guys in the sense that I am not willing to apologize for my power or competitive urge. I wouldn't want to train with anyone, male or female, who is female-identified—if "female-identified" means self-effacement or stopping short of what I can do. I'd have to make too many concessions, as if it made no difference that Lester can bench hundreds of pounds more, or that there are women out there who can bench hundreds of pounds more than I can. This requirement of self-effacement is routinely associated with female athletes who adhere to emphasized femininity. "The command and control structure of management," Jere Longman writes when describing the U.S. Women's Soccer Team, "typically male and symbolically represented by football, was being replaced by a more pragmatic, consensus-building style, traditionally female . . . everyone becomes a peer. Parts are interchangeable."[13] But athletes, people, are not interchangeable. Call me male-identified, but I love being "one of the guys" in the sense that as one of them I don't have the pressure to be a nice girl, little Miss Congeniality pretending she's the same as everyone else. I'm not the same as everybody else. Like it or not, feminist or not, men are still the only ones culturally sanctioned to be so self-assured. In the boy space of our training group, bravado is a lusty joke—"I'm going to kick your ass today, you wuss." Verbal sparring establishes comraderie, and I am a good deal more comfortable with this mode of relating than the "you go first, no you go first" group-therapy style you are expected to use if you're a woman. The gym is the one place in the world I don't have to put my ego on the shelf (I was voted "Biggest Ego" in high school, and it was not meant as a compliment). In the common critique of masculine codes of relating to self and others, cultural feminism can come across as if self-assertion and pride in achievement were bad things, mirroring the traditional definitions of gender that feminism set out to transform in the first place. The way the guys and I joke with each other and participate in constant one-upsmanship is, paradoxically, a form of respect. Each of us is confident that each of us has abilities. We respect each other, so competition poses no threat to anyone's identity or self-worth.

I hear the voices of my critics already: subsuming successful, strong women under the category of "one of the guys" implies that women are not as good as, less-than. Or alternatively, I will be critiqued for embracing the kind of Rambo feminism that Burstyn warns against. Within the third wave of feminism, however, as well as in queer studies and poststructuralism, there is little agreement that women are or should be "feminine" or "masculine." In fact, to some, these terms have little currency and are seen as limiting stereotypes. Consequently, a revaluation of the masculine within feminism is currently taking place within a younger generation that is sometimes dubbed postfeminist, though more accurate names for it are "gender studies," "queer theory," or "third wave feminism." There are differences between Generation X and Y feminists and their second wave, boomer mothers, but not a clean break. Forms of second wave feminism (like Burstyn's work) that use an oppositional rhetoric that condemns masculinity and extols the virtues of femininity might find a smaller audience than expected in third wave ears, for some of us highly value the masculine as well as feminine parts of ourselves (especially when we are not stigmatized for doing so). In the words of Analee Newitz, Ana Marie Cox, Jillian Sandell, and Freya

Johnson in their essay, "Masculinity Without Men" in *Third Wave Agenda*, "each of us thinks of herself, to a certain extent, as male-identified, and each of us is resolutely feminist."

> The idea that some women might want to assume certain "masculine" traits or consider themselves as "male-identified" does not suggest that women are becoming "like men," but rather that the relationship between gendered social roles and biological sex is more fluid than we have been taught to believe. . . . Neither does such a shift automatically signal a regressive step for feminism.[14]

Is it a sign of regression for feminism that in the months after his birth, "Lester" became both a term of endearment and the code for everything that signified achievement and value? I can't see it that way, because the advent of Lester established some unbreakable bonds. Billy is still my training partner—5 feet 6 and biceps the size of roast hams. He works at a used car lot fixing trucks, polishing Trans Ams. On weekends in the fall he hunts. He gives me bottles of whiskey for Christmas. During the spring and summer, he's NASCAR-crazed and often goes off for the races or has get-togethers at his trailer before the big races on TV. He is one of my closest friends. He shows up every day we're set to train, religiously. I never doubt him. He's the first person I'd trust if I needed anything. It's been seven years. We've seen each other through divorce, the tenure process, the death of his brother, the near-death of his son. We've both got alcoholic fathers and explosive personalities, and we both see facets of our lives in the skeletons of those upstate New York winter trees. Except for the latter, he's the poster man for what looks from the outside like simple machismo. But machismo often isn't anything like what it's said to be.

Machismo, like femininity, can be many things. It isn't solid or stable, but it can be what binds you together after a shattering fall, some life event that leaves you staggering, ace bandage to hold in a sprain. It can be the sense of joy you feel after a well-placed shot of a soccer ball into the net, that sense of mastery that says "yes!" It can be what you need— the sense that "I am this person, I do exist"—to be able to open to others, see others, find a sense of connection with them. Masculinity can be ugly, big bluster in reaction to fear. I once heard a playwright describe masculinity as a "shivering pretense." Theorist Kaja Silverman calls it a "hollow fiction," a denial of the fact that "lack of being is the irreducible condition of subjectivity... if we were in possession of an instrument which would permit us to penetrate into the innermost recesses of the human psyche, we would find not identity, but a void."[15] Here masculinity is the illusion of self that covers over a void, a lack, an absence at the center. But it is a fundamental pretense, what the modernist poets called "necessary fiction," an illusion without which most of us could not live. The illusion of a powerful, bounded, wholly independent "self," for one thing, the cowboy strut alone into the distance dear to the American dream from the Daniel Boone frontier days to the "cowboy politics" that sometimes surface in the present day. A very limited thing. If that's all one is, one would fit the personality profile that researchers have found characterizes athletes in competitive sport: "low interest in receiving support and concern for others, low need to take care of others, and low need for affiliation." "This is a personality profile," Burstyn writes, "of a narcissistic individual who will have a difficult time understanding the importance of prosocial public policy, or what it takes to build and maintain strong communities."[16] But it isn't all one is.

At one point, when I was most frightened, unsure I had a place in the world or existed at all, masculinity was everything to me. Empty, for a time I was my bluster, achievements I'd racked up: race times, academic degrees, pounds pressed. I've since come to see masculinity as a stage, not one you get over, but a resource you can draw on when you begin to forget the small part that is you cast adrift among rocks and trees and global warming, disappearance of species, suicide bombers, the corporate destruction of the earth's surface, the injunctions on Americans to buy, buy, buy. The disappearance of fossil fuels, the large bright whirl of nightly news, friends losing jobs or family members, endless radio broadcasts about war and natural disasters, and the confusingly counterpoint glamour imagery of MTV. Lester's a reference point through all these things, a refuge, pause, a clumsy, quirky joy.

Lester was recently put to the test when I became pregnant. I was more anxious, I think, to tell Billy than anyone else, for here was one irrefutable physical sign (though not in my view, I knew that it was in many people's, and I was afraid it was in Billy's) that I actually was female, different, diminished, not part of this brotherhood of which I'd temporarily been granted a share. The common cultural assumptions that pregnancy stands for femaleness and marks a period of physical limitation and debilitation haunted me, who had relied so absolutely on physical prowess for my sense of identity and place in the world. As

Jane Gottesman writes, "athletics is a catalyst for girls' and women's self-creation, self-knowledge, and self-expression," and Lester is one part of my self-creation, the "masculine" identity that has been part of my world for as long as I can remember.[17] Despite what people see when they see a female body and the long freighted train of assumptions that go along with that, I never felt those assumptions—weakness, softness, a nurturing instinct—had much to do with me. I'd always used my body to prove this difference, running faster, being stronger, physically outperforming most of the men and women around me. Now, suddenly, I was perhaps going to have this means of self-expression taken away, have people see me as this other strange thing? I panicked. And I dreaded telling Billy and put it off.

But one day I did tell him. I could hardly avoid it. He laughed, was a little uncomfortable, shrugged, and then we picked up and went on as always. The pregnancy didn't make me weaker or slow me down. Even late in the game, I was still down on the bench struggling under 225 pounds, except now I could pop it up there more than once. None of the terrible debilitating things that the pregnancy books assert as a certainty plagued me. I was not exhausted or nauseous. I was not clumsy and awkward. I did not have to scale my training back. I was not weaker in the least. And Billy and I trained, just as we'd always trained. We made jokes about how the morphology of pregnancy actually made our bodies more alike—his beer belly, my protruding stomach. He told me how to compensate for the stomach with squats—take a wider stance. How to bend to lift the plates. Lester didn't vanish in the irrefutable "fact" of biology, and Billy knew it. Lester wasn't dependent on the specificity of my form, or on outmoded ideas about ways biology supposedly limits women. Lester was there the whole time. He is always with me, part of my teeth, my bones, my brain, my breath.

## Talk to the "Animal"

Lester is but one version of female masculinity. There are many others, one of which is the ectomorphic yet muscular "Animal," Shari. Don't let her fool you. She might, when you look at her. If you read the size of the muscles as the measure of the power behind it all, I guess you could be easily duped by the lean, wiry 5-foot-4 112-pound build. I (Shari) was a little boy-girl child that breathed fire from the very start. Innocent blue eyes to hide the wild underneath. Loud. Talked back to you, for sure, and, since infused with "patriarchy," agreed with the male head of the household, who didn't like the realm of the emotional and "irrational." Important days ahead, age six. Climbed to the top of the tallest trees in the back yard, charted out how to lead the neighborhood kids through forest expeditions, told the squirrels who were dancing in the treetops how they too could participate. Chased streams for miles, caught frogs in the mud, tossed fireflies into jars all night. When boys mouthed off, I tied them to trees, beat up some others when they annoyed me, while big brother laughed at skinny sister in disbelief and held a stopwatch to gather data on the hangtime of their cries. I know, I know, not very nice. But it was surely more empowering than sitting quietly inside with that Barbie doll—threw her in the toy pile, never looked back, witnessed lots of her type later on in college.

Other times, uh oh—perfect devaluer of femininity and patriarchal protector here—my best (female) friend and next-door neighbor gave me binoculars to watch her and her brother execute lengthy dance performances and skits in the house (one way we could still play when our tyrannical parents wouldn't let us out of the house). But technology serves multiple purposes, and it made me into a male superhero. When I sometimes viewed her parents interrupting the skits, entering the room to yell, to rampage—when the play faces across the way turned to stress, nothing made more sense in the world to me than extracting her from the situation. Dropping the binoculars, hurling open the front door, I ran through the woods, climbed the balcony, flung her sliding glass door to the right and "saved" her superhero-style from parents caught in the very act of verbally abusive mantras. She appreciated the protection. Was I a young super-peeper, therapist savior to be? Patriarch with bologna curls in stretchy pants? Hypermasculinist hegemonic masculinity with no cape, stuck as a Shirley Temple look-alike? What to make of me?! How would I—and how couldn't I—grow up to be called "Lats" by Penn State Division I football players, beat them at pushup contests, offer myself up to college football coaches as a prop at practice to push "their guys" in the weight room into doing more? How would such a tiny kid, who grew up into a not-much-bigger adult, eventually race past the biggest flexing male thighs when cycling in biathlons, get nicknamed "Animal" in cross-country races while whipping past competitors, and then eventually revel in the safety of the weight room while hurling huge plates, nearly bigger than I am, on hammer strength machines?

Small independent thing overvaluing the masculine, wriggling away from maternal, white, middle-class 1950s mommy? Title IX alpha femme in the making, only possible from second wave feminist fights? Sweet femme trapped inside a highly sporty butch swagger? Butch girl stuck inside idealized fit girl body who dips below 115 pounds unless eating at 3 and 4 A.M.? I am all of these. I am living third wave.

Certainly, gender fluidity was always the name of the game, so Judith Butler and her "gender trouble" never seemed indecipherable to me. Kindergarten, big class performance. Kids were told we could "choose." Pink tutu and ballerina show on one side. All the girls went there. Indian headdress and Native American (racist) war scene. Yep, all the boys. Not hard to guess who crossed the line. Emphatically yelled to mom that night that I would *not* be wearing the tutu or dancing like a ballerina with the rest of the girls. Honestly, I thought I chose what any sane child would choose. The rush of the running, legs stretching, lungs filling with a fight for life, chasing, screaming, wild smiles, curious laughter, definite winners. No contest. Gladly put on my chief hat. White and Asian middle-class suburban mommies happily packed the room, their smiles slowly turned to horror-laden stares one fine afternoon in the middle of small-town New Jersey. When repeatedly asked why, I was glowing, so pleased with the award-winning performance I wasn't really in the mood to discuss it, or to feel confused, and luckily, I didn't have to be. My strong Jewish mother intervened and responded to the questions and admonitions very simply: "that's what she wanted to do." That's that. Barrie Thorne's ethnographic work reveals how adults can lubricate children's school and playground gender transgressions. She was right.[18] Oh, choices. I had choices! There was that liberal feminist discourse starting already that would eventually convince me to buy Nike! Choices at age five for another soon-to-be white, middle-class beneficiary of Title IX! Look out! A powerful voice! If I had only known that she/he life was not going to be so simple.[19]

Sure, I've spent the rest of my life "doing what I've wanted to do" to an extent that I am certain is not enjoyed by much of the female population, and is certainly not enjoyed by my immigrant, inner-city, rural, and third world sisters. College. Business school. A Ph.D in the social sciences. Good health. Lifting four days a week for eighteen years. Track practices. A racing bike that allows me to taste the wind like wine. Endless gym memberships. Showing the world, yes, that girls can do it, too, especially the white, middle-class "masculine" ones? Because we don't have to help financially support a family that continually labors for low wages, we can stay in the weight room an extra hour. Screw the world for putting thoughts of devaluation there to begin with, but haven't many sisters of color and sisters in the working class always rejected the frailty line? I'm not angry on the outside. I just do pullups, dips, and bench. Yes, that's my body project. It's come down to pretty base-level victories that still somehow get labeled as masculine in 2003, and you must know that the battles are carefully selected.

One particular battle was on a sunny morning during graduate school, when I noted that ROTC met on the track/football field once a week. Lines of shaved heads, muscular frames, disciplined, normalized move-ments, male sounds, postures. Eyes straight ahead. No blinks. Very nice pullup bar off to the side of the track, I thought to myself. One of those mornings, with backpack loaded up with heavy books, dressed to teach, I decided to say good morning in my own way. Left the backpack on. Jumped up to the bar, and hit the pullups like the tree climbs—one-two-three-four-five-ten—fifteen—twenty pull-ups that day. Easy. Felt like laughter for the first dozen, the next five were with wishes that Title IX stayed alive. The last three, I have to say, my soul went dead, and it was only the fire lit inside that made me press it out so that girls would not be erased, silenced, diminished, or seen as weak. And voila, it was so, if only for a moment in time. Mary Jo Kane suggests that men and women offer a "continuum of overlapping physical performances by gen-der"—I was evidence of it.[20] At around pullup number ten, the ROTC "soldier" audience stopped looking straight ahead, broke the rules by checking out the situation. I knew it, they had to. So did General Jack, standing at the front of the pack in hierarchical form. He did a no-no and turned his head to the right. Never saw a girl do that, eh? The male gaze took on new meaning here in the silent rays of light that had not yet crept along to meet the rest of the campus that morning. Not sexu-alized or objectified, I was instead an object of wonder. A variation on these themes continues with similarly discerning choices. I'm not sub-tle. I do frequently pick out the strongest man in the gym and chal-lenge him to dip contests. I like to use strategy by making him go first, so I can assess the competition.[21] I like to watch his bulging, huge mus-cles, and then I like to surprise him. I always thank him for the competi-tion, appreciate it with real sportsmanship. Did I mention I like to win?

Sure, there are a number of other more institutionally politicized day-to-day activisms I also carry out, but I perhaps naively think that this brand of individualized work—repeatedly highlighting a continuum of overlapping bodies and performances by gender—might also help to change the world in its own small way.

So it's been quite a stint of time now, enjoying the benefits of cumulative battles fought for by liberal and radical feminism, the gay and lesbian liberationist movement, and queer activism. Yeah, there's a little more room in the world for someone like me, perhaps coupled with some white privilege, some class privilege, Nike needing some more cash from my demographic, and a healthy dash of my own ambiguous signifiers that keep everyone confused. Add a solid dash of warmth, laughter, sincerity, and I might sway you. It's okay if she's . . . you know . . . one of those women who are a little different . . . you know . . . she can play sport really well, but she might look a little like those who are erased from media coverage and don't keep their endorsements very well, even when they play really well. Female masculinity means something different to me than to Lester, carries different baggage, weighs on me with a little more trepidation at night. We share a rejection of emphasized femininity that meant no fear of being devalued or reprimanded for being a girl who wasn't quite competent or valued enough. We both will never, ever get accused of being a girl who didn't push hard enough, do enough. True, society embraces a greater mix of signifiers now than before, and I am a powerful performative of sorts, but my response does depend on a context of gender inequality, with weighty demands for compulsory heterosexuality. Carrying female masculinity as a badge doesn't always mean empowering things when one quick accusation can end it all. The femmy butch who can't gain much some muscle mass? The butchy femme who is finally allowed to gain some muscle mass? Lesbo? Dyke? Strong hetero, bi, or tranny girl who went too far? Not real. Not a real woman. Real women aren't that strong. Don't train that hard. Don't study that hard. Don't know strategy or competition so well. Are more obsequious, don't have so much to say, don't climb for or hunger for the top so profoundly. Real women don't sound so confident in job interviews or at conferences. Real women wear tutus and dance. Play with Barbie. Don't threaten anyone. If that's the definition of "women," then we are both real men, I suppose.

We're macho—always have been, on some level. The gym is one of the only spaces where that's okay, so that's one of the only places we feel comfortable. It wouldn't be too much of an exaggeration to say it is one of the few places we feel seen, solid, good. We know—good feminist women and grrls aren't supposed to want to be men or be "like men." We're not supposed to identify with elitist, retro bonehead ideologies of physical superiority or with anything that claims one person is "better" than the next. We're supposed to affirm ourselves as women, all equal, and to redefine "woman" and "girl" to encompass value and strength. We're supposed to be creating "alternative femininities," but to still see ourselves fundamentally as women. We're not allowed to do both. That we are these other things too, boy things, has gotten us called bitches. It's made a lot of people not like us. It's made many people suspicious about our politics. But we're spots along that continuum, more gruff than some, and we feel strangled by and sometimes angry about the idea that everyone with (or without) boobs is essentially the same.

With our aggressive insistence that we also live for ourselves, not just others, we are the horror figures in popular culture, the crazed career women of *Fatal Attraction,* the bloody extremities of *G.I. Jane.* Whether we're het, hom, bi, or trans, regardless of the extent we perform the femme, some of us are either born with more testosterone than others, or carry out plenty of cultural practices (from a young age) that inter sect with biology in ways that are turning your heads. Among many other factors, this all has concrete effects on our bodies and personalities, and it shapes your ideologies. That's not necessarily good or bad, it just is. Testosterone, like gender, exists on a continuum, and social and cultural practices unquestionably intersect with the biological to produce new physical forms.[22] Whenever the media (or some wings of conservative Christianity, or radical, essentialist feminism) wants to evoke ineradicable biological gender difference, they write about testosterone as if only men have it. But everybody's got it to one degree or another, some men have less of it than some women, and what we *do* shapes it. It, along with values that we embrace and practices we foster, makes some women more aggressive and competitive than we are "supposed" to be.

Lester and Animal aren't a matter of misidentification or lack of reflection.[23] Even though they were publicly named in moments that involved the demonstration of physical strength, bench-pressing and cross-country running, they have always been with us, the core of our determination, part of our expressions of anger, hurt, and aggression. Like the All-American with which their traits are linked, they were the parts of us who believed in competing ferociously. Anyone who has been raised and has excelled in intercollegiate Division I athletic culture or any other culture that emphasizes individual achievement (academia or corporate America, for instance), for better and worse, will have their own versions of Lester and Animal. All of us need to admit this and to create some public endorsement for the complicated joys they bring so that parts of ourselves we value, that motivate us, can be publicly and institutionally validated for women along with the kind of cooperative traits associated with femininity.

This acceptance of female masculinity is starting to be validated in contemporary imagery of female athletes, especially in advertising and in popular mediums such as film. In a recent poem, Nellie Wong, an Asian-American activist famous in international circles as a radical poet, comments on this in "Resolution":

Lucy Liu kicks butt in *Charlie's Angels,*
And there's Michelle Yeoh
in *Super Cop 2,* her quiet fury
taking care of herself
and the Hong Kong cops
who try to be chivalrous
thinking this petite woman
needs a man's protection
because she's that, a petite woman.
But watch out! Women are signing
up for martial arts classes, learning
discipline, respecting their bodies,
unleashing their minds to say "hands off!"
through their eyes and throats
to abuse, wandering hands, domestic violence
Perhaps Hollywood, for once,
gives us fighting women
who fly from the ground
to rooftops and ricochet off walls
Perhaps Hong Kong's treatment
of women in film reflects feminism
of a kind that Hollywood emulates
Perhaps it is not too much to imagine
that being physical is just as important

as being intelligent,
that the 100-year-practice
of foot binding was a terrible prelude
to all this kicking and chopping,
this resolution roaring
in women now.[24]

From an Asian-American perspective wherein emphasized femininity has long been the dominant stereotype, the "fighting women" who "kick and chop," demonstrating a physical power previously associated with masculinity, mark an important development in popular imagery. So many women, if you talk to them, have their own versions of Lester and Animal, find them an inspiring, much-cherished part of their lives, and find inspiration and comfort in mass-cultural imagery that speaks to this.

We don't know to what extent Lester and Animal—our muscles, attitudes, drive—are the product of a culture that values masculinity, a product of competitive environments, or to what extent they are the result of the hormone levels in our blood. It's an interaction effect, maybe. As the Wong poem suggests, we also don't know to what extent they are defense mechanisms, warrior personas responding to the warlike domestic environment in which one of us grew up, or to the adversarial dog-eat-dog world of American corporate culture or violence against women more generally. We don't know whether Lester and Animal mark a cultural condition, an adaptive response to what Peggy Orenstein refers to as women living in "a half-changed world."[25] We think they—and all the versions of them out there—are all these things. Like Wong's identification with "fighting women who fly from the ground," what we do know is that Lester's benchplay, Animal's backpack pullups, move the world, and Lester and Animal are names for human longing.

# CHAPTER FOUR

## Bodies, Babes, and the WNBA

Predictably if not paradoxically, some of the same critics who argue against female masculinity are adamant in their arguments against emphasized femininity in athletes as well. The seeming obverse of female masculinity is emphasized femininity, and the most obvious place that emphasized femininity has been present lately has been in representations of female athletes who have posed in ways that some call "pornographic." A major issue that continually resurfaces in the discussion of women's sport images and seems to argue against the claim that the female athlete images have been functioning in a way that counteracts the objectification thesis is this so-called babe factor in the representation of women's sports—the phenomenon of women posing for men's magazines in ways that call attention to their sexuality, specifically their heterosexuality. The necessary point of departure for a phenomenon like the recent debates about top female athletes posing nude for calendars, *Sports Illustrated, Life,* and other widely circulated magazines is the social context of the mass media in which such representations appear. While social critics like Jean Baudrillard argue that the contemporary world is constituted by images, a hyperreal in which the global communications industries have erased the distinctions between global and local, real and unreal, these crimes also make the case for the seductiveness of the image and consumer culture, and the fact that the economy of signs is so pervasive that it structures existence as such. For Baudrillard the content and form of our lives in the symbolic economy of late capitalism is reducible to the "collective sharing of simulacra," and our experience is necessarily that of seduction by mass reproduction and its attendant homogenization and manipulation. Media and its images then become not "just" representations we can turn off but reality itself, indisputable facts of life within which we are inextricably caught up.[1] "Images 'R' Us"... It is only within the context of such a world that images matter enough to generate pages and pages devoted to discussions of pictures of naked, sexualized female athletes like those, for instance, that filled newspapers and listservs in the summer and early fall 2000.

You know the ones: images of tennis player Anna Kournikova in *Sports Illustrated* lounging in Lolita-like longing on a bed; high jumper Amy Acuff with only the computer-generated wash of an American flag, placed strategically, to distinguish between her image and some of those on Kara's Adult Playground; swimmer Jenny Thompson standing on the seashore in bright red boots, sporting magnificent thighs and a stars-and-stripes brief, fists clenched over naked but not visible breasts in *Sports Illustrated;* images of soccer player Brandi Chastain in the buff behind and around soccer balls in *Gear,* swimmers Dara Torres, Jenny Thompson, Angel Martino, and Amy Van Dyken naked behind the American flag in *Women's Sports and Fitness,* and Amy Acuff again in *Esquire's* "Girls of Summer." And while one might get tired of the seemingly endless debates about such images—and the fact that female athletes get a lot more press for such images than for their athletic performances—the production and consumption of these images has real effects: visual texts like these help shape people's everyday experiences, identities, and thinking. But what effects, exactly, and according to whom?

## Creaking Old School Feminists versus New Age (Post-) Feminists

Recent media discussions of female athletes buff and in the buff seemed to fall into a polarized debate that is both predictable and symptomatic. Offering commentary on this recent "overexposure" of female athletes, in one corner we have Camp 1 (according to Sally Jenkins in the *Washington Post*), the "creaking old school feminists." In the opposing corner we have Camp 2 (according to Melissa Isaacson in the *Chicago Tribune*), the "so-called new age feminists—read women in their 20's who haven't a clue about real feminism and from whence it sprung."[2]

As feminist athletes and professors who by birthdate and ideological orientation straddle these two camps, otherwise known as the second and third waves of feminism, we sometimes feel like we spend a good deal of our intellectual life trying to translate between two hostile war-ring camps speaking very different languages.[3] The same debate is repli-cated again and again whenever the question of body image or beauty culture is raised. For Camp 1 the position seems to be: the media is al-ways bad, the product of evil capitalist patriarchy, and its representation of women is the worst. For Camp 2 the position seems to be: the media is the air we live and breathe, and we manipulate it for our own ends, and aren't we so clever and aren't we hot babes? For the first camp, fe-male athlete nudity confirms the "normalcy" of heterosexuality and tries (offensively to some) to show that these babes aren't "dykes"—"a back-lash against women, a way of diminishing their power, trivializing their strength, putting them in their sexual place";[4] for the second camp, the athletes have "worked their asses off" for their bodies and are proud of them, and see it as their God-given, MTV-culture-driven right to ex-hibit them, along the lines of the generational maxim, "I'm all over the media, therefore I exist."

Polarization indeed. Yet both positions make sense, both have limita-tions, and where one is located demographically helps determine one's response. Given that in the mainstream sports media outlets women's sports receives such a disproportionate amount of coverage (a recent study released by Michael Messner found that ESPN reports on male athletes still outnumbered reports on female athletes 15 to 1), the fact that so much of the coverage female athletes do get draws attention to their (hetero)sexuality clearly indicates a continuing unease—at least in baby boomers and older—with women's attainment of "male"-coded attributes such as self-sovereignty, athletic prowess, and power.[5] But it is also true that if ESPN hasn't embraced the female athlete, other forms of popular culture have. The image of the athletic female body, like the one seen in a spring 2001 Nike ad for the teen-plus mag *Jane*—ten-nis player Mary Pierce with well-developed triceps, biceps, quadriceps, shoulders, and abs, pictured in the weight room with a medicine ball, sweating, hair pulled back—visually demonstrates the sense of ex-panded possibility the athletes themselves often cite: through their ath-leticism and strength, they get to be girls and boys both, demonstrate codes of masculinity and femininity simultaneously. But it is also the case that as long as femininity is defined as (hetero)sexual access (as it

You're going to go through hell.
You might want to dress on the cool, comfortable side.

Weight rooms are places
of pained faces and
burning tissue. Tennis
courts are fiery pits of
torment and anguish. Mary
Pierce is not afraid. Her
Dri-FIT tennis shirt gets
rid of her sweat by moving
it away from her body
where it evaporates.
She keeps cool, dry and
confident. While her serve
continues to be lethal.

NIKE·FIT

the
evolution
of
skin

Best of both worlds: boundaries in gender codes come down. Mary Pierce in Nike ad, *Jane* (March 2001).

was in the Kournikova *Sports Illustrated* spread), and as it has long been the case with female bodybuilders and fitness competitors, we have a problem.

Quite typically, the "catfight" staged by the media pitting "creaky old feminists" against the "so-called young feminists who don't know what feminism is in the first place" is an inaccurate representation of the actual positions. For instance, the Women's Sports Foundation's position' on the issue is nuanced and not at all "old":

> The Foundation believes that there is nothing wrong with portraying female athletes as feminine, physically attractive, or in ways that seek to represent an artistic study of their bodies. . . . The question . . . requires an examination of context. When a female athlete appears . . . she should be portrayed as respectfully as her male counterpart, who is most often portrayed as a skilled athlete.[6]

It is the context of the image, not whether there is nudity, that is important, as the naked male and female images such as those of Mary Ellen Clark, Gwen Torrance, Gail Devers, Holly McPeak, Carl Lewis, and many others appearing in *Life* magazine in 1996 demonstrated—images that communicated power, self-possession, and beauty, not sexual access. The *Life* spread was one of the few that featured male and female athletes together photographed in similar ways, and this is important because there is also the matter of equality of image. As Mary Jo Kane, director of the Tucker Center for Research on Women and Girls in Sport, says: "I'm just asking for equal treatment. When Tiger Woods is on the cover of *Sports Illustrated,* naked, holding a golf ball with the Nike swoosh in front of his genitals, I'll be quiet." In fact there was such an image of the 1996 men's water-polo team, balls clutched over genitals in *Life,* and this 1998 Nike ad of Michael Johnson is pretty close to what Kane calls for, but such images have been proportionally fewer and farther between than the images of female athletes. Furthermore, the female athletes are usually positioned in ways that seem vulnerable, such as an image of Gabrielle Reece that was on the next page from Johnson's ad.

Kane's was our response—show us the male version of abs, buns, and pecs if you're going to show us the T&A—when working the debate surrounding female bodybuilders and their pornographic representation in magazines like *Flex* in the mid-'90s. At the time, it seemed that bodybuilding was one of the few retro sports left in a positive, changing cultural context for female athletes, and that both the debate

Equal opportunity bodily exposure? Michael Johnson and Gabrielle Reece for Nike, *Condé Nast Sports and Fitness for Women* (March 1998).

and the silliness of the imagery would die in the pages of *Flex*.[7] This interpretation was far too optimistic, it seems. Still, there has been a host of positive representational changes that are often obscured by the "naked women" debate, and those changes bolster the Camp 2 position and deserve mention here. A recent poll that showed that young peo ple—men and women—now give the athletic female body a higher rating than that of the anorexic model, and our own focus group research, featured in chapter 6, shows a wide spectrum of responses to athletic bodies.[8] As we discussed in chapter 1, the increasingly mainstream nature of the female athlete appeal is so widespread that even *Vogue* magazine, that diehard propagator of the waif model ideal, featured Marion Jones on its January 2001 cover, calling her "the new American hero" and giving her a ten-page feature within.[9]

Suddenly the athletic body has become an ideal for both sexes, problematizing traditional gender codes in the popular imagination. Or, as Judith Butler puts it in a more theoretical language,

> in challenging the categories by which we sort men from women, Martina [Navratilova, who is now marketable enough to be featured in a Subaru ad] produced the crisis that allowed us, in turn, to love her accomplishment all the better. And this greater capacity on our parts not only expands the field of play, allowing greater participation, but it allows the

category of "women" to become a limit to be surpassed, and establishes sports as a distinctively public way in which to enact and witness that dramatic transformation.[10]

As we have argued, contemporary gender codes cannot be so easily polarized as they once were in that there is a definite trend in the ideal image repertoire that emphasizes male femininity and female masculinity. The appearance of such images points to a larger cultural shift, a shift that must be taken into account—though it most often is not—by our models of critical analysis. As Toby Miller writes, "the commodification of sports stars across the 1990's has destabilized the hegemonic masculinity thesis."[11] Miller reads this change as one potentially positive but unintended consequence of the heightened commodification characteristic of late capitalism and its voracious need for new markets.

> These challenges and inconsistencies make sports exciting at a political and analytical level. Clearly, sports continue to be a space of heteronormative, masculinist white power, but they are undergoing immense change, with sex at the center. Objectification is a fact of sexual practice within capitalism. Excoriating evaluations of women's bodies has long been the pivotal node of this process, with the implied spectator a straight male. Now, slowly in many cases but rapidly in others, the process of body commodification through niche targeting has identified men's bodies as objects of desire and gay men and straight women as consumers, while there are signs of targeting lesbian desire. Masculinity, understood as a set of dominant practices of gendered power, is no longer the exclusive province of men as spectators, consumers, or agents. "Female masculinity" can now be rearticulated as a prize rather than a curse.[12]

The shifting context that Miller describes here, especially that of male objectification alongside the idealization of female masculinity, makes the standard objectification thesis at least partially inadequate. For part of the context that informs the debate about female images is that female athletes in the generations after Title IX have come to redeem the erasure of individual women that the old *Playboy* model of sexualization performed, rewriting the symbology of the female body from empty signifiers of ready heterosexual access, blank canvases, or holes on which to write one's heteronormative desires, to the active, self-present sexuality of a body that signifies achievement and power and is in that sense "masculinized" or "queered" if you follow the traditional equation of masculinity with power and heteronormativity. The athletic body,

DRI-FIT BASE LAYER ●●●●● WICKS AWAY SWEAT. ATTRACTS STARES.

Messing with sex: masculine/feminine athlete for Nike, *Condé Nast Women's Sports and Fitness* (September/October 1999).

when coded as athletic, can redeem female sexuality and make it visible as an assertion of female presence, and make that presence amenable to a range of sexualities.

Of course, bodies, muscular or not, can and are coded as vulnerable and/or granting heterosexual access. But it's more complicated than the simple reduction of a woman to a "piece of ass." As Susan Bordo writes,

the old feminist fear of "objectification" seems inadequate. . . . The
notion of women-as-objects suggest the reduction of women to "mere"
bodies, when actually what is going on is far more disturbing than
that. . . . Often, features of women's bodies are arranged in representations precisely in order to suggest a particular attitude—dependence or
seductiveness or vulnerability, for example. . . . We're not talking about
the reduction of women to mere bodies, but about what those bodies
express.[13]

The reduction of women to sex objects or "mere bodies" sounds
anachronistic in an equal opportunity exploitation culture that sexual-
izes everything. Using Bordo's template as a guide to read the latest crop
of controversial images of female athletes, the Jenny Thompson photo
expresses neither seductiveness nor vulnerability, but is a mixed bag,
combining the powerful thighs and strong stomach of a great athlete
and the cartoonish red boots and striped trunks of Wonder Woman.
That this image appeared in *Sports Illustrated,* where the rest of the coverage was of male athletes, none posed similarly, reflects a "sexist" context, but many did not read it that way. In a poll taken in an AOL chat
room in which Thompson was discussing her photo, 80 percent of the
participants thought that the message behind the picture was strength,
not sex. The Brandi Chastain photos in *Gear* of Chastain crouched naked
around a soccer ball do express triviality and vulnerability, not strength.
The Anna Kournikova photos, despite the fact that she is clothed, express
seductiveness, triviality, and vulnerability given the facial expressions
of Kournikova with imploring eyes and pouting, pursed lips, and a body
language that is withdrawing and inviting rather than assertive. The notorious track calendar shot of Amy Acuff expresses feminine triviality
and heterosexual availability, with her striped socks signifying little-girl
vulnerability while her Kate Moss–like body stretched naked on the
locker room bench suggests fragility and easy access. Given the bodily
stances and direct gazes of the Olympic swimmers that appeared in
*Women's Sports and Fitness,* the Annie Leibovitz draped-with-a-flag
photo of Dara Torres, Angel Martino, Amy Van Dyken, and Thompson
expresses a self-conscious parody of exploitative shots, and what Judith
Butler would call "gender performativity": Martino with a traditionally
male crossed-arms-revealing-big-biceps pose, Torres with a cynical here-
I-am, whatever, look, Thompson with a more femmy side shot of butt
and leg, and Van Dyken with a smart-ass expression that can only com-

ment on how posed the whole thing is. Taken together, we can see that the images are not easily reducible to a single formula.

## Why'd She Do It?: The Disappearance of the Subject/ Object Dichotomy in the Hyperreal Meets the Post–Title IX Empowerment Narrative Meets the Bottom Line in Women's Sports

With such a diversity of images, it is clear that the second wave feminist critique of the objectification of women's bodies cannot encompass that diversity, nor can it account for the way female athletes seem to understand the production of their images in the contemporary context (nor can it account for the ways in which the male body has become objectified). In the images of female athletes in question here, it is no longer simply the case of naive women who buy into a false sense of power when they pose for the camera and we need to educate them about their mistake. Instead, athletes already know the criticisms and reject them. They know exactly what they are doing. They know, and they do it all the same, both because they do not experience themselves as manipulated and powerless, and because like many others in the MTV generation who are fighting high debt-to-income ratios and diminished permanent job prospects, they see rightly visibility in the media as the only "real" outlet for the achievement of selfhood this culture offers. According to Jeanette Lee, the women's world billiard champion, who has a vibrant, sexual media presence,

> I've heard numerous times about how many years I've brought the sport back by being too sexy. I completely disagree with their argument. Michael Jordan is incredibly sexy and you don't hear other men complaining. I think it's a very shortsighted view. Although some women disagree with my using my femininity to attract the media or whomever, I feel as though it's brought quite a bit of attention to our sport that wouldn't have been there otherwise.[14]

For Lee, as for other athletes, the bottom line is more name recognition and therefore more existence in the hyperreal sense, and since the sexualization of image is now a both-genders proposition, the critique of women as "sex objects" no longer seems to wholly describe what is happening. That critique further underestimates the relationship between cultural valuation, visibility, and marketing oneself that is part of the increasing dominance of the hyperreal.

If conditions of hyperreality have become the dominant way post–Title IX athletes like Lee experience and understand the world, then it becomes more than an academic point that within the hyperreal, the distinction between subject and object is not as clear. This point helps in revising the objectification thesis—the idea that female athletes, not male athletes, are reduced to their heterosexuality in dominant imagery. This imagery influences gendered experience. According to social theorist Richard Lane,

> in perspectival space, there is still the play of the opposition seeing/being seen; with hyperreality . . . the active seeing and the passive being seen are one and the same position . . . it becomes impossible to locate the traditional nodes of power and subjection with the collapse of perspectival space; instead, there is a circulation of positions . . . the notion of total involvement or immersion combined with alienating detachment.[15]

In the current context, athletes, whether male or female, occupy this paradoxical space where they are both subject and object simultaneously—both active subjects who perform their sport and market their image, and commodified objects who are passive, who exist to be ogled in the classically "feminine" position of being seen. As Toby Miller writes of Olympic swimmer Duncan Armstrong, he "shifts between the unstable position of the body on display, defenseless before the gaze, and the administrative figure of shrewd self-commodification, in control."[16] Furthermore, the idea of an athlete's "total involvement combined with alienating detachment" can help us to understand the position of the contemporary female athlete and her willingness to pose pornographically. Like all athletes, she is both totally involved with and curiously detached from her body simultaneously.

But there *is* a gender-specific modality here, even if it is not that of the objectification thesis. The second cultural context at issue is that the women posing in these "pornographic," highly sexualized images are also part of a generation for whom, as post–Title IXers, the right to play sport and be rewarded for it has always been part of their experiences.[17] There are ways in which serious athletic training disassociates or alienates an athlete from her body, a way in which athletes, male or female, are taught to regard their bodies as productive machines from and of which they are both separate and in control, both completely immersed in and alienated from, and this experience is largely unique to the generation post–Title IX. Serious athletic training paradoxically produces a profound (and only partially mistaken) sense of the self-authorship of one's body. This sense is one of the benefits of sport—you get beyond a culturally mediated sense of your body and tend to forget the cultural fetishization of female breasts and nudity because that isn't how you experience yourself. And you feel that, through your labor, you've made yourself.

Beyond the generational naivete of which these athletes are some-times accused, this is where the often-expressed "I worked hard on this body and I'm proud of it!" statement comes from. The athlete is used to the contradictory experience where she is simultaneously connected to and disassociated from her body, making her more vulnerable to ma-nipulation by images, precisely because she sees herself as invulnerable to and separate from them. Sport teaches a self-possession that creates a sense of immunity from exploitation: "it's my body and I've shaped it" is the rallying cry because the athlete thinks her body is *her* body. No matter how it is posed, she feels she has a strength that transcends cul-tural labels, even as her only possible reference point is precisely those labels. Here we can see why both feminist and postfeminist positions are applicable, and why contemporary critical frameworks need to in-corporate both.

Gabrielle Reece expresses these contradictory sentiments directly in her January 2001 cover and photo layout for *Playboy*. "Gabby's concep-tion of her body as a performance machine informs her attitude to-ward these photos," the introductory text to her photo spread reads. "'I don't think of the images as sexual,' she says. 'Our goal was to shoot the body as a form. . . . No big deal. I'm not trying to say, "Check me out.". . . I [also] wasn't trying to create layers between myself and the pictures. The only things I had on were mascara and sunblock. In a sense, they're more me than any pictures I've ever taken.'"[18] To Reece, there is a dis-tance between herself and her body, a "performance machine" that naked or not, in *Playboy* or not, is a "form," a work of art, an achievement that one relates to as to a sculpture or to a painting. And yet she sees no "lay-ers between myself and the pictures." The *Playboy* spread to Gabby both is and is not her identity. And the pictures, it must be said, are not your standard "come hither" cheesecake. The other "fuck me" photo spreads in the same issue form a frothy (if chilling) contrast to the stark, serious, breathtakingly beautiful (in any context) images of Reece. The images occupy different visual registers informed by different codes, showing again how difficult it is to make generalizations. Even in *Playboy*, all is not intrinsically bad.

In the summer of 2001, Lisa Harrison of the WNBA's Phoenix Mercury was voted the "Sexiest Babe in the WNBA" through a poll on the ESPN Magazine website. A lucrative offer to pose in *Playboy* followed, which Harrison, who makes $36,000 a year in the WNBA, considered. The usual media attention and controversy followed, prompting Harrison to say, "it's really sad that I get all this attention because of possibly being in *Playboy* as opposed to what I do on the court every day." She also said the lack of attention to the quality of women's play bothers her more than being considered a sex object.[19] But Harrison conversely expressed a common assumption about this issue when she equated "femininity" with sex appeal: "it's nice to be recognized as feminine and not just being stereotyped as a tomboy" (code for lesbian?). In this often-repeated cliché, "masculinity" is defined as "being a tomboy," which conceivably means constructing oneself as an athlete who achieves regardless of her physical appearance. "Femininity" is defined as "being a babe"—in other words, successfully creating an image that viewers interpret as (hetero)sexually attractive. Femininity = sex appeal, masculinity = achievement, as if never the twain shall meet.

Yet perhaps the cultural understandings of masculinity and femininity have not kept pace with the visual codes of popular culture, which seem to deconstruct the boundaries between these terms in a way that should drastically affect our understandings of them—and that do affect the understandings of younger generations because they are experiencing the images in an entirely different context. The 1990s saw the normalization of the commodification of bodies of both genders, the development of the body as the hottest fashion accessory, the most valued personal asset, and the normalization of porn that occurred with the internet, Calvin Klein and Victoria's Secret ads, among other factors. These changes, coupled with demographic factors like the closing of the entry-level gender wage gap in this generation, along with the decline in real wages and high debt-to-income ratios, means that both women and men come to read cultural images from a position that is mostly structurally equal vis-à-vis each other (neither young men or young women are well off financially), and that there is no longer much structural reinforcement for images that make either gender read like sex toys for the other. Furthermore, posing for sexualized images no longer carries the social stigma it once did. For much of the younger demographic, exhibiting a hot body is an intense sign of valuation and does not signify as devaluation.

These factors address an older demographic's recurrent question. For the images of female athletes that clearly are reducible to the conventions of soft porn and nothing else, there has been much speculation about why famous female athletes—our contemporary icons of power and achievement—would pose in ways that express the giving up of one's will, achievements, and personal power. While it may be at least partially true that some young women now think they are equal and can "have it all," including the right to present themselves as "babes" at no cost to themselves or how seriously the world takes them, the advent of female Olympians posing like Playmates runs much deeper than this expression would initially suggest. The November/December issue of *Sports Illustrated for Women* states that two dozen female athletes polled at the Sydney Olympics "said they felt that women should be proud of their bodies, and saw no problem with putting them on display [in a sexual way]" (121). There are cultural and historical reasons for the athletes' claim that reveal their perspective to be more than naive. The largest of these reasons is the fragmentary, surface-oriented, image-based cultural mood or state known as postmodernism, which is reflected in the pervasive context of the mass media invoked earlier.[20]

Though the connection may seem far from self-evident, it can be argued that part of the reason female athletes may be willing to pose in sexualized ways that might seem degrading to some is that their experience of themselves through sport gives them a sense of invincibility that makes them feel immune to degradation. While those athletes not indoctrinated by university humanities programs may not formulate their views in precisely these terms, the general cultural drift that characterizes postmodern subjectivity can be seen as a context for their attitudes and actions. Part of that context is the general agreement among cultural theorists that the human subject is born into systems of meaning that serve as the reference point for any self-conception. Such a postmodern self-conception can feel destabilizing in that it questions the modern sense of self associated with humanism, the idea that the subject has inborn, essential qualities that can be expressed as one's given, essential "self" independently of his/her social and historical context or position.

Like others in this paradoxical historical moment, athletes might experience the "postmodern condition" of struggling to form their selfhood and identities in a cultural context where "image is everything" and there seems to be nothing essential about oneself beyond whether one chooses to wear Diesel or Armani jeans. At the same time the fluidity of consumer symbols seems the only means of self-construction, the old humanist view of the essential self is still offered as the dominant mode of understanding, causing a disjunction between frameworks of meaning and experience. We would argue that sport, which is still very much a "modern" form that supports the humanist view of the essential self, and functions according to cherished mythologies such as individualism and the level playing field, can be seen in the contemporary context as a protest against or way of bolstering oneself against what is experienced in consumer culture as the postmodern erasure of the self. Ironically, although it is part and parcel of the consumer economy, because of its modern form and the way it fosters illusions of authenticity, sport often enables the athlete to see him/herself as the origin of meaning and action, as a fiercely individual actor who achieves in his/her own terms independent of any larger system of meanings.[21] Sport may be one of the last contexts left in which one can foster this illusion and seem to experience oneself as a "true self." This is important to many because the erasure of the self as the source of its own meaning is also an erasure of the cherished American ideal of self-sovereignty. Though we may not necessarily know we are missing this ideal, sport is one of the few places in the contemporary scene where one can preserve that sense of self-sovereignty in concrete ways. Or, put a little differently, sport is one of the few concrete outlets we have for this older, less fragmentary, more stable experience of the self—an experience that is paradoxically dependent upon highly contingent foundations such as winning your next game or race.

Contemporary athletes may be using sport to bolster a modern conception of the self in a postmodern context that challenges that sense of self. This point has sometimes gotten lost in the postmodern critique of the "Zeitgeist of the modern era."[22] Though writers such as C. L. Cole, David Andrews, and Genevieve Rail have powerfully and productively used poststructuralist theory to read sport, postmodern theorists writing about sport have not always been attentive enough to the ways in which sport is still effective in preserving Enlightenment ideals of individuality, at least in preserving those ideals as a kind of modernist "necessary fiction."[23] For instance, Judith Butler claims that female athletes contribute to a gender crisis that destabilizes all the old tropes of masculinity and femininity, and thereby identity itself:

> that reconsideration of what we claim to know as gendered life can take place only by passing through an unstable and troubled terrain . . . a situation of not-knowing. . . . When we witness muscularity and contour, the corporeal effects of a ritual of athleticism, are we not for the moment seduced by the need to know which gender it is? . . . What we witness is the very contingency of this categorization; at that moment, we enter into precisely the kind of epistemic crisis that allows gender categories to change.[24]

While Butler is making an argument very familiar to anyone schooled in postmodern thought, examined from the point of view of the female athlete rather than that of her image's consumer, we might find that it is precisely this sense of contingency that the female athlete fights on some level through her identity as an athlete—not just the contingency of gender or sexuality, which would be positive, but also of the self, which would be negative in some ways. Often, what she wants is just not an expanded gender or sexual norm but the permanent public recognition of her value, presence, or being as an individual that isn't changeable. She strives to step out of the historical shadows of the traditional feminine (as in Hegel's formulation that the being of woman is a shadowy nonbeing) and into the province of "masculine" being—which, of course, calls those various categories into question and places them in a state of flux. But she is motivated by a desire for stability, not flux.

This is the ultimate irony that is part of a very contemporary struggle: for women and "others," the old model of the sovereign self is only possible through the postmodern fragmentation of this very model. The conditions of possibility for her being are, then, nonbeing in the sense of a decentered self, for can the ideal of self-sovereignty incorporate a notion of decenteredness and fragmentation? According to most theorists it can't. Butler writes that "there is no centered or directed athletic activity without a . . . cultural idealization of that body, a perspective on one's body situated in relation to a set of cultural norms."[25] So while it is true, as Butler points out, that these norms have shifted enough that a woman—exemplified by the figure of the female athlete—can now be muscular and competent and strong, what exactly does that muscularity and strength signify? Not a fluid self but a solid self, a solid symbolic return to the model of the self as a fixed, unquestionable presence, an "I am" that no theoretical word-trickery can mess with, but an "I am" that simultaneously represents historical change since before women, nonwhites, gays, and others were excluded from precisely such assertions of self. This paradox is what people see when they see, for instance, Marion Jones, this solidity is what they admire along with Jones's incarnation as pomo flux. The "category of 'woman'" that Butler claims female athletes surpass is surpassed precisely by their both surpassing the indeterminate flux or softness and vulnerability that was traditional femininity and assuming the rigidity of the hard, athletic contour that invokes precisely the imaginary of centered self-presence, the sovereign individuality that is dear to mainstream American culture to this day.

Butler's formulations about female athletes only tell part of the story because the athletic experience is based in a wild and contradictory confluence of modern and postmodern assumptions about the world, self, and how we live in that world. The postmodern notion, promulgated everywhere in the media—that you can construct your own identity and body however you might like, that there is no necessary, determinant given—is also a cherished tenet of athletic culture. "Failure is not an option," blares an ad for Max Lean from *Muscle and Fitness Hers*, "From a size 12 to a size 3 . . . in just 16 weeks." Kelly Ryan tells you how to achieve "pec perfection." Universal Nutrition features Monica Brant, posed by a roadway construction sign reading "Body Construction Ahead."[26] An ad for PHYS.com tells you that you can veto the vote your genetics cast, using their website to help you construct yourself "from the outside in." If sport culture is all about control of the self and the body, postmodern culture, with its velocity and fragments and constant change often has the effect of making one feel out of control. One easily accessible way to feel in control is through the idea of self-construction. The notion of constructing oneself becomes literal here. So although sport is a modern institution whose grounding philosophies rest on the idea of the individual who achieves independently and for whom achievement and value are part of his/her essence, the paradox is that this individual simultaneously believes that he/she is completely constructible and in

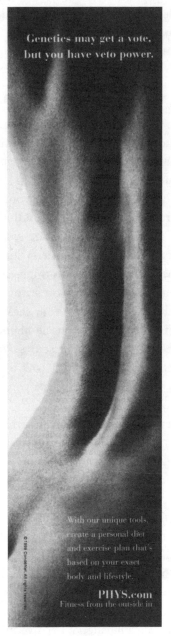

Genetics may get a vote,
but you have veto power.

With our unique tools,
create a personal diet
and exercise plan that's
based on your exact
body and lifestyle.

**PHYS.com**
Fitness from the outside in

Postmodern subject, construct thyself! PHYS.com, *Condé Nast Sports and Fitness for Women* (April 1998).

control of his/her destiny precisely through athletic performance. A postmodern performativity through sports is undergirded by a belief in a centered, controlling individual who is the agent of said achievement, and that achievement is thought to be the expression of individual essence.

This is not, however, entirely a misrecognition. The athletic experience is an experience of self forged through a tangible, physical dimension, contradictory though that experience may ultimately be. For someone engaged in serious training, the feelings of competence, development, and well-being are unmistakable, grounded in the flow of the blood and the beat of the heart, the rising heat as your muscles stretch and you become taller, stronger, more fully present than before. Your body's outlines gain shape, dimension, and you are asserted into the world, taking up space. Your shoulders back, flushed with endorphins and fast-pulsing blood, you begin to think that nothing, no one, can mess with you here, in this magical place where you swing at a ball and the bat connects, your shoulders perfect arcs, your legs a ground-devouring blur. This place where you contract muscle fibers down deep in your chest and behold, 200 pounds of iron rise over your head. This place where you gain the crest of the mountain with a steady stride, amazed by the expansion in your lungs. This place you do things you never thought you could do.

Take this magical experience, one that can be repeated over and over, whenever one wants, of this splendid body in motion, self in control, brain sending messages to dendrites, neurons, across myelin sheaths, muscles responding in perfect bursts, and tell this person she is manipulated by imagery, exploited, and reduced to sex by photographers and corporations and capitalism, that she sets the women's movement back when she steps in front of the camera and takes off her clothes. Tell her that whether she realizes it or not, she is part of a patriarchal structure that oppresses her. She will snort in derision, shake her fiery head, extend her long sculpted limbs and breathe in. This—her creation—exploited? This, her five minutes of fully realized postmodern existence, the end toward which all things tend, her five minutes of fame—this she should not do because it sets women back? This will be a language as utterly foreign to her as her body is dear, something meant for somebody else, perhaps, but not her. The words simply make no sense. It is her body, her best creation, and it is an inexplicable, marvelous source of strength. She wants you to see it. She wants everyone to see it. She wants you to see her.

The ways in which sport can bolster a modern illusion of self-sovereignty, the self as the origin of its own meaning, help explain why female athletes might experience themselves this way and therefore feel immune to the sexual objectification. For those Title-IXers schooled in the vagaries of mass-mediated selfhood, athletes both are and are not their images, both are and are not the "cultural objects" we see. Our argument is that female athletes operate from a strong, centered sense of self that they have developed in athletics and hold on to that modern sense of self even as they negotiate the postmodern context of existence by and through image. "They look at us with almost unimaginably self-confident calm: they know that we admire them and they know we have good reason to do so," Glenn W. Most writes, describing statues of Greek athletes from the fifth century B.C. "Standing before us naked causes them no embarrassment, for they have done this many times before and are proud of their bodies . . . they know what they do they do supremely well, better than anyone else. It does not even occur to them that we could want to do anything other than admire them."[27] The same sense of self-possession is operational in many female athletes today. So what if some stupid guy wants them to pose in corny retro-feminine poses like those of synchronized swimmer Heather Olson and three-time Olympian swimmer Dara Torres in the September 2000 issue of *Maxim* magazine? Who cares? These are just a few of the images of them that have been in the media, images of all different kinds. Such retro poses are just that—poses—and have nothing to do with who they are, what they've accomplished. Anyone can see it isn't them. They're just using the system to get what they want—the paradoxical postmodern existence where being derives from name recognition (though they know it doesn't really), as well as greater support for and recognition of their sports.

Which leads to a third and more prosaic explanation for why women pose for these pictures—the basic economics of gender inequity in sport.[28] They want to play, women's sports are still underfunded, and "[hetero]sex sells." In a 1999 report for the Women's Sports Foundation, "Addressing the Needs of Female Professional and Amateur Athletes," athletes on all levels reported that they play under conditions that are sometimes less than desirable. Issues like inadequate funding and gross pay inequities are part of most athletes' everyday experiences. Except for a few sports, groups reported problems with basic funding in terms of travel, accommodations, and training expenses. In the words of one team, "I think as a team we all did our part—maybe we could get a little something back. Like room and board for a week."[29]

In 2000, the Matildas, the Australian national women's soccer team, posed nude for a calendar to raise money for their sport, which was both chronically underfunded and unattended. The calendar raised a lot of money and attendance did go way up.

Amy Acuff cited the same reasons for her notorious USA Track and Field calendar, as well as her frustration that after five years of record-breaking high-jump performances, still little or no attention was given to her sport. While critics accuse athletes like Acuff, who jumped in an Anne Klein–designed fur tube top for some of her meets, of setting women's sports back, the athletes see themselves as making their sports marketable and therefore viable, a legitimate part of the cultural horizon where they have the opportunity to do what they love most: play their sport. Clearly, we have a blending of contexts and responses here— the still-existent equity issues of second wave feminism, responded to by third wave feminist athletes who use third wave strategies to fight for equity in ways that for some second wavers only reinstitute that inequity because the athletes are forced to sell their status as sexual objects in order to be athletes. But in a context where everything is sexualized and all athletes are commodities selling themselves to greater and lesser degrees, is there even such a thing as a noncommodified, nonsexualized space for sport? However, we need to still ask why men's teams are usually not forced to make "hot bod" calendars to raise money for equipment while this is much more typically a route of survival for women's teams.

Whether or not the athletes who pose in sexualized ways are "setting their sports back," in our critical analysis we also must take into consideration the fact that the recent wave of pornographic images are not the only images of female athletes available to us. All ranges of possibility are contained in the hyperreal, and the incessant drive for the "new" necessitates a restless movement from code to code. To select just a random few images from similar media outlets (Sports Illustrated for Women and Teen People), in a similar period to the one in which female athletes dropped their bras and briefs, we have shots of Stacy Draglia, getting ready to make a leap, concentration and muscles solidly in place. Brazil's center midfielder Sissi poised for a kick. Ding Meiyuan of China, gold medalist and world recordholder in women's weightlifting, poised with hundreds of pounds held triumphantly overhead. Cheryl Haworth, bronze medalist in the same, demonstrating a glam girl–coded but extremely powerful physique for *Teen People* as she stands looking with a clear, level gaze at the viewer—all 300 pounds of her mighty and gorgeous in a black dress. Gymnasts Brook Bennett and Ed Moses sharing similar statue-like muscle poses and amounts of exposed skin. And softball player Crystyl Bustos in an extraordinary photo of strength, beauty, and athleticism that focuses on her developed biceps, shaking up *Teen People*'s ordinarily gender-rigid codes.

Similarly, Jane Gottesman's traveling photography exhibit and book *Game Face: What Does a Female Athlete Look Like?*, produced in conjunction with the Smithsonian and featured on the *Today* show in July 2001, marks the triumph of the ideal of gender fluidity as a primary visual mode in the contemporary scene. The book is a stunning collection of photographs that covers everything from Olympic athletes to little girls swinging from their backyard trees. And it's there: the female masculinity we have been describing is there, shining out from the eyes of "Nancy with Fins," post-workout shoulders squared, swimming cap tight around her head. In "Eleven-Year-Old Vanessa Noble with Her 9mm Ruger P89," skinny Vanessa with braces and a girly-girl smile, gold jewelry against her blue turtleneck, Ruger in hand, ankles bowed out to the side. In Julie Krone astride her thoroughbred, covered head to toe in mud: "As an athlete, I have an insurmountable amount of desire. I'm ruthless, cocky, self-assured, and almost always unbeatable." In the 4×100-meter gold-medal Atlanta Olympics relay team at the end of their victory lap, legs raised in a jig, gorgeous six-pack midriffs tight, heads thrown back in laugher and unmediated joy: "We do things that give us more of a sense of power than the average woman." In "Corvallis High School Runners, Valley League Championships," collapsed in a circle at the end of their run, four abreast in each other's arms, soaked hair straggling from ponytails, mud streaks over their uniforms and chipped blue-painted nails, fingers lain on teammates' arms like those arms are the world's precious things. This is what a female athlete looks like. This is what female masculinity looks like. Sometimes. Sometimes that masculinity is compromised and disguised by a pornographic sexualization that feminists rightly critique, but we hope we have clarified some of the reasons why female athletes might willingly participate in this sexualization such as the sense of immunity sport gives them.[30]

At the same time, feminist critiques that focus on sexual difference, are critical of the masculine sport nexxus, and see women as less competitive, more cooperative, and more "moral" than men (in the sense of not falling into the "masculine" sport model) can work to take away what contemporary athletes might experience as hard-won gains. This chapter has attempted to demonstrate why the sense of "masculinity" defined as self-sovereignty is a positive thing for female athletes who, but for their athleticism, might not otherwise experience themselves in this way. Both the traditional prescriptions of "the feminine" that mitigated against self-assertion and the postmodern experience of subjectivity, which is an experience of self-authorship but also fragmentation, work in the contemporary context to erase the "self." Masculinity has always been equated with achievement and has been connected to the male body as a fundamental part of the formation of modern sport, which was to some extent a reaction to what was seen as the "feminization" of turn-of-the-twentieth-century culture. But masculinity is not at all the property of men. It's a quality, spirit, bright within that shines and shines and shines. Why can't we own that spirit, fire, shining grace that is and always has been with us? When and where will individuality, cockiness, wills to power be seen as part of us, our blood our teeth our bones? By symbolically incorporating "masculine" codes like individuality and self-presence, female athletes can and have been photographed in ways that are beginning to form a new iconography that is an alternative to codes of easy sexual access and vulnerability, and that doesn't necessarily cater only to the heterosexual gaze, although that is still too often the case, as in the pornographic imagery discussed earlier.

The female athlete is a powerful presence in the contemporary scene, and her sexuality, though it often is, is no longer simply coded as male active/female passive, or as exclusively receptive to men. Critical analysis needs to give credit to these emergent symbologies and complications, as well as to the fact that theorists working within the postmodern context, to quote C. L. Cole, "work from positions and locate change and movement in strategies other than the resolution of contradiction."[31] In this case, contradiction can be seen as a source of change or at least as a necessary thing.

In the culture of images we are always dealing with a mixed bag, both/ and, not either/or, and there has been some progress and there is some cause for hope—the kind of hope Toby Miller alludes to when he writes that "an unintended, potentially progressive consequence of capitalist marketing [is that] . . . the new consumerism is generating a sea change in gender norms principally evident in sports."[32] Or, as Joli Sandoz, editor of *A Whole Other Ball Game*, writes:

> Why aren't [women sportswriters] focusing more frequently on the sportswomen who choose to resist? There are many such stories out there, on the court, and in videos and essays and fiction produced by sportswomen. Instead of critiquing the media as an end in itself, shouldn't we be offering or asking readers about other ways to think about the problem? Publicizing strategies that might be more effective in the long run?[33]

We think Sandoz is right—why focus exclusively on the half-empty glass when half-full is alive and vital and in our faces? Why persist, like so much of disciplinarily based academia, in utilizing critical frameworks that incorporate an either/or kind of frame—images are either oppressive or empowering, setting things back, or moving them forward, proceeding either from a material or a hyperreal base—when all of these things are operational simultaneously? We'd much rather live in a culture that idealizes Marion Jones as a gorgeously ambiguous hero than a culture that tells us that our being is either reducible to sex or to power, and that for women the two can't mix. We must emphasize, however, that all is not equal in the land of the image, and female athletes are more often presented in ways that reduces them to their "sex appeal." Yet, as we will argue in the next chapter, the male body as a sexualized commodity is a trend on the rise, and though equal-opportunity sexploitation is a dubious development, it still suggests a new cultural context and the need for different forms of critique.

# CHAPTER FIVE

## Body Panic Parity

> Struggles over culture are not a weak substitute for a "real" politics,
> but are central to any struggle willing to forge relations among
> discursive and material relations of power, theory, and practice, as
> well as pedagogy and social change.
>
> —Henry Giroux, *Impure Acts:*
> *The Practical Politics of Cultural Studies*

### Boys Will Be Girls, and Fight It: *Fight Club*

If there is increased gender flexibility in popular cultural images, if female athletes can now in some ways own "masculinity," a parallel trend marks the male body as a "feminine" object of beauty. In terms of traditional gender codes, male and female bodies are now sometimes presented quite differently than they were in earlier decades. Female athletes and their fantasy counterparts in female action heroes, along with the overt commodification of the male body in advertisement and popular culture, have destabilized the polarity that formed the cornerstone of earlier feminist theories of objectification. This polarity argued that men were represented as active agents in the world while women were represented as passive objects valued only for their appearance. But as Susan Bordo writes in *The Male Body: A New Look at Men in Public and Private*, "nowadays, the 'act/appear' duality is even less meaningful."[1] The historical development that the male body is now a similarly commodified object, valued for its approximation of cultural ideals of male beauty and the fact that men, like women, have their own "body projects,"

Just for you: Abercrombie & Fitch catalog (spring 2000).

is a profound one, for such a development necessarily changes the whole critical framework.[2] The codes, they are a-changin', and our interpretive templates have got to keep pace.

"I'm hot, I'm for you, and you've got to live up to me" is the complicated set of messages to various audiences purveyed in this September 2000 VW ad. That a buff topless model is being pictured here as an omnipresent reminder of the new body ideal for men is clear from his looming image placed next to a generic, kind of geeky regular guy, who gazes dully out into the street as the new VW Jetta passes him by in a streak. The ad both comments on the commodification of the male body, since the ad is for Jettas and not Jardon Clothing, and makes a connection between the ideal body and the Jetta, which is described as having a "laser beam–welded, fully galvanized steel body. Just one of over 40 standard features on the Jetta." But, since it is singled out, the "fully galvanized steel body" of the Jetta that is anthropomorphosized by the model's body is clearly the most important feature, as is, by association, a "steel body" for men in general. That the clueless man standing next to the model's image is being passed by the Jetta, so fast that it is only a streak, suggests that in this cultural moment, men without steel bodies will be left in the dust.

But for all the emphasis on steel, the model's image simultaneously looks vulnerable because it is so overexposed, bright white in a dingy tan

In the dark: an ideal for men and eye candy for whomever might want him, *Women's Sports and Fitness* (September 2000).

street, naked flesh surrounded by all things covered and dim. Similarly, the model's expression makes him look gentle and even a little pleading, as if he is offering himself up to those who view him and he knows it. This is a nice guy, his eyes and mouth say, no Schwarzenneggerian Terminators here—do with me what you will. His figure is at once a reminder to men that their bodies are inadequate compared to his, *and* that he is nonetheless open and available. He's eye candy, in the moment of this image, his value resides in that fact, and he knows it. This body of steel is also the body of the boy-toy, existing for the pleasure of his consumer's gaze. The body of steel is, in this way, *like a woman's.*

The development of a cultural context in which the male body was rendered like a woman's through its sexualized, commodified status generated enough anxiety that it soon found expression in other forms of popular culture. In the fall of 1999, for instance, one major "struggle over culture" was expressed in movies such as *Fight Club,* which forwarded the male body and its status in consumer culture as one of the movie's main themes. This was an unprecedented focus, because at least since early women's liberation protesters threw their bras and eyelash curlers into the Freedom Trash Can outside the Miss America Pageant in 1968, we've been a culture that is semi-conscious of the fact that, for better or for worse, the female body is one of our most commodified economic assets. For thirty years women have pointed out ways the idealized images of the female body in the mass media are problematic, promoting insecurity in young girls and a ceaseless striving after an image of perfect thighs, breasts, and skin that is more computer-generated than real. In the late '90s, with the arrival of the female athlete as a new ideal image on the cultural stage, the feminist critique took the idealized image of the female athlete as its focus, with everyone from university professors to your next-door neighbor commenting on Brandi Chastain's sports-bra exposure of her ripped abs and the fact that the blondness of the Women's World Cup soccer team got them so much media play. Bad, bad, bad, according to these commentators, athletes should be athletes, not beauty icons. We're just subjecting women to the beauty thing again.

But it wasn't just the female soccer players who were mass media's revered and fetishized objects. Michael Jordan and many others have clearly joined the club. Commentators who interpret the whole beauty thing as a "woman's issue" forget that when Marky Mark first put his six-pack on display for Calvin Klein and the female office workers ogled Lucky Vannous's lats and ass in that Diet Coke ad of the early '90s, American culture saw the mainstreaming of the male body as a new commodity trend—a commodity trend with consequences, according to Harvard medical researchers Harrison G. Pope, Katherine A. Phillips, and Roberto Olivardia, who have recently coined the term "the Adonis complex" to describe the kind of body obsession in boys and men that used to characterize only women: exercise compulsion, binge eating, and a nearly 50 percent dissatisfaction rate with physical appearance (a full 38 percent of men surveyed said they want bigger pecs). According to these researchers, "the Adonis complex" names the "secret crisis of male body obsession" arising from "the media's powerful and unrealistic messages emphasizing an ever-more-muscular, ever-more-fit, and often unattainable male body ideal." Men can no longer get by on their achievements, as has long been the case, their appearances less important than their activities. Goodbye to all that. Boys just gotta be hot. As Toby Miller puts it, "beauty is as much a part of male sport discourse today as toughness, while grace is an avowed compatriot of violence . . . their relationship

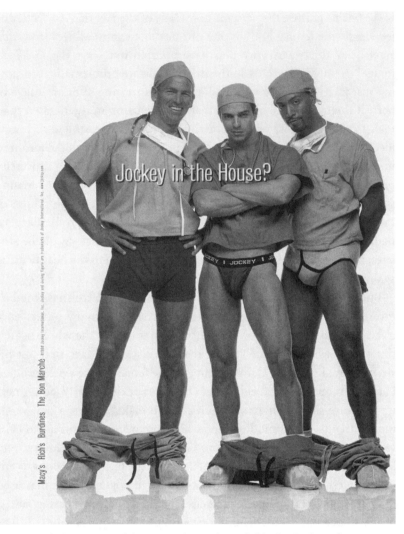

Dropping their pants: model surgeons in scrubs and skivvies, Jockey ad,
*Women's Sports and Fitness* (June 2000).

has become crucial to marketing both individuals and sports itself in
ways that were occasional and casual in earlier times."[3] So the commentators who are so quick to cry out against sexualized media representations of women forget that boys and men have become the object of the
same desirous, product-buying inducing gaze that the girls and women
have, and that our analyses should accommodate this change and its
consequences.

Men as sexualized boy-toys and a female beauty that's been reformu-
lated as the muscular, ripped torso of Brandi Chastain? Some of us aren't
complaining a bit, but in the fall of 1999 some boys were waging a war
against the image, a campaign to take back the gaze. American culture
delivered a raft of media productions that focused on the so-called
emasculated position of the American male. Among them was a movie,
*Fight Club,* that fast achieved cult status and spawned imitators. *Fight
Club* offered raw flesh as a refuge from the simulacrum of consumer
culture, the gym and muscular physicality as a retreat to the real of masculinity that's been stripped away by the omnipresence of mass media
and consumer fluff. In that context of commodification and consumption, boys were being treated *like girls,* and as recent media conversations have shown, they didn't like it a bit.[4]

## The First Rule of Fight Club Is: *Occupatio*

When analyzing the context for and meaning of *Fight Club,* three things
come immediately to mind: modernism and its prissily obsessive horror
of feminized mass culture, watered-down Baudrillard (the "real" is now
a commodity sign, the media, the hyperreal) and *occupatio.* Occupatio
is the rhetorical device by which a speaker says he will not talk about or
tell us what he does in fact end up telling us. *Fight Club* is organized
around just such a premise. "You do not talk about Fight Club" because
its activities—men getting together on weeknights in the male-only space
of tavern basements to literally beat the shit out of each other, slamming
each other's faces into the concrete, pair by ecstatic pair—supposedly is
antithetical to the passive, consumer-based pastimes of late twentieth-
century capitalism. The brutal activity of the fight redeems the emasculated male from the historical displacement that is his construction as a
feminized consumer. Na na na na na na, "it's for men only," the film's
initially hapless and unnamed narrator (Edward Norton) quickly sneers
at Marla (Helena Bonham Carter), his "sportfuck," when she asks what
Fight Club is. There seems to be a lot at stake in keeping Fight Club a
male-only space, and a lot at stake in not talking about what's at stake.
Rhetorically, the whole film makes use of occupatio, for the redemptive
power of the retro-male Fight Club, what you're not supposed to talk
about, is in fact what everyone talks about.

Such talk about not talking, however, is manly talk, and invokes Baudrillard's mass-media appropriatable formulations about the unreality

of consumer culture. The narrator, an insomniac made into the walking dead man by his empty addiction to material things, tries to explain his and other men's needs for Fight Club by offering up (with eyes requisitely glazed), pseudo-philosophical neologisms like, "everything's a copy of a copy of a copy," or "this is your life, and it's ending one minute at a time." Norton's character seems a contemporary Charlie Marlow (Conrad's beleaguered narrator in *Heart of Darkness*) expressing his horror of a world based on consumption that is nothing, the unnamed narrator insists, if not a simulacrum. In the world before they created Fight Club, they were all "slave[s] to the Ikea nesting instinct. . . . I flip[ped] through catalogs and wonder[ed] what kind of dining set define[d] me as a person." Real men don't define themselves through dining chairs—get it?

Real men, in fact, don't like women at all, superficial Starbucks-chugging, new VW Beetle–driving, liposuctioning-our-hips-off idiots that we are. In one scene, Norton and the film's Subject-Presumed-to-Know, Tyler Durden (Brad Pitt), are smashing cars and reserve a special sneer of contempt for the Beetle, which is obviously much too much the girly car. In another scene, they raid the garbage bins behind a liposuction clinic to get the fat they need to make the soap they sell to department stores for absurd sums, "selling," Durden says in his superior, fuck-it-all-I'm-too-cool-to-care-about-anything growl, "rich women's fat asses back to them."

While explaining why things like relationships and marriage are farcical and empty and sounding more than a bit like the post–World War II "Momism" of writers like Philip Wylie, Tyler proclaims that "we're a generation of men raised by women and I'm wondering if another woman is really the answer we need."[5] Women, apparently, are connected to the unreality of consumption that *Fight Club* redeems, for the answer that we do need, according to the film, is men brutalizing other men and themselves in order to truly reclaim their lost masculine identity and to be "man enough" to face the darkness of the world of violent brutality that lies just underneath consumerism's passive, shiny surface.

After the initial framing device, the film opens at the point when Norton's character, unable to sleep, becomes addicted to support groups where men stand around holding each other and crying and repeating mantras like, "Yes, we're men. Men is what we are," but the film makes this an easy satire. By the film's logic, they are not men because they are acting too feminine and are too far from the "essential" violence at the hearts of their natures. Unlike the feminized pap of self-help workshops, Fight Club works as an answer because, according to Tyler, he and his Fight Club brethren are

> an entire generation pumping gas, waiting tables. Slaves with white collars. Advertising has us chasing clothes and working jobs we hate so we can buy shit we don't need. We're the mental children of history, man. No purpose or place. We have no great war. We have no great depression. Our war is a spiritual war. Our great depression is our lives. We've all been raised by television to believe that one day we'd all be millionaires and movie gods and rock stars. But we won't. We're slowly learning that fact. And we're very, very pissed off.

Oh, but you are a god, man. It's just the messed-up world that won't let you be. Except, of course, you are a movie god. . . . Put another way, in a consumer, entertainment-driven economy, only a celebrity is allowed individuality, and in a culture that worships the individual, our raison d'etre becomes celebrity magazines. In his discussion of the power of celebrity, P. David Marshall writes,

> In the public sphere, a cluster of individuals are given greater presence and a wider scope of activity and agency than are those who make up the rest of the population. They are allowed to move on the public stage while the rest of us watch. They are allowed to express themselves quite individually and idiosyncratically while the rest of the members of the population are constructed as demographic aggregates. We tend to call these overtly public individuals celebrities.[6]

As Tyler puts it in another of his ironic tirades, ironic because the celebrity Brad Pitt is the ultimate consumer object and subject, "we are by-products of a lifestyle recession. Murder, crime, poverty—these things don't concern us. What concerns us is celebrity magazines, television with 500 channels, some guys' name on my underwear."

Horrors. Having some guy's name on your underwear is just a little too . . . proprietary. Suggestive. Let the chicks have some guy's name plastered across their chiseled stomachs, but not (heterosexual?) men. Let women define themselves as consumers. "You are not your fucking khakis," Tyler admonishes both the camera and his sheepish male audiences at Fight Club who are now ashamed they had accepted the consumer code. Real men don't wear Calvin Kleins or khakis. Real men "lose the tie" and the DKNY, strip down to their pants, and confront the same blood-and-guts morality as Hamlet in his "alas, poor Yorick" speech

by slamming each other's faces into the concrete, destroying the beauti-
fied image that has canceled their authentic identities as smelly, brutal
men. In one of the film's most violent scenes, the narrator goes over the
edge and won't stop hitting the typecast Jared Leto, who, bleached blonde
and graphically beautiful, becomes the film's literal whipping boy as the
narrator destroys half his face to the extent of extreme disfiguration
and punching out one of his eyes because "I felt like destroying something beautiful." Poor pretty boys. Poor narrator. Poor Tyler, righteous
angry victims of the feminizing maw of consumption, and their emasculated place within the economy at large. It's no coincidence that the
Fight Club guys have service jobs that make them seem unimportant,
cogs in a machine: waiters, copy boys at Kinko's, low-level execs subject
to the whims of sniveling bosses with soft flabby guts.[7]

Though their violence and "rebel" masculinity is clearly a response to
the social conditions in which they find themselves, the film romanti-
cizes the brutality it constructs as the reality of the (male) human condition, the antidote to the prettified surfaces of the media scene (to which
those low-level jobs are linked): "when the fight was over, nothing was
solved. But nothing mattered. Afterwards, we all felt saved," explains
Norton's character, after one of the bloodiest fight sequences. "Reject
the basic assumptions of civilization," instructs Tyler, "especially the importance of material possessions." Please. If you're going to try to elevate
your disempowered white-boy angst to the status of metaphysics, at least
read your *Cliff's Notes* version of metaphysics first. And cop to the fact
that you are directly implicated in all the things you critique.

This is the source of *Fight Club*'s bad faith: its claims for difference
reinforce the very thing from which it claims to be different, giving the
same old modalities of rebellion a new wardrobe, the way it ineluctably
participates in the very structures it claims to stand outside of and reject. No longer a slave to his Ikea or his DKNY, the Norton character
proclaims that for the members of Fight Club, "we all started seeing
things differently. Everywhere we went, we were sizing things up. I felt
sorry for guys packed into gyms, trying to look like how Calvin Klein
and Tommy Hilfiger said they should look. Is that what a man looks
like?" Norton gestures to the model, with the requisite chiseled pecs and
detailed abs, in an ad for Gucci underwear posted inside the bus he and
Tyler are taking. Tyler smirks and delivers one of his omnipresent max-

ims: "Self-improvement is masturbation." But in the very next scene, Tyler rises triumphant from his latest fight, his pecs even better developed, his abs even more detailed, than those on the Gucci model he's just dismissed. Pitt's body is, in fact, in better shape for this movie than for any of his others, his muscular development so pronounced that at first it only seemed possible that this was a body double, not Pitt. So while Pitt may not have been "packed in a gym" because he had his own exclusive facilities in which to train, by Tyler's logic, Pitt's *Fight Club* body is the product of some serious, serious masturbation. A body that looks like Pitt's in this movie is the product of no less than nine months of serious gym time of the six-day-a-week, three-to-four-hours-a-day kind, as well as following a diet so restrictive as to be downright scientific.

But like his movie character, Pitt is the voice of bad faith when, in the *Rolling Stone* feature "The Unbearable Bradness of Being" that appeared at the time of *Fight Club*'s release, he insists that the look of his body is natural, that he hadn't trained much for the role, and that "I eat crap. I'm one of those guys you hate because of genetics. It's the truth." Please. The first rule of serious weight training is: genetics are only one-quarter of the picture. Diet, nutritional supplementation, cardiovascular training, and specific, focused lifting make up the rest.

Because of its need to make protestations to the contrary (I don't care about my image at all, nope, not me), *Fight Club* needs to make use of occupatio in order to make the argument it makes in talking about the feminization of the contemporary male that no one wants talked about in the first place, because talking about it would be to admit that such a thing—feminized men—exist.[8] According to Pope, Phillips, and Olivardia however, "men of all ages are preoccupied with the appearance of their bodies. They almost never talk about this problem, because in our society, men have been taught that they aren't supposed to be hung up about how they look."[9] Leave that to the women. Men almost never talk about the problem because if they do, they will sound like women (or, perhaps, gay men). This is the real truth that *Fight Club* hides—not that we have to be "man enough" to face the dark brutality of masculine "nature" that's denied by all this prettified consumption, but the truth that, like it or not, the tough guy is dead, and there's no way out of the circle of globalization, economic instability, and consumption that makes "women" of us all, except maybe the CEOs of the multinationals.[10]

## Body Panic Parity: Social Contexts for *Fight Club*

Perhaps global shifts in the economy account for the changing unstable status of men in workplaces, with more and more low-paying jobs on the one hand and increasingly unstable and rapidly disappearing high-paying jobs on the other. These changes are linked to men's increasing concern with their bodies and images. Though many discussions of body-image issues exclude them, increasingly male value is judged by the male equivalent to T&A: abs and pecs. Susan Bordo writes,

> It used to be a truism among those of us familiar with the research on body image problems, that most men (that is, most straight men, on whom the studies were based) were largely immune ... but a decade later ... [when] men were asked how they would like to see themselves, three of men's top six answers were about looks: attractive, sexy, good looking. Male "action" qualities—assertiveness, decisiveness—trailed at numbers eight and nine.[11]

In mass-media imagery, the male body is increasingly divorced from personality: just who was that Diet Coke guy? Who are the Jockey underwear guys? Those Abercrombie and Fitch guys? The male ideal is a ripped, athletic image, all about six-packs and chiseled shoulders. It is an ideal based solely on looks: who cares if this guy can make conversation, what does his butt look like? This ideal is having an effect. Like Naomi Wolf's early 1990s treatise *The Beauty Myth,* which helped to document and create a widespread awareness about the negative effects of beauty culture on women and self-esteem, Pope, Phillips, and Olivardia cite a growing number of men like Scott, who is 26 years old, 5 feet 9, 180 pounds, 7 percent body fat, 31-inch waist, 46-inch chest, and has the requisite six-pack. But despite his exact approximation of the new male ideal, Scott constantly fears he isn't big enough and is too fat, doesn't think he is big or masculine enough to appeal to women, and "puts all his hopes and dreams into his workouts and not his daily life." He is obsessed with his body, and is quoted as saying that "if you could see what I was thinking about during the day, 90 percent of the time it would have something to do with either my weightlifting, diet, or the way I look. I can't go past a mirror without posing just for a minute to check out my body." Scott has feelings of panic if he can't get to the gym and would ask his girlfriend several times a day whether he looked big or muscular enough. "Over the last several years," Pope, Harrison, and Olivardia report, "we've interviewed many men with Scott's condition."[12]

In an article for the Adios Barbie website, Chris Godsey asks himself,

> Why do I spend so much time in the mirror, flexing and twisting and prodding and scrutinizing every part of my body that I deem less-than-perfect? Why can a Polo sport ad inspire me to denounce all fat and commit every waking moment to some sort of muscle-building or cardiovascular activity.... I don't want to say it, but it's true. It's like I'm a woman. My sense of self-esteem too often depends on how I see my body... and I'm not the only guy going through it.[13]

Being "like a woman," of course, is also being "like a gay man" due to the feared supposed narcissism of the (often white, middle-class) gay male community. Straight men have been sold the same bodily objectification to which gay men and women have long been subject. The codes are merging. According to Peter Arnell of the New York advertising agency The Arnell Group, "the male torso reigned as the most powerful crossover image [of the '90s], appealing to men, women, gays, and straights alike."[14] The naked male torso is ubiquitous in ads, and men's magazines now focus on how to achieve the "right look" in a way that parallels similar invocations in women's magazines and results in body panic parity. Research on the effect of this panic on the lives of ordinary men reveals a parity of issues that used to be "women's issues": "chronic depression, compulsive behaviors, and often seriously impaired relationships with family members and loved ones" (25).[15]

Though we hadn't had a name for it yet, the "Adonis complex" made perfect sense to us. We'd seen it in the gym, and Leslie saw it even more graphically at the athletic department at her university. In the weight room where Leslie served as a strength-training coach for intercollegiate athletics, the male athletes spent more time scrutinizing their bodies in the mirror than did the women.[16] At first it made her laugh to see them splitting their bodies into parts and anxiously cataloging them, one criticizing his lack of deltoids, the next distressed by the size of his pecs, the next agonizing that his abs weren't as cut as the guy's next to him. One day, when the wrestling and track teams were lifting at the same time, stretching the small gym to capacity, one group of men in the corner started lifting their shirts and scrutinizing their abs, the male body part most often focused upon in advertising and movies. The men's conversation sounded exactly like the conversations we've all heard for years in women's locker rooms, only with the focus on a different part: "my abs aren't flat enough. Yuk. Look how fat I am. You can only see four squares, not six. Look at all this garbage!" (he was grabbing his "love handles," clearly loved no more).

The conversation started with one group in the corner, but within a few minutes it had spread through the whole gym and any onlooker would have been treated to the previously unlikely spectacle of at least seventy men, cute boys all, eighteen to twenty years old with some of the most beautiful bodies you've ever seen, anxiously pulling up their shirts and simultaneously discussing their bodies' shortcomings. A spectacle for our times. "It used to be I'd have to tease the women," the track coach of one of these anxious male teams said, "about how much they worried about their appearances, how much time they'd spend in the locker room in the mirror, fussing with their hair. But now, the guys are worse than the girls are!" And as if to prove him right, at just that moment one of the male sprinters, who had just been debating with his teammate whether the shape of his gluteus maximus was up to snuff, turned and said, "I've gotta have a bubble butt for the ladies—am I right?" Our current aesthetic standards demand no less and it's a rush: after years of having our own bodyparts cataloged, dissected, evaluated for their adequacy or inadequacy, now the male body is up for scrutiny, too.

So now we're all judges, equally scrutinized and scrutinizing. Trying to live up to images that for men are only achievable through steroids and digital manipulation, and for women are most often produced only through plastic surgery and digital manipulation. We know this. We are cynics, savvy critics, we know the media's tricks of the trade, but we try to live up to the images anyway. Body image is the great equalizer, related to a new equality of anxiety about image that makes traditional gender-role stereotypes based on the idea that women are the sole object of the gaze ("men act, women appear, men look at women, women watch themselves being looked at," as John Berger famously put it) more obsolete. This obsolescence is the "truth" *Fight Club* strives to cover with its hymns to smashed faces and hot boy blood.[17]

Intoxicated though the world of advertising slogans and other forms of mass media are with the ideas of self-determination and control, cultural theorists such as Susan Bordo have argued that the very insistence on these themes shows that they are increasingly unavailable to us.[18] An older generation's critical models insist that we do have control, that we can just "turn off the t.v." if we don't want to be part of image culture and the body panic it prescribes. But if our lives are lived even partially in Baudrillard's hyperreal, a critical model that assumes there is a safe haven to which we can escape is in bad faith. Like the characters in *Fight Club,* claiming a self-determination that eventually backfires and ends in utopian silliness (blowing up the buildings that house the credit-card companies), critical models that assume an outside "doth protest too much." Why not begin from a critical model that is honest, that admits to some complicity with images, to just how much of our own lives, our pleasures, our griefs, our very selves, are bound up in the construction of our bodies, hair, accessories, clothes, from a model that addresses how we're all "women" in this way? Let's not pull another occupatio like *Fight Club.* Let's talk about what we're talking about. You are your fucking khakis, the male body is becoming more "beautiful" even as we speak, and you, gentle readers, have got a lot to live up to.

## Girls Will Be Boys: *Girlfight, Tomb Raider, Killer Woman Blues*

Heeding the call of the image and its structuring power, however, is not something many academics like to do, from right-leaning traditionalists who still insist that popular culture is just so much "fluff" to left-leaning politicos who do the same in their materialist mantras that see cultural images as somehow irrelevant and divorced from structural realities or "the real." In Henry Giroux's words,

> orthodox leftist criticism mirrors the increasing cynicism and despair exemplified in its endless invocation of such terms as "reality politics" and its call for a return to materialism. In the end, its rhetoric appears largely as a high-minded puritanism ("the only true members of the church") matched only by an equally staunch ideological rigidity that barely conceals its contempt for notions of difference, cultural politics, and social movements.[19]

There is a definite difference at play in the images and trends analyzed here, a shift in cultural politics, a coming to fruition of some of the earlier tenets of the (liberal feminist part of the) women's movement such as the right to individual development for women, a change in the expectation that a woman live only for her husband and children and sacrifice her self-development for theirs. Old feminist mantras that criticize the "objectification" of women or criticize beauty culture for its promotion of unattainable ideals have to expand to include men, for whom beauty culture is now a pressure. Few would argue that women should be self-sacrificing in the sense of trading all their individual development for service to their families (there is some flexibility about what kind of families we form, or whether we do so). Whether the image always reflects lived reality is a real question, but the strong woman icon—of whom the female athlete is the most obvious example—is much more widely visible than she once was, and she is often taken as a sign of differences in gender roles. Yet for some critics, these differences that have developed in the last thirty years, and especially the last ten, don't take the "right" form.[20]

In *Killer Woman Blues,* for instance, cultural critic Benjamin DeMott decries the cultural ascendance of what he calls the "killer woman": "the entire culture industry appears obsessed with reducing feminism itself to a venture in wish fulfillment, an expression of the presumably universal desire of women to think, feel, and behave like stereotypical men." DeMott's book is focused on exactly the double-stranded cultural trend we have been tracing: the "feminization" of men through consumerism and the "masculinization" of women through iconic figures like the female athlete. But while we argue that this trend can be a positive step toward gender fluidity and equity in representation, a destabilization (not a reversal) of old polarities that place the individual self, competitiveness, and achievement on the side of masculinity and self-sacrifice for others, consensus-building, and caretaking on the side of femininity, DeMott argues that what he calls "women-becoming-men" is actually an endorsement of and a cover for "corporate aspiration . . . seen clearly, the killer woman functions as a . . . new savior for the country's profit-maddened." He sees the iconic figure of the powerful woman as a betrayal of feminism and social justice, as the scapegoat and figurehead for corporate bottom-line mentality—for DeMott, she stands in for the inhumane values of the corporations, which are then absolved because it's a woman arguing for those values. Throughout the book he makes it sound as if he is a supporter of feminism, at least the transform-the-world by introducing a "woman-centered" perspective form of feminism, which is the only kind of feminism DeMott seems to accept as valid.[21]

Keep the sexes in their "essential" places, but "listen" to each other and things will change for the better seems to be the bottom line *Killer*

*Woman Blues* argues, in a more sophisticated version of the "men are from Mars, women are from Venus" argument. He attacks the idea of women taking on "masculine" attributes, claiming that for women to do this means that "utopia equals agreement, by both genders, that victory in the global competition is the big thing and the only thing" (206). While he is also critical of men acting "like women" ("males . . . take up effeminacy or ditsiness as modes of charm or 'style,' or by adopting the sulky manners of the cunt-tease") (xiii), his main mode of contestation seems to be that men are properly ruthless corporate raiders. It is women's job to change this "nature,"[22] and so women's emulation of this stereotypical male role is devastating for everyone. "Who's going to be gentle and love the children?" seems to be his implicit background cry. Never once does he suggest that women or men could be "masculine" and "feminine" simultaneously, that each could be guys in one context and girls in the next depending on the situation. Despite his calls for "gender flexibility," his argument relies on white middle-class and binaristically opposed notions of gender essentialism, for it is women's job, according to DeMott, to critique masculinity, not act it out. But what about men critiquing masculinity? If DeMott is so antimasculine/corporate, why only attack the representations of women who seem to embody this ethos? Why not simultaneously attack the countless representations of men who do so? What masquerades as an argument for "social justice" too often sounds like an argument for a return to traditional gender roles with classic inequities in power and privilege. At base, his argument seems rather Victorian: women "really" are kinder and gentler and they're just being duped by mass-media representations that suggest they should be tough. It is their responsibility to see through this current sham and through their innate "ethic of care" make the world kinder and gentler because no one else is going to do it (though he does cite a couple of examples of men who do). While DeMott notes that "a prime element" of the "killer woman" persona "is the air of having escaped into freedom and self-sovereignty," he seems to see such ideas as contributing to a bad, corporate mentality, but never suggests that men's freedoms are also troubled (or that both men and women's "natures" are made more complex given intersections of race, class, and sexuality).[23]

One of the best features of the iconic female athlete is precisely this suggestion of self-sovereignty, but DeMott doesn't like the idea of self-sovereignty, at least not for women. Indeed, his argument is not unlike the old arguments of female physical educators and their corollary in more contemporary spokespersons like Varda Burstyn: it is women's responsibility to counteract the immorality and ruthlessness of men's sports and transform sport into a more humane practice. As Colette Dowling points out in *The Frailty Myth*,

> female teachers of physical education envisioned a world where "women's sports" would be different from men's . . . they wanted to see difference in men's and women's sports, not sameness, in part to assure that their jobs were unique and would not be taken over by men. . . . Basketball was pruned into a scaled-down version of the men's game. . . . Stars were not allowed.[24]

The "star," the ultimate figure of competence, the one who stands out, the individual elevated above the rest, is the ultimate bugbear for critics like DeMott and Burstyn because a "star" is the representative of masculine, individualist, antidemocratic values. The star is the antithesis of sameness, and women athletes are often criticized for taking on the star persona. Venus Williams, for instance, was initially criticized for being "too cocky" and celebrating her victories over her rivals much as male stars do (her marketing reps persuaded her that such behavior was not in her best financial interest).[25] Mia Hamm was always given kudos for being self-effacing, for insisting that her performances were no different from those of her teammates. Men can be stars, women can't—both mass media and cultural criticism seem to want women to be different, "team players."

But such criticisms forget the fact that, if the goal is really social change, the icon or star is a crucial figure in a culture almost entirely driven by the star system, and that making stars of female athletes can have positive effects. Dowling writes that "girls began following their new, athletic role models the way groupies used to follow rock stars," with the result that "today's young women are developing ways of standing up— with their bodies, if need be, for their rights . . . female strength, courage, and competitiveness are providing women a new way to live in the world."[26] There is a connection between the star system and the sense of individuality and possibility it confers on girls that has a different effect than it does on boys: while the latter confirms a traditional masculine role that is based on the devaluation of the feminine and women, the former stages a fight against that devaluation in a way that is necessarily linked to the concept of individuality and strength. This is not to say that "masculine" values such as individuality and strength are the only values that are of value, but rather that one has to have a sense of self-worth, value, and strength, and be recognized as such before one can be of value as a team player or supporter. Notions of innate difference that draw absolute binaries between individual/group, star/supporter, self/other, and male/female, and that want women to follow the ideology always associated with the second term in order to supposedly "transform" or "humanize" the corporate world or men's sports and fight for "social justice" do a fundamental disservice to the very categories of people they would claim to support.

What DeMott and others forget in their eagerness to keep women from acting like men is that, in Dowling's words, "without difference you cannot have hierarchy. . . . Hierarchy is how social inequality is maintained, and 'masculinity' and 'femininity' are about hierarchy. Supposedly 'natural' differences between men and women are used to validate the differences in the amount of social power they had" (48). Anti-star, team-oriented, properly and "naturally" self-effacing women reinforce the concept of innate gender difference and symbolically keep women, even at the peak of their achievements, from being able to claim the priority and precedence that would deconstruct gender hierarchies based on the idea of difference. Women being "like men" in the sense of being proud of their individual achievements and calling attention to them isn't necessarily or exclusively about perpetuating "bad" masculine, corporate values as DeMott and some versions of radical feminism would have it. It can also be seen as a refusal to step aside, a refusal of a secondary, supportive role, and as a move toward real equality in terms of whom, in the most basic sense, is valued in a given culture and who isn't.[27] An equality of valuation that results from the demonstrable erosion of gender difference is something that the female athlete and the "killer women" associated with her are beginning to approach.

It is precisely this erosion of difference that *Fight Club* and *Killer Woman Blues* protest and that the 2000 movie *Girlfight* (the winner of Sundance Festival awards) celebrates. If *Fight Club* demonstrated cultural anxiety about the feminization of men, and *Killer Woman Blues* protests the advent of the tough girl, *Girlfight* is an example of what De-Mott identifies critically as the new cultural celebration of strong women. *Girlfight* shares some of the same values that *Fight Club* holds dear, but articulates these values from a very different perspective. They are what have traditionally been "boy" values, like the sign hanging on the wall of the boxing gym that reads, "when you're not training, someone else is training to kick your ass!" But unlike *Fight Club,* which tries to keep the rough stuff for the boys, *Girlfight* argues that not only are these values adoptable by women, they represent human potential and development in a dog-eat-dog world where victimization is the norm and everyone has to fight for a place. Access to the world of such values is necessary to even get in the game, to signify in the film's cultural context at all. In what has become something of a cinematic norm in the last few years, the film concentrates on a gender reversal in which Diana Guzman (Michelle Rodriguez) is treated by others (especially her father) as if she is a stereotypical girl when she is actually a natural at the "guy stuff" like boxing, an activity in which her brother (a "sensitive artist" type) only half-heartedly participates, much preferring his more "feminine" activities, drawings and artwork, to the rough-and-tumble of the gym. Eventually Diana's brother gives her the money his father gives him for boxing lessons and lets her take them instead. This move is meant to indicate that left to their own devices, the "true selves" of this brother and sister do not conform to established gender roles.[28] When a boxing trainer, sounding a bit like DeMott, says, "Boys are different from girls. What's so wrong about saying it out loud? Boys are different from girls. No girl has what it takes to be a boxer," he establishes the gender "difference" position the movie contests. Though one might raise the question of whether "what it takes to be a boxer" is ultimately of any value for either men or women, for *Girlfight* women's participation in sports like boxing is one of the few ways to gain respect from those around them.[29]

This is important, because the film is very clear that before Diana became known as a boxer and was perceived as a girl, she was nobody, had no real identity in the terms of this world. At the beginning of the film, she sits in school, staring off into space, not at all part of her surroundings, like she's waiting for her life to begin—and she is. She has nowhere to fit in, is invisible as "somebody" because the only "somebodiness" that seems to be offered to the women in this particular world (working class, urban, most of the characters multiracial) is the "nobodiness" (or all-bodiness) of the sex object. As Diana puts it derisively, referring to one of the school's most popular girls, "always with that damn mirror of hers [puts on a feminine voice]—'ooh, just a second. Let me get my mouth just perfect so I can suck on your dick, which is all I'm good for anyway.'" Diana knows that physical appearance and sexuality qualify as the only value markers for women and wants to be "good for" more than this. She knows and can talk the bottom-line, no-romance language of the guy world: "Guess I'm not prime trim, huh?" she says to Adrian, a fellow boxer for whom she develops feelings. "How'd you get so fucking crude?" he asks her. "How'd you get so fucking polite?" she responds, turning gender conventions on their head. A clear example of DeMott's excoriation of the "killer woman" as a naive stand-in for corporate values, *Girlfight* equates politeness with "ladylike" decorum and subsequent vulnerability to devaluation and abuse, and the ability to stand up for oneself with Diana's adoption of guy-action and guy-speak.

The movie shows the traditional female role to be one of limitation and victimization. Diana's now-deceased mother had been continually abused by her husband, Diana's father. He is always shown in a biceps-emphasizing, wife-beater tank top swigging a beer, taut as if ready to strike, physically threatening. Juxtapositions are used to make the point in *Girlfight* that there should be and is a choice for women outside of the limitations of traditional roles. After a scene where Diana is shown at the dinner table, cleaning up after her brother and father, she looks despairingly out the window at a young mother abjectly trying to console her crying child. With an expression both sad and determined, Diana goes immediately to her father's room and takes money out of his wallet for boxing lessons. The only time we see her smiling with joy is when she's watching boxing. While boxing is for her boyfriend Adrian an escape from the "nobodiness" of the limitations placed on him as a working-class white male with no future, for Diana it is an escape out of the nobodiness and self-cancellation of the female role. Sitting together in a bombed-out urban park, looking despairingly toward the tenement apartments where they live, Adrian says "in places like this, no one matters ... that's not going to be my life man. I'm going to run pro and I'm going to move far away from here. Somewhere where I'm not going to get killed doing my laundry." "Right," Diana says, "or raped in your own fucking stairway." They both fight the idea that "no one matters" and the physical violence that seems to characterize their neighborhood, but for Diana it's also a matter of refusing the victimization that seems to accompany the quiet self-effacement of the traditional female role.

This scene where Adrian and Diana calculate their worth or lack of it in the urban world in which they live is juxtaposed with a scene from

Diana's gym class. There, we see what "regular girls" are like and why they might be vulnerable to such physically intimidating postures as those Diana's father strikes, and why Diana doesn't want to be one of them. In their President's Council on Physical Fitness test they are the poster girls for incompetence, as none of them, with the exception of Diana, can do a single pullup, pushup, or run a lap. White girls, black girls, Hispanic girls, racially mixed girls alike, they are completely ineffectual, uncoordinated in their movements, lacking in will. Diana's physical prowess forms a stark contrast, as she does one-legged pushups with ease and can do as many pullups as they can't. But the movie is careful to show that the difference is Diana's refusal of social definitions rather than anything innate. When Veronica, the movie's traditional girly-girl sex object (though there's a twist in the tradition in that Veronica is black), says to Diana, "looks like those hormone treatments really do the job," she calls attention to socially constructed ideas about what's "natural" in men and women. But the movie is clearly critical of Veronica's idea that a woman has to take hormones in order to be strong. Instead, it presents gender on a spectrum, and masculinity and femininity as qualities shared by bodies of both genders. It is polarization, notions of innate, essential difference, that are shown to be outmoded cultural assumptions that can result in degradation and abuse—assumptions that, according to Sherrie A. Inness, "bind women to the cult of femininity and separate them from authority and power."[30] It's "boys" like Diana who deny that separation and refuse those assumptions and abuse.

One of the climactic scenes in the movie is the scene where not only does Diana refuse her father's abuse, but gives it back to him once and for all. When, in a confrontation after her first boxing match (her father doesn't want her to box), Diana starts calling her father out about his treatment of her mother, he tries to cut her off with "Hey, I'm your father," as if that appeal to his authority will just shut her down. "Yeah, some father," she responds. "the only thing you had the heart to love [her mother] you practically beat into a grave." He tells her to shut up but she just keeps talking, at which point he shoves her into the refrigerator and hits her. Then, in a stunning sequence, she sends him staggering with a blow to the face and soon knocks him to the ground, stepping over and beginning to choke him. Both the father and Diana's brother beg her to stop as she tells him, "I could snap your neck right now if I felt like it. I could kill you if I felt like it—Did you stop when Mom begged? Did you stop when she said 'please'? You belong to me now. How does it feel to see so much of yourself so close? How does it feel?" This scene is a perfect example of what DeMott excoriates as the new pop-culture tradition in which women now act as brutally as men, but what he misses in his plea for the "social justice" of gender difference is the power of the mirror effect. By physically overpowering him, by being as threatening as he ever was, Diana holds a mirror up to her father where he can see what abuse looks and feels like, where he can experience first-hand the devastation of "belonging" to someone else, having yourself erased in this way. There is no more potent cure for abusive behavior than this, and Diana's father is transformed by this experience in a way that no "feminine" pleas on Diana's part for the recognition of her "different" perspective could have produced. If observing the social roles of femininity leads women to hopelessness, sexual exploitation, and suicide as it does in *Girlfight*, observing the social roles of masculinity has for women the power to redress those wrongs and to make people see women as something rather than nothing, as beings-in-themselves rather than as solely beings-for-others.[31]

Diana's ascent from nobodiness to somebodiness is clearly linked to her physical development and prowess. "All these years," she tells her father after she's left him incapacitated on the floor, "you just looked right through me," with the implication that now he's going to have to see her, take her seriously as a person. "Looking right through" women as if they didn't matter, as if they weren't there, is what *Girlfight* argues the culture of gender difference does to girls, and is what physical abuse does to them more particularly—makes them invisible, erases their personhood, wipes them out. Again juxtaposition in scenes is key, for the scene where Diana kicks the shit out of her father is immediately followed by a scene in which Adrian says, "As a matter of fact, I feel pretty fucking small around you, so be nice," prompting Diana to ask, "So I'm someone, huh?" and he says, "Yeah, you are." Unlike his conventionally attractive girlfriend who follows the standard female narrative, Diana becomes "someone" because she insists on being seen in her own terms—as a boxer, as a fighter, not a "girl."

Diana is a good example of what M. Ann Hall calls "the reshaping of feminism into individualism, self-growth, and the commodification of everyday life, with an increasing focus on the body and women's physicality."[32] Diana's "growth" in the movie is an individual growth, and her body is the agency of such growth. If for men, athletic achievement has always been a standard for "somebodiness," Diana uses that same standard to redeem her status as generic girl. Does her individual growth, then, help the status of the generic girls to whom she is contrasted, or does it merely serve to reinforce those conventions because she is presented as different? The movie seems to suggest that her form of ascendance is available to all girls, but is this particular form actually an ideal in terms of everyday experience? This points to perhaps the most problematic paradox of the athletic female icon. "Next couple of weeks," her trainer tells her, "I'm going to train you so hard you'll be wired like a machine." "Machine" status is the precondition for "somebodiness" in athletic culture, and while this is now one of the available avenues of somebodiness for women, an identity that is dependent on athletic performance and treating one's body like a "machine" is just as problematic for women as it has always been for men. It is still an externally based form of valuation, dependent on performance and training practices that are not always in the service of health. What will boxing gain for Diana in the long term? Permanent cultural valuation, or permanent brain damage? The film stops short of confronting such issues and underemphasizes the fact that race and class status make discussions of girls and women, boys and men, all the more complex.

A more complicated psychology to the argument in *Girlfight* has reference to the everyday. Though some feminist critics didn't like what they saw as a conventional romantic ending where it is clear that Diana and Adrian will be together (didn't like it because Diana is learning to be independent of men and isn't supposed to be going for a traditional lifeless life of marriage and kids), this is a romance with a difference. While the romantic ending could also easily be read as trying to make Diana heterosexually appealing to compensate for the fact that her sport "masculinizes" her—makes her "abnormal" as noted above regarding Veronica's comments about hormones, therefore placing her sexuality under suspicion until we are reassured she is a "real girl" because she's with a boy—that reading would also have limitations. Again a strange logic of gender essentialism would come into play in such a reading. For if, by the usual rules, Diana would be "one down" in the conventional boy/girl romance narrative, giving him power over her, since she is not represented as one-down, the cultural (il)logic of homophobia dictates that if she's one-up on a boy she's got to be a dyke. Perhaps addressing this all-too-widespread view, the movie would then be reassuring viewers that Diana is a "true girl" after all in that she chooses a man for a romantic partner.

But the romance-with-a-difference is this. The movie's climactic boxing match is between Diana and Adrian, due to the new rules of "history in the making—New York's first gender-blind amateur boxing final." Predictably, given the trajectory the movie has set up, Diana wins, which leads Adrian to question whether or not he then suffers a loss of face in their relationship. "So now I lose respect, huh?" he asks. "No," she shouts. "You boxed with me like I was any other guy. You threw down and you showed me respect. Don't you see what that means?" The movie argues that their fight, and her win, her one-upsmanship, paves the way for a relationship (albeit, heterosexual) based on respect for and even the recognition of her physical superiority. Diana's clearly one-up at the movie's end. Adrian comes to her, and his body language—hesitant, small, careful movements—recognizes her as the "big dog." If the movie were only including this heterosexual romance to reassure viewers that Diana is "really" a girl, this would presuppose the traditional inequalities and power differentials characteristic of that romance's typical narrative, but Diana is shown to be "the man" in the romance scenario as well. In order to be "the man," does Diana have to be cast as a lesbian? To say so would be to replicate the very logic of homophobia and its fixed gender-role prescriptions in the first place. Though the movie can be read as a reassurance to heterosexual viewers, it can also be read as an argument for new heterosexual femininity that includes power of the female athlete as icon, as a challenge to assumptions about innate male superiority based on physical strength, a challenge that helps to establish a kind of flexible power differential that laws and claims for women's innate "differences" often cannot.

If *Girlfight* is a drama that stages the ascendance of the female athlete icon, the same ascendance is visible in the action movie genre. While the generic conventions of the drama speak to narratives of "real life" and "things as they are" (engendering their own fantasy structures and identifications), the generic conventions of the action movie directly speak to the powerful structuring mechanisms of fantasy and desire. If the action movie in 2000–2001 was any indication, women as action heroes were a good deal more interesting and spoke much more directly to viewers than men. Repeatedly, in movies like *Charlie's Angels, Crouching*

*Tiger, Hidden Dragon,* and *Lara Croft: Tomb Raider,* it was up to the women we love who kick ass to save the day. Just as DeMott suggests, in 2001 women took on every male action hero attribute imaginable. Like *Girlfight,* these movies marked a paradigm shift from the "killer women" movies of the late '80s and early '90s *(Basic Instinct, Fatal Attraction, Thelma and Louise, To Die For)* in which, according to Inness, "women who adopt the masculine attributes of toughness are literally insane . . . killer-women films are all about punishing women who aspire to toughness" to a period of movies in which "toughness and its relationship to women is changing . . . chang[ing] the assumption that toughness is primarily a male attribute," decentering men as "predominant power-holders in a culture where toughness is strongly aligned with leadership, authority, and power."[33]

In *Tomb Raider,* for instance, Lara Croft (Angelina Jolie) is presented as Arnold Schwarzenegger's Terminator, Harrison Ford's Indiana Jones, and any of the Batmans and James Bonds simultaneously. The movie opens in a museum setting reminiscent of *Raiders of the Lost Ark* and zeroes in on Lara in black t-shirt, combat boots, and shorts, wielding big guns in the midst of a shoot-out with a terminator-like robot (the terminator once his human exoskelton has been stripped down). It's woman versus machine, and the woman wins. She's got the Terminator's big-gun demeanor and moves, and it turns out that the robot was programmed by Lara's much more diminutive, computer-geek brother to give her a real challenge. Shift to Lara's Batman-like mansion, where her butler brings her a feminine outfit to wear, admonishing "a lady should be modest." Lara agrees as she strides off in her black jeans and shirt: "yes, a lady should be modest," making it clear that she both refuses the designation of "lady" and the "modesty" or self-effacement that this designation implies. Lara has many of the signifiers of the ultra-macho. She's a trick motorcycle rider clad in black leather, she strides into rooms with dark Terminator-like sunglasses over her eyes, she walks shoulders back like the typical guy. Her brother is anything but the typical guy, easily incapacitated by the bad guys while Lara outfights all twenty or thirty. She drives her motorcycle and Hum-Vee in a way we've all been trained to recognize as the body language of a bad-ass heroic individual who will undoubtedly save the day. In fact it's part of the movie's tongue-in-cheek, awareness-of-audience-saturation-with-genre-conventions-commentary when Lara's brother asks her blithely, "Time to save the universe again, is it?" and she replies, "Absolutely." Saving the universe is this boy-girl's day job.

Her big guns and space-taking stride don't necessarily mean that there aren't people out there reading Lara Croft as a typical sex object who just performs a few extra tricks—after all, much cultural commentary was reserved for the size of her breasts, much bigger than actress Angelina Jolie's usual chest. But like the shift from punish-the-killer-woman to glorify-the-killer-woman movies, there is also a shift underway from movies in which women's "tough attitudes and actions fail to interfere with their primary role as sex objects for men" to a period where sexuality is either self-consciously exploited *(Charlie's Angels)* or deemphasized *(Crouching Tiger, Hidden Dragon, Tomb Raider).*[34] Though she's got a big chest and leather gun-holsters on her thighs, Lara is not presented primarily or gratuitously as a sex object any more than the Terminator is. Female action heroes partake of the same complicated iconography as female athletes, and their status is similarly dependent on their physicality. And while they are usually framed as heterosexually desirable and therefore "beautiful," they are not in any way reducible to that beauty. Lara Croft is no more a sex object in *Tomb Raider* than is her sometime lover, who is featured in a parallel shower scene to Lara's own and is even more deliberately (hetero)sexualized by her gaze as she surprises him, gets the information she wants, and leaves him with a pointed downward glance and remark, "always a pleasure."[35]

It would be impossible to say that there aren't those who read female action heroes like Lara (as well as kick-ass female athletes) as glorifying retro-male values of domination and control. As with any text, many readings are possible, and audiences tend to generate those readings in the service of their own desires. But there is also something more powerful and fundamental about the giddy joy and/or activist viewing a viewer can experience watching women knock out their abusive fathers, fly through space with dominion and certainty, and wield swords and guns with the skill and finesse of any male action hero than critics like DeMott allow for when they read scenes such as these solely in terms of women's unquestioning emulation of destructive male values that eliminates the possibility of social justice from the world. Watching them, the same kind of roaring joy may be experienced as that of the millions at home watching the decisive goal in the 1999 Women's World Cup, our voices mixing with the voices of 94,000 fans in a sold-out Rose Bowl.

The cultural turn toward "women we love who kick ass" is simply not reducible to the women's unquestioning mimicking of male values or selling the ideology of the corporate bottom line to the hopelessly naïve.

Of course either male or female omnipotence in action films is a transparent fantasy structure, produced by corporate marketing strategies in order to best target female as well as male demographics in order to make the quick sell. *Tomb Raider* was not even a particularly good movie. But female action heroes, just as male action heroes have always done for boys, have a way of making you feel more bold, like the world is (perhaps) as much yours as anyone else's, that you have a place in it. And fantasy identification with powerful figures doesn't necessarily end there, doesn't necessarily stop at a retro, bone-headed "masculine" egotism capable only of recognizing the self. Recognition of self is only a first step, but it is a necessary, long-denied step for many social subjects. For it is only through having a sense of belonging and place that one can feel confident enough, secure enough, have emotional resources enough to give to, recognize, and see oneself as fundamentally connected to others. As with female athletes, there is a double-sidedness to the female action hero that critical models like DeMott's do not address. Sherrie Inness best addresses this more complicated picture in *Tough Girls:*

> What must be considered is whether it is desirable for women—either in popular media or in reality—to ascribe to the same tough images as men. Do we want female characters who are as brutal as the Terminator? Are we hoping to see women who are as merciless as Dirty Harry? Are we secretly longing to cheer for women who are as violent as Rambo? These are disturbing questions with no simple answers. The tough woman is sometimes guilty of the worst excesses of her male cohorts, but she also suggests that women can be strong heroes and leaders, roles that have long been considered the province of men. The tough woman demonstrates that it is acceptable, even desirable, for women to be physically strong—a positive message in a society that is still ambivalent about women developing physical power equal to that of men. Finally, the tough girl shows the ability of women to be strong, autonomous individuals who are not dependent on men. We need to recognize the positive messages that the tough girl embodies, but, at the same time, recognize that her increased popularity might have a negative impact.[36]

While there can be a "negative impact" of the female action hero or the female athlete who "selfishly" acts like a male athlete and thinks "only" of her own career (God forbid), who seems to unproblematically endorse "male" values, or who is not socially stigmatized for being independent of men or choosing something other than heterosexuality, this impact is somewhat mitigated by the fact that she signifies differently than her male counterpart. She is not only "like men," in becoming a powerful individual but is also fundamentally something else. Like her counterparts in the icons of gay and lesbian and ethnic and racial cultures, she stands for the larger, previously devalued group as well as for herself, because of the fierce identifications she engenders in her fans who have found themselves devalued as a group and feel redeemed and supported by a positive representation of someone who belongs to that group.

Furthermore, female action heroes are rarely presented as only masculine individuals who stand alone in the world using everyone and everything around them. She reflects typically "masculine" values of domination and control (a fantasy that enables as well as prevents engagement with others), but she also is connected to the struggles of everyone who identifies with her to be accepted as "someone." Though Lara Croft, for instance, is James Bond and Indiana Jones and the Terminator, she is also emotionally connected to her brother, for whom she is a kind of protector, her father, and to her sometime lover, even though he has put the bottom line first and betrayed her ("she's in it for the glory whereas I'm in it for the money," he assures Lara's archrival) in order to close a deal. She isn't only an isolated individual, mowing down the rest of the world to stand alone (though she is the only female character in the film, a problem). Like Xena, her even more compelling counterpart on television, she combines a kick-ass indomitability with a recognition of others and their worth. Female action heroes and female athletes give us an iconography through which we can more fully recognize both the individuality of subjects and their many connections to others—both masculinity and femininity in both men and women. Easy gender polarities simply do not have the signifying power that they once did.

If, as we have argued, female athletes and female action heroes are much more common on the cultural stage, providing an alternative ideal, this ideal is not without its problems. This is an ideal that, like its masculine athletic counterpart, is extremely difficult to achieve. While it is true that there are significant health benefits to the weight training, dieting, and cardiovascular work that it takes to achieve this ideal, the irony is that all of us—from the dean in the School of Management to the bus driver to what seems like the entire student body, high school and college, female and male—are now training and eating like professional athletes though we haven't a game or a contest in sight. The athletic aesthetic has become mainstream, and though seriously training to achieve it does bring health benefits like greater cardiovascular efficiency, control of stress, increased energy, and less depression, it also raises the greater risk of body image and eating disorders and compulsive training that athletes have always had. If we all look like athletes, we are all susceptible to the same risks.

But the media and even sport advocacy groups rarely, if ever, elucidate and discuss those risks. And, as anyone who has lived their lives within a certain version of athletic culture knows, those risks are pervasive. Sport researcher Helen Lenskyj writes, "it could be argued that training regimens for high-performance sport both produce and reinforce obsessive/compulsive behavior in the two related areas of eating and exercise. The social context of competitive sport is an ideal breeding ground for the development of eating disordered behavior . . . self-deprivation— physical, social, sexual—is valued and enforced, and it is not coincidental that similar self-depriving behaviors are exhibited by individuals with eating disorders."[37]

For all their benefits, the psychology and sociology of sports, like eating disorders, can transform people into one dimensional, robot-like freaks. One of sport culture's most popular mythologies is that peak athletic performance is only attainable through an individual's single-minded dedication to his/her sport. In *Glory Days*, his memoir about his days as a competitive high school and college basketball player, Bill Reynolds writes, "I believed that being a player had to monopolize all of your time, that the very act of thinking about other things, doing other things, having any other interests, somehow detracted from being a serious player."[38] When you are in an atmosphere where athletic achievement is the highest honor, winning is the only thing that's valued and is therefore often the sole basis for an athlete's sense of self-esteem, he/she will do whatever it takes to be "serious" and win. For many athletes, this means serious forms of weight manipulation and attention to diet (gaining weight for sports like football, losing it for sports like wrestling, cross country, and gymnastics), as well as what can easily become compulsive training. In other words, if they follow the one-dimensional attitude that runs deep in sport culture, athletes will sacrifice their humanity and live only to eat restrictive diets, sleep, and train. Yet at least athletes have a goal in mind—winning the next game or meet. What can the gym rats, men and women on the cardio machines and hoisting weights for three hours a day, six days a week, obsessively counting their grams of protein and fat, say they have to train for besides perfectly chiseled abs and hips and lats?

Nothing in this cultural moment is simple or one-sided. Our bodies are the kind of gender performativity Judith Butler speaks of to a certain extent, sets of signifiers that we do have some control over (some of us more than others), signifiers that categorize us. This culture gives us few opportunities for creativity, and our body projects are one such opportunity that we both agonize over and take pleasure in every day. We're not saying we shouldn't do cultural critique, especially when it comes to the issues, like body image, that hit us closest to home.

For better and for worse, male and female bodies are in a process of resignification. It is a profoundly important historical development that men now have their body projects, too, for that changes the whole critical framework. Guys aren't against us, they are with us—we are all "women" in the sense of being judged by appearances. "This is complicated stuff, man," Chris Godsey writes on the Adios Barbie website.

> Why do so many people obsess about body image? Do we want to look good for other people, or for ourselves? Are we trying to attract a mate, or prove our dominance over the competition? . . . One thing I do know: body image is no longer an exclusively female problem. . . . Men are also consumers, and we're just as receptive to the suggestive sell. . . . Body image isn't limited by race, sexuality, culture, religion, social or financial status, education or geography either. It's a human problem, and it runs remarkably deep. And since we caused it, I'd like to believe we have the ability to fix it—where do we start?[39]

Where do we start, indeed? Most of us know we are manipulated by a culture of images, but this knowledge doesn't fix the problem, for the problem runs so much more deeply. So this is where we will leave you— with this fundamental, definitional question: once we reach a point of understanding that we are not these images—that we don't have to look like Gisele or Jennifer Lopez or Gabrielle Reece, or Lenny Kravitz or D'Angelo or Brad Pitt in *Fight Club,* or even like Michael Jordan or Jason Kidd or Lisa Leslie or Anna Kournikova to be "beautiful"—then what? While iconic female athletes and beautiful guys with cut abs offer some flexibility in the realm of ideal images, they still function as an ideal from which there is no easy escape. It's no longer a matter of "just turning off the TV." Images 'R' Us, at least partially. How do youth interpret the iconography of female athletes who are built to win? We'll leave it to the kids to tell us this, as they do with some eloquence, in the next chapter.

# CHAPTER SIX

## She Will Beat You Up, and Your Papa, Too

It's late afternoon on the school grounds, recess is over, and mounds of buzzing bodies begin to shuffle, maneuver, and make their way into a maze of classroom seats. Young boys and girls approach the door, peer in, hesitate, smile, then zoom by, as others begin to yell, "Are we gonna talk about soccer today?!"[1] Boys sitting far away from one another begin to yell, "Soccer! Yea!" and madly shuffle through their pockets, take out the most recent schedule for the WUSA, slap it out onto the table, excitedly reciting when the next televised match between the CyberRays and Freedom is, arguing over which team is more worthy of being named their favorite.[2] Girls whip past classroom chairs with bursting enthusiasm, wipe their foreheads, yell, "We just played soccer!" and glisten with beads of sweat. The girls are not as likely to participate in the talk of sports teams, champs, and timetables that precode our focus-group discussion on media, women, and sport. However, the sweat is invariably theirs—sweat earned not from passively watching on the sidelines in the heat of the day, but that which represents the rush of their own kicks, runs, muscles bursting across grassy fields that are frequently filled with co-ed play at this age level.

### Been There, Played That

It's 2001, nearly thirty years after the passage of Title IX, and boys finally enthusiastically argue over when Brandi Chastain and Mia Hamm might play head to head later in the week. Girls rush onto soccer fields at recess, and although many more girls than boys hesitate to hop onto the field and are generally more cautious on the field of play, one cannot ignore that a shift has likely taken place. A shift has also potentially occurred in the sports students play. When asked in focus-group discussions to describe their current sporting activities, grade-school boys rallied off a rather traditional list that represents the triad of hegemonic masculinity in sport: baseball, football, basketball, while also offering handball and soccer as popular. Paying attention to some of the race and class detail revealed that young African-American boys more often mentioned basketball, Latino boys more often listed soccer and boxing, and kids from more privileged backgrounds shouted out that they also played tennis, swam, did rollerblading and skateboarding. High-school boys also added in an occasional bowling, snowboarding, break dancing, and water polo to the mix.

Grade-school girls made shorter lists of sports than did boys, but frequently offered pairs of sports that challenged the notion that kids self-select into sex-typed sports, describing pairs of one masculine and one feminine activity such as basketball and jump rope, soccer and aerobics, or baseball and cheerleading.[3] Young girls stated that they played soccer and football nearly as often as did boys, a few girls wrestled, and a handful played street hockey. Still, girls also participated in many more traditionally female activities than did boys such as four square, jump rope, and an occasional ballet or dance class. At adolescence, the lists of sporting activities became shorter for girls while fitness activities and those that reinforce emphasized femininity (such as cheerleading) increased for high-school girls. This may highlight a combination of factors including fewer sporting opportunities or encouragement for girls than boys, and/or how a shift might occur in the transition from preadolescence to adolescence that leads to increased pressures for femininity (that will be read as heterosexual) and therefore more sports attrition,[4] more sex typing of sport at that age, or shifts from sport to fitness.[5] Here, high-school girls frequently listed sports such as cheerleading, gymnastics, swimming, and volleyball, but also offered a dose of softball and track, with yoga, fitness, Tae Kwon Do, and kickboxing reserved for the more wealthy.

## If You "Let Her Play," Will They Know Her Name Some Day?

Despite some potential loosening in the gendering of young kids' activities, tremendous increases in adult female athletic participation at all levels,[6] and an increasing emphasis on female athletes within the popular cultural realm, students had difficulty when asked to name a popular female athlete. Fully 13.4 percent of 152 students, made up of an equal percentage of boys and girls, could not think of a single female athlete. In two of the groups, 100 percent of the students quickly thought of a popular female athlete and wrote down her name.[7] Of the remaining groups, fully 20 percent of students could not name any female athletes. We then asked these students if they could think of a male athlete, and numerous names were called out with speed, including Shaq, Kobe Bryant, and Michael Jordan. Only one high-school girl found this situation problematic or remarkable. She showed a self-reflective moment when she remarked, "See . . . huh . . . I think that's funny, strange . . . huh . . . I can remember the names of sports players who are guys, and they have a very big impression . . . but . . . not the girls . . . hmmm not the girls." Indeed, it appears that much of the sports/media complex works to reinforce the association of sport with masculinity, and this is coupled with far less women's print and visual coverage when compared to men's sport. These trends lead to name recognition problems of even famous female athletes. Time will tell as to how much this trend will shift both in larger popular forums and within sports/media, but the obstacles are challenging.[8]

Names of the first female athletes who came to mind depended on class background, as the majority of students from lower socioeconomic classrooms listed either Chyna or Molly Holly from the World Wrestling Federation, Marion Jones, Venus or Serena Williams, or Lisa Leslie from the WNBA. Jones and Williams were also mentioned by students from more elite groups, but ice-skaters Nancy Kerrigan or Michelle Kwan, tennis star Anna Kournikova, and Women's World Cup soccer stars Mia Hamm and Brandi Chastain were mentioned most. This is consistent with researchers who reveal how gender, race, and other social locations affect what programs one watches (and how these are read).[9] Difficulty with recognition of female athletes was also exemplified through the fact that a handful of students within each group stated that they could think of someone, but they "didn't know her name." Among these students, we then asked for "a description of her sport or who she was," and in most cases, students were thinking of either Marion Jones, Flo-Jo (more often the case in the high schools), the Williams sisters, Mia Hamm, or Brandi Chastain. The way in which students described athletes also indicated the power of media to construct audience recognition of athletes. For instance, one girl shouted, "she was a soccer player, and I remember that she won the World Cup," while in another group two girls chatted aloud, "What's the girl that ran . . ." " . . . in the Olympics?" "Marion Jones?" was then called out. We often had to probe to flesh out whether students meant Hamm or Chastain when referring to soccer players and, when asked, we were frequently met with "the one that took off her shirt," highlighting the degree of public consciousness about the sports-bra controversy that ensued after Chastain showed the world her inspiring arms and abs and fell to her knees in pumped glory at the 1999 Women's World Cup Championship. That Brandi Chastain was most identifiable as "the woman who took off her shirt" while male athletes were very easily recognized by name and sport team provides evidence that sport/media plays a vital role in building audience demand, recognition, and types of recognition of female athletes.[10]

Recognition of the six images of female athletes we showed during focus groups also met with mixed success. The 1999 U.S. soccer team victory, currently televised WUSA games, and the "sports-bra controversy" clearly aided the recognition process for Chastain, who was by far the most well known. Very few students knew who Jeanette Lee or Marion Jones was. In one uncomfortable silence as to who Marion Jones was, one girl let out her knowledge, stating "she is the fastest woman in the world." At the high-school level, a few confused Marion Jones with Flo-Jo, and again used not sport, but feminine signifiers when asking, "Is that the woman with nails?" Several other students wondered aloud if Marion Jones was the apparently more popular actress, also of color, "Rosie Perez." Perhaps highlighting how actresses and models are more salient within the consciousness of youth, students in more than half of the focus groups asked if Jeanette Lee was "their favorite actress," "Lucy Liu." Whether or not this reveals how actresses have more celebrity impact on students, are more widely shown, or if students tend to simply connect women of color with other women of color due to a process of racialized "othering" is difficult to ascertain. But one thing is certain: there is a disjuncture between the fact that many students, including many of the girls, play aggressive, physical sports, but they do not seem to be immersed in a sea of everyday cultural iconography that widely includes female athletes. This underscores the need for children's, adolescent, and adult popular culture to continue to increase the quality and quantity of women's sports coverage and to more actively infuse media with a range of images of strong, fit, and athletic women. Only when this disjuncture is narrowed, enforcement of Title IX is more pronounced, coaching and administrative jobs are distributed more evenly by gender within sport, and pay gaps for athletes are smaller can we truly interpret positive student reactions to the images of female athletes that follow as more profoundly culturally empowering.

## Querying Youth on Female Alphas, Betas, and Balphas

We asked a total of ten questions and were mainly interested in the meaning youth derived when reading images of athletic women. As noted in the introduction and throughout this book, female athletes are increasingly ubiquitous in the public eye. We are facing a post–civil rights, post–second wave feminism, postindustrial consumer culture that provides a unique historical context in which to consider some of the cultural work images perform, particularly when considering the power of consumption and the fractured nature of identity. Consistent with Krueger's guide for categories of questions, we used a combination of opening, introductory, transitional, key, and ending questions.[11] We began by asking students introductory questions such as age, race, and gender, and moved to request that they describe the sport and fitness activities they do now, have done in the past, and might consider for the future. To transition into the key questions, we asked students questions about recognition of female athletes (covered earlier in this chapter). We then showed the groups six recent images of female athletes from sport and fitness magazines (see the appendix for a full discussion of the method). We strategically chose Brandi Chastain, Women's Professional Billiards Association champion Jeanette Lee, a female hockey player in a Nike ad, a female bodybuilder, a muscular blonde fitness icon, and Olympic track star Marion Jones, so as to ensure that we did not reproduce discussions of a monolithic female athlete. We also chose these six to ensure coverage of different kinds of sports (team versus individual), and to elicit a wide array of discussions surrounding multiple signifiers of race, class, gender, and sexuality.

## Not So Naive Know-It-Alls: Critique and Consume

Many students were schooled in civil rights and feminism by their parents, and were savvy consumers of products, practices, services, and trends. Indeed, analysis of popular culture cannot simply argue that students are assimilable to dominant ideologies. Rather, students offer both liber-atory and reactionary narratives that define, make, and contest culture, some of which are not always easily explained or predictable.[12] We were humbled, entertained, hopeful, and saddened by many student conversa-tions that moved with shocking rapidity between Ph.D.-level critiques, humor-laden wisecracks, simplistic optimism, or, among preadoles-cents, touchingly naive statements.

Highlighting an in-depth understanding of consumer culture, the prevalence of infomercials, and the way in which political issues are now "wed to the celebrity sphere," one high-school boy began a conver-sation with "What's she selling?" when viewing an image of a fitness icon.[13] "Clothes," called out one male student in response. "Her body," called out a female peer. "Fitness centers," added another woman. Students were seemingly not expressing positions of those who were "duped," as some suggest when emphasizing more traditional Marxian analyses that consider the "false consciousness" of the masses.

At the same time that students were actively making and constituting culture, there were also moments where "hegemony" appeared to be alive and well, with uncomplicated stereotypes about race, gender, and sexuality indubitably lingering. For instance, numerous focus groups discussed the image of Marion Jones as a racial "other" with comments like "frightening" or "tell her to lighten up."[14] Female bodybuilders were discussed primarily for being "like men," and "ugly," and the image of Asian-American Jeanette Lee elicited discussions about "mystery" and "evil." Simultaneously, however, the image of Marion Jones elicited dis-cussions of beauty and physical power, and female bodybuilders were viewed by some as "independent" and as having the profoundly impor-tant ability to self-defend. Without question, images of women in sport can be crucial in constructing new ideals of youthful, adolescent, and adult female subjecthood. But we cannot simply report narratives as indicators of some unfettered pure knowledge or "truth," nor can we view culture as always already wholly inscribing social actors. Individuals make meaning, but even as it is made, it is ever confined by the weight and levity of this social, historical, political moment. In the coverage that follows, we have tried to present a balanced version of social reality that is not reducible to simplistic categories, but rather attempts to cap-ture the complex and multifaceted voices that reveal the "messiness of lived reality" with integrity.[15]

## "I Like the Aggressive Feelings I'm Getting" and "I'll Just Run Away and Watch Her Score": Title IX Blasts Binaries

Powerful, focused Chastain, hair pulled back, staring pointedly, face serious, brow furrowed in concentration at a ball heading straight at her, certainly captivated students. Muscular arms propel Chastain, strong thighs pushing against the earth, her body is torqued to one side, right leg raised with intent to stop the ball from getting past her, only one pointed toe touching the grassy field. Consistent with researchers who find that principles of liberalism and liberal feminism echo throughout American institutions,[16] combining notions of individualism with ideologies of freedom, opportunity, choice, and an assumed positive outcome derived from one's hard work, it was common across schools for students of all ages to state that Chastain was a "hard worker," "persevered," was "achieving," or had "determination." Responses that emphasized the above principles were expressed more frequently from students in higher socioeconomic classrooms when compared with students from lower socioeconomic status. This is possibly due to the fact that those who benefit from and succeed within the current system tend to believe in and tout its ideals.[17] Also extremely popularly touted by students were a combination of liberal feminist studies and ever Nike-like "I can do anything," and "I can do whatever I want," with younger kids more often imitating the commercial, "When I grow up . . . I wanna be a pro soccer player," or "I wanna be pro at a sport some day," than older ones. While some might view these responses as offering a cultural shift for possibilities for hope, agency, and upward mobility, other researchers highlight how such views are reflective of Nike successfully capitalizing on and selling Horatio Alger myths and liberal feminist ideals while negating the fact that major economic, social, cultural, and political inequities exist inside and outside of sport (some of which Nike helps sustain).[18]

Still, the image of Chastain was viewed as positive, offering an alpha female role model for boys and girls to view powerful, physically competent champions who commonly described her as "sporty," "healthy" "powerful," "talented," and "making a nice shot." A sprinkling of mostly female students appeared to be well seasoned in the critical surveillance of women's bodies at age nine, reporting that Chastain was "old" or had either "big legs" or "turkey thighs." Both boys and girls cited that their reaction to the image was that they "wanted to play soccer," but girls more often than boys stated that they loved the image because it made them feel "strength and power," were "excited," or "wanted someone to teach" them so they could play or play "better." Far from running the other direction, or "asking to play,"[19] however, several girls stated themes of power and agency, stating that they had an "aggressive feeling" when viewing the picture and that they "liked it." For the somewhat more shy, they expressed that the image "made them feel like trying." Other common responses surrounded respect for the tenacity that Chastain represented, since she was perceived as "really going for it" or "really in the game." Both boys and girls linked athletics to competence when they stated that they "admired her athleticism" and liked that she "represented confidence." Surely, such images of women in sport help to extend new understandings of the possibilities for girls' and women's bodies stretching historically, constraining definitions of masculinity and femininity.[20] Whether or not and how the sport/media complex will work to contest or reinforce the currently powerful televised sports manhood formula—and the effects this has on youth perceptions of female athletes—should continue to capture the interest of future researchers in gender, bodies, media, and sport.[21]

## Girls Will Be Boys and Boys Will (Run or) Step Aside (or Not)

Young boys were much more likely than girls to feel concern with Chastain's athletic performance, for instance, boys stated that "she's asking me: can you kick as hard as me, and I feel funny," or another who noted that the image of Chastain seemed to be "saying I made a goal and you didn't." Indeed, a handful of boys seemed threatened but simultaneously recognized a continuum of overlapping athletic performances by gender when they identified excellence in girls' sporting performance. Common themes were "I'll just run away and watch her score" or "she'll beat me," while other boys reported that "I would get out of the game because she would knock me down." At the same time that boys produced mixed narratives about Chastain that revealed what might be considered tenuous boundaries around "masculinity," both boys and girls often picked the image of Chastain as one that made them most want to do sport. The most popular reason offered (for both boys and girls) as to why the image made them most want to sport was, thanks to media featuring the U.S. women's soccer team, or their playing the sport themselves,[22] that they "loved the game."[23] Another popular reason for liking the picture the best was the activity implied in the shot, with boys in particular stating that "she actually goes up to the ball so it looks like she's playing it." While boys were more likely than girls to offer "action" as a reason for liking the shot, both boys and girls were very likely to express that other more passively posed images made them least likely to want to do sport.[24]

## Powerful Postmodern Pout? Revisiting Emphasized Femininity

While we chose Chastain's image to explore one type of iconography of women in sport, we chose the image of Asian-American world pro billiards champ Jeanette Lee, given Lee's unique status as a world champion pool player and as an icon of the intersection of emphasized femininity with racialized code. Clutching a pool stick in her hand, with long, straight, black hair swaying well below her exposed collarbone, Lee stands in a black, sleeveless, tight-fitting dress that emphasizes her slim, curvy figure. Upon viewing the image, the majority of boys and girls read the image of Jeanette Lee as being "sexy," "hot," "seductive," or "pretty," and stated that she indeed signified emphasized femininity through naming her a "model," "prostitute," or "singer." Some students felt that she was "snobby," "cool," or read the image as offering a combination of gendered and racial codings such as "clever," "mysterious," "evil," "smart," or "dangerous." Consistent with Espiritu, who analyzes how Asian-American women are often reduced to one-dimensional caricatures in Western culture—either the "Lotus Blossom Baby" or the cunning, not-to-be-trusted, desirable "Dragon Lady," many of the students' comments fell into the latter category. Espiritu argues that given U.S. history of immigration exclusion laws, economic exploitation and sexualization ideologies of sexism and racism work together to produce imagery of Asian-American women as mysterious, "exotic others."[25] As stated by one ten-year-old girl: "It looks like she was smoking and wanting to have sex, and saying come, join me!" Indeed, this image also elicited numerous sexual comments from boys of all races, and most boys and girls agreed that the image of Lee was the "most attractive" of the images.

Boys of all ages seemed to "do heterosexuality" in the same way that researchers highlight the performative elements of "doing gender," when yelling "She's hot!!" "I love you," "Rarrr!" or asking to "pleeeeeeease see

The black widow: Women's Professional Billiards Association champion Jeanette Lee.

the picture again."[26] Numerous girls stated that Lee was a "sexy mama!" or made comments that linked attractiveness to a perceived form of power, such as "she holds herself with the attitude of 'you want me and you know it.'" Girls, too, openly "did heterosexuality" and yet highlighted its constructedness through attempts to ensure their peers that they were not gazing at the picture with desire. This was accomplished through reads such as "if I were a man, I would find her very attractive" or "I would want to go out with her if I was a guy." Through claiming the subject position of a heterosexual man, girls and women safely uttered confirmations of a heterosexuality at the same time that such proclamations can be viewed as offering paradoxical moments of fissure. Imagining such a subject position and acknowledging it through public utterance can complicate dominant relationships between fantasy, desire, action, and identity. High-school girls were somewhat less willing to take on a male subject position in this way, perhaps indicating an increased pressure for heterosexuality found after puberty, with girls asking more contested questions about the image, such as "what if you don't check girls out," or "I'm not attracted to women," and "where are the pictures of the guys?"[27] Other students usually stepped in to suggest that "the topic is women athletes today" or pushed students to comment on the photo anyway with statements that one "doesn't have to be attracted" to an image to comment on what first comes to mind. It is not simply the case that one's race, class, gender, or sexuality identity impacts how images are read.[28] Simultaneously, difference is accomplished through active public utterances, performances, and readings of media texts that are drawn from available, circulating public discourse.[29]

At the same time that sexuality was clearly infused into the discussion of Lee's image, important reminders that she was a world champion who challenged cultural norms about women's abilities emerged. This included numerous girls who felt that the image meant that "girls are equal to" or "better than" boys, while several others recited the infamous song from the Nike ad where Hamm taunts Jordan with "I can do anything better than boys." Boys from lower socioeconomic backgrounds more often noted than any other group that Lee was a "champion," and that she "inspired" them to play. While some high-school girls thought that the picture "showed that one shouldn't doubt that women can do it," others highlighted that "women can come out on top in a male-dominated world."[30] A small group of students seemed to offer more exasperated reads with "Do you have to be beautiful to win?" or stating that the picture is "weird because she has to be sexy to come out on top." Grade-school girls asked the simple, yet still critical, "How come she dresses so fancy just to play pool?" Indeed, students recognized what might be considered by some to be broader cultural constraints that require women's sports to be pleasing to a male audience in order to succeed.[31]

While there is some suggestion in the available research that images of Asian-American women exist in this way to affirm white male virility, this does not consider the ways in which images might serve a politicized function across various social groups. For instance, several Asian-American high-school boys stated explicit recognition of themes of structural agency and constraint (perhaps coupled with Horatio Alger myths) when they made comments such as, "She overcame racial obstacles, too, not just gender." Simultaneously, an equal number of other high-school boys seemed to rely on old classifications of sportswoman as ugly, masculine woman, when they pleasingly expressed that "you don't have to be ugly to play sport." Young boys were again concerned that they might get beaten literally or figuratively, with one eleven-year-old reporting, "I feel that she can beat me. I feel that she would hit me with the stick," while another reported, "I wouldn't want to play her because I know she will win. . . . My friends that are boys will laugh at me for losing to a girl." Similar to the response toward Chastain, several girls noted that the image led them to want Lee to "teach them" or thought that Lee "could teach" another person pool. For instance, one grade-school girl stated that "what I got from the picture was that she is really sure about her skills. And that she's really good. It's like she is saying she could teach you."

While tropes of race, emphasized femininity, and sexuality may have led students to vote Lee's image most attractive very often, it is vital to note that she was simultaneously voted as the image that made students least want to do sport. In the words of one fifth-grade girl: "she looks lazy . . . just standing there . . . wearing pretty clothes . . . looks like she goes to places where there are a lot of men and she doesn't look too happy about it." Another Latina fifth-grade girl noted that muscled imagery elicits her desire to do sport, when she stated that "she doesn't look like anything . . . there are no muscles," while another girl of the same race added that "she doesn't even work out," and a Latino male stated that "she is not even doing nothing." Despite Lee's world championship status, ideologies of a productive, active self tended to be valued as most important in eliciting a desire to do sport. At the same time, muscle acted as a positive signifier of sports performance, and a lack of muscle perhaps linked emphasized femininity to "lack" of movement or action. Such frames had a negative impact on students' stated desire to participate in sport. These preliminary findings with youth offer a solid argument for why images of powerful, muscular female athletes should proliferate—to counter the multitude of passive modeling shots that circulate much more widely than do female athletes within popular TV programs and beauty magazines. It also might run counter to marketing tactics that prefer the more passive, feminized version of Lee so as to, in one fifth-grader's words "attract spectators." While some might view Lee's "token" status cautiously as one of a few women on top in a sport typically dominated by men, it appears that this particular representation elicited a multiplicity of discourses. Such reads were not easily reducible to femininity as powerlessness, or Asian-American woman as simple sexual object. Imagery also offers powerful opportunities for youth to view women in a previously all-male realm, to create the terms of the struggle over how representations were read and serve to constitute youth identity across several simultaneously intersecting social locations.

## "Girls Can't Play Hockey!" Rough Innocence, Don't Hold the Pink

Broad shoulder pads take over much of an up-close Nike ad showing a young girl wearing a hockey jersey. The athlete is featured with a pensive look on her red flushed face, gaze averted as if she is thinking about the recent game. Light, long, sweaty strands of blonde hair peek out from underneath her helmet. Upon closer examination, one sees that Nike has positioned the words "I like pink" near her cheek, accompanied by a tiny Nike swoosh. Either suggesting that "feminine" girls could try a rougher tougher task or assuring the viewer that this sporty girl really does also like pink (femininity). Nike provoked divergent student views. First reactions to the shot seemed both reactionary and politicizing, with shock and surprise ripping through the room as boys and girls yelled, "Girls play hockey?!" "Girls can't play hockey!" or "Is there a women's professional hockey team?" Angry girls yelled back, "Yes they can!" or looked to us with pleading faces to be mediators and authoritative voices on the question of the existence of a women's pro team. Such an uproar was another sign that the sea of available images in the sport/media complex rarely involves certain women's sports. Perhaps unaccustomed to seeing female athletes play this usually male-dominated game, girls frequently declared that she looked like workers in male-dominated occupations such as "an airplane pilot," a "football player," or "an astronaut."

The challenge that women pose when venturing into male-dominated occupations and sports was clear. Seemingly displeased with seeing the image of a girl in a sport typically played by boys, boys more often than

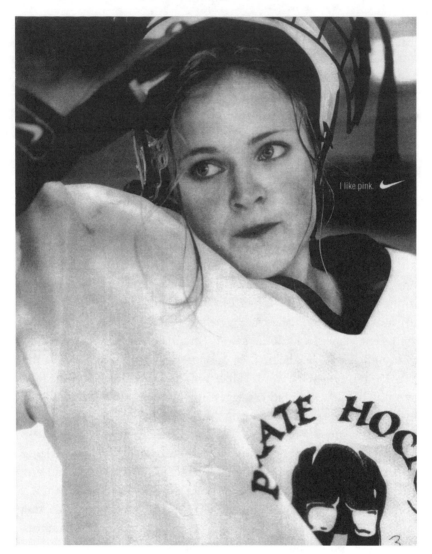

I like pink.

Masculinity and femininity all shook up: Nike ad, *Sports Illustrated for Women* (April 2001).

girls warned that the athlete was "tired" or "irritated" in the image, that hockey was "too rough" for girls, or offered similar strands of protection-ist discourse. Such discourse can be enacted historically to reinforce cate-gorical male physical superiority and female physical inferiority, which all too easily translates into keeping girls and women out of sport.[32] This was expressed within focus groups as "hockey and football are too dangerous for girls." Boys were not the only ones who touted this, as a small number of girls also agreed that hockey "was not a sport that girls should do," or "I don't think it's okay for girls to do such a rough sport." No student argued that some boys might also find hockey too rough, reinvigorating ideologies of absolute gender difference.

At the same time, several boys and girls argued that this image performed important cultural work through shifting their perceptions of women in sport and also broader society. Numerous students reported that it was "pretty cool to see a woman play hockey," while girls more often than boys stated that "girls can do things that boys can do." Some students read the image as indicative of a co-ed venture, commenting that participation in such a venue made them feel "powerful because she plays against boys and girls." The relationship between student beliefs, the day-to-day realities they will face, and actual behaviors are much more difficult to discern than the struggles we witnessed when making meaning out of imagery. Invariably, having access to iconography that challenged the assertions made in the outset of the discussions ("Women can't play hockey!") serves to open up the field of fathomable possibilities for girls and women.

But images never operate in a vacuum, and in addition to the agency that audiences have to make and create meaning, there are historical, political, and cultural contexts that help to provide images with highly specified fragments of meaning. Furthermore, words or text often work in conjunction with images to help produce a "preferred meaning." Preferred meanings do not overdetermine the meaning of the image and are not wholly hegemonic, but refer to meanings that producers of media images build into imagery and text with the intention of shaping the meaning derived by the audience.[33] At the same time, individuals bring "lived experience" to their readings of images, given their social positioning.[34] Most students didn't miss the text next to the athlete's face that read, "I like pink," and stated it aloud when gazing at the picture. This led to other students reflecting aloud on the text. Here, students' comments were consistent with research findings that tend to uncover that feminine markers are often drawn upon to help mediate historical tensions between femininity and sport.[35] This was expressed through discussions that the hockey player was "rough and tough but cute," or "serious about her sport, but also pretty and feminine." A large handful of boys also stated that they liked the picture because she was "tough," "but still innocent," or that she "looks natural" or "not afraid to be a girl."[36] Perhaps this was an indication that sports performance often gets equated with "being like a man," or, as argued by Ann Chisolm in her work on female gymnasts, "resonances of androgyny are tempered by associations with" a more child-like image.[37] It was telling that these replies were elicited during the discussion of the text that accompanied the image, leading readers to negotiate the "preferred meaning" that Nike privileged in the ad. At the same time, it was noteworthy that the hockey player elicited comments of being "natural" while the bodybuilder (who was shown next), with musculature showing, was almost always seen as "unnatural." This highlights the arbitrary nature of masculinity and femininity, and how signifiers of muscularity that are seen as excessive work to police the boundaries of "natural" femininity.[38] Also noteworthy was the fact that it was white boys from more elite classrooms who tended to offer read of "innocence," pointing to powerful historical associations between purity and elite white womanhood that emerged during the late nineteenth century.[39] It is also important to note that discussions of the innocence of a white female hockey player stood in stark contrast to those elicited when reading imagery of Asian-American Jeanette Lee, previously discussed as signifying exoticism and desire. The meaning of focus-group discussions about innocence are also particularly intriguing given the designation of hockey as an aggressive, team, contact sport with a high risk of injury, body checking, and "some degree of intimidation and retaliation," all of which are often viewed as antithetical to innocence.[40]

Some girls agreed with boys' characterization of the image as "innocent," but more than a handful protested this theme, especially at the high-school level. One angry high-schooler summed up resistant themes when she explained that the image seemed to declare the message, "I may be in a hockey shirt but I'm really an innocent confused girl who likes pink," while another argued, in a heated fashion, "Why can't she look gross and musty, she has to look like a girl?" Younger girls protested much less often, but when they did, they expressed that "girls are better" than boys at hockey.[41] Approaching what might be considered a third wave stance concerning how the most privileged girls view consumption as power, one white girl noted, "She has a great attitude, she's pretty, has confidence, she gets into it, she's sweaty and I like how she's in a typical man's hockey jersey—that gives me a lot of power to know that we can wear a man's hockey jersey and look damn good."[42] Finally, a small segment of boys did not make public remarks about the image, but instead wrote down for us that they read the picture as a way to devalue girls in sport, or the meaning attached to feminine signifiers. These boys indicated in written comments that "she shows no sports skill, she's just a pretty face" (one has to wonder if an "ugly" face would have signified sports skill?), while another wrote "I like pink? She probably lost," perhaps pointing to how femininity continues to be infused with ideologies of female physical inferiority, even in an era of obvious female athletic competence, increased participation in women's sport, and new iconography of female athleticism.[43]

## Not Ready for Love?: Bodybuilders Shake Up the Heterosexual Order

More than twenty years after the introduction of bodybuilding for women, participation in the sport was highly stigmatized across classrooms. At the same time, contestatory, heated exchanges were the norm, and no other image stirred up as much controversy. Arms positioned on hips in a tight fist, the model's whole body was in a near flex. Dressed in a tight spandex top and short shorts that revealed bursting muscles, she sported red lipstick, earrings, makeup, and clearly plucked eyebrows. Hair cut short, she offered just a slight smile, stared directly at the camera, and sported large biceps and shoulders, a ripped four-pack set of abs, and well-muscled legs. At the top of the ad, the text read, "To build a body like this you have to make a few sacrifices."

Consistent with a vast literature that highlights assumptions of natural linkages among a sex, gender, and sexuality triad within Western cultures, large muscles were often viewed as leading to tensions and contradictions with femininity and were then conflated with sexuality.[44] Students overwhelmingly offered the terms *ugly, nasty, grotesque, gross, strange, manly, a man, unnatural, unacceptable, too strong, inappropriate,* and they clearly stated why—"too much" muscle. Clinging tightly to conceptions that the gender order was unnaturally disrupted by a woman who had massive muscles, many students cowered when the picture appeared, pretended to take cover, yelled, "Ahh!" or, in one young boy's words, "I turned the other way." Younger students were more likely to state and write down shorter, simple thoughts such as "disturbing," "fake muscles," "not real," "turkey," "go to the hair salon" "very very very very strong and ugly," or "doesn't look right." One tiny girl stared closely and pointed carefully at the picture with her pencil, raised her hand hesitantly, and quietly declared, "it says that she made sacrifices. I think she made too many." When asked what sacrifices she thought were made, the girl replied, "I think she sacrificed her family... and her work." At the same time that this student associated women with the disproportionate care of their families, she was extremely aware that bodywork takes a tremendous amount of time.[45] While her comments might seem reproductive of assumptions that it is women's job to take care of the family, she simultaneously challenged notions of bodybuilders having "unnatural" bodies by highlighting that all bodies are the result of numerous time-consuming and ongoing practices.[46]

Older students wrote and spoke of longer and somewhat more complicated criticisms of female bodybuilders. Still, these harsh criticisms often categorized the imagery as either a masculine and therefore assumed to be "ugly" woman or a chemically induced "freak." Similar to academic researchers who have shown how it is assumed that men are more often seen as naturally muscular, (even when on steroids) while women are seen as unnaturally muscular and require "unnatural" means to acquire such a body, one high-school male wrote that "with the money she got from this shot, she can go buy more steroids."[47] One white woman from an elite high school asked, "What was she thinking?" while a white male from another high school offered that she looks like "Martha Stewart on crack." Numerous young boys reported that they disapproved of such a look, stating that her "chest looks like a man," and implied that she had lost heterosexual desirability when one commented that "she might like attention but she is not going to get it." One lone high-school boy offered that she was "the strongest babe I've ever seen," offering the possible "desirability" of "female masculinity."[48] Those students who commented on the athlete's looks did not comment on athletic function or performance.

Such declarations did not always go unchallenged. For instance, one high-school girl yelled, "Nasty! What a bitch! I hate her!," while another yelled, "Why are you so quick to jump on her just because she lifts weights? Why a bitch? Why do you say *hate*? I'm *serious*! *Just* because she works out a lot ... what?" At times, it was surprising that younger students were brave enough to offer resistance amidst a constant string of thoughts being yelled (perhaps performed in front of one another) in succession. At one grade school the string went "ugh!" "ew!" "weird!" "sick!" "woaahhh!" and "plastic surgery!," when one angry hand then went up and a girl added, "All she did was exercise a lot so that she *can* look like a man.... Hey, women and men are equal and she has a right to look like ... to be as strong as a man." Though her hesitancy to offer women the "right" to "look like a man" was replaced with the statement that women have a "right" to be as strong as men, her comment highlights the way in which students contest, struggle over, and constitute meaning. They clearly do so in a context of a larger gender order that presumes that biological sex is equated with socially constructed definitions of masculinity and femininity, that become all too easily conflated with sexuality.[49]

Finally, some students pointed to vivid understandings that there is overreliance on a binary gender order where hegemonic masculinity is fissurable, and that boys will have powerful negative feelings if they're not "on top." "I think that boys are intimidated by her ... that's all," said one fifth-grader of the pose. Some grade-school boys offered an admittance that "I don't want a woman to be buffer than me," or that the image of the bodybuilder "intimidates men and women should leave the muscles to men." Questions as to what "might" happen to the heterosexual order if women don't "leave muscles to the realm of men" also emerged, highlighting the constructedness of sexuality and the role that (also constructed) bodies play in signifying it.

High-school boys and girls offered more indepth comments that revealed the tenuousness of a heterosexual order that relies on binary gender oppositions for its existence. "Well, yeah ...," one boy began, "she would intimidate guys ... and if you cover her face up ... and put more clothes on her, a guy would not wanna be with her, because it would remind a guy about another guy." Actively constituting their own heterosexuality through reliance on a dimorphic gender order, boys in particular discussed the role that muscularity plays in signaling or disrupting gender and sexuality.[50] Similar to the previous comments from girls on the image of Lee, some girls offered that they could only comment from a boy's point of view, stating, "if I were a guy, I wouldn't want to date her." Whether or not such statements are read as powerful indications of compulsory heterosexuality at a young age, or as expressions of how gender and (hetero)sexual identity are actively constituted and constrained among peers, heterosexual male identity as a subject position for expressions of desire was the rule.

There were also resistant responses that slid out of the mouths of youth that offered either solid recognition that physical strength and musculature did not categorically belong to boys, or that weightlifting helped women to achieve independence or self-protection in daily life.[51] Boys openly recognized that size and strength are not reserved for male athletes while noting that she "has huge shoulders and is stronger than me." Several boys of color from lower socioeconomic classrooms stated themes that the bodybuilder image was "bulky, ladylike, brave, and bright," or that they "wanted to be like her when I grow up." Others touted that they liked that she appeared to be "independent," that she could "take care of herself," or that she looked like she "was proud of herself and that was a good thing." High-schoolers more often read the image with what might be deemed a "stealth" or "Rambo" feminism than younger students, equating muscularity with violence. For instance, there were themes from high-school girls that the image was read as an invitation to fight on one's behalf. One girl proclaimed, "She will beat you up, and your papa, too." One high-school boy from an elite classroom also assumed that muscularity meant physical violence, stating that he "wished like, she was my aunt or something, so like if I did get in a fight, I could call her up." Other high-schoolers agreed, when one girl added to the discussion, "It'd be great if you wanted someone nearby to help you kick someone's ass." This is consistent with Heywood (1998), who argues that weightlifting can be seen as a third wave feminist strategy to physically self-empower, ward off attack, heal past bodily victimization and abuse, and shake up assumptions surrounding gender and the body. Why muscularity was automatically linked to violence was never specifically discussed, and whether or not this interpretation was due to linking muscularity with masculinity and violence or a unique form of female empowerment through the ability to self-defend was not clear.

At the same time that students recognized that the image of the female bodybuilder might signify physical independence or power, muscularity meant "ugliness" and disruption of the heterosexual and gender orders seemed to win out. In fact, the image was frequently chosen in several schools as the *overwhelming* choice of an image that made students least want to do sport, particularly among girls. Here, young girls touted that they "did not want to be all yuckey," or did not want to "look like a man" and thought that she was "gross," while boys stated that she was "too muscular" and the image made them "want to look away." This may be consistent with previous analyses of media which find that for women's sports to be popular, it has to appeal to a male (heterosexual) gaze.[52] While this image certainly has the potential to offer powerful resistance to such norms or even points to their constitutive components, it appears that students found that the image simply "took things too far." Why and how the definitional ceiling on muscularity for women continues to shift (or not) in certain contexts will continue to prove to be a fruitful area for future research.[53] Indeed, our current sociopolitical environment should demand it.

## "... This Weight Is Heavy, Am I Done Yet?": Weights Meet Barbie in the Third Wave

Our selection of the next image was made given that it represented the complexity of one contemporary icon of (racialized, classed, gendered, sexualized) fitness: a cut, well-muscled white woman with long blonde hair, lipstick, a tiny pink sports bra and blue short-shorts. The fitness model has her head tilted in a classic modeling position, yet holds a gigantic dumbbell in her right hand, revealing a clearly vascular, muscled, capable arm. Her left hand is resting on her left knee, and her left leg is positioned resting on a dumbbell near the ground, her bulging calf muscles are visible to the viewing audience. The response to the image might be summed up best by work that considers how dominant fit ideals now include substantial muscle mass for women, but not "too much."[54] While some students equated the image with the more muscular and substantially physically larger, yet also blonde and feminized Molly Holly from the World Wrestling Federation, most students immediately associated the image with fitness, calling out the names of several popular fitness clubs. One boy called out that she "just left Jenny Craig," perhaps accurately challenging the fact that the model's body signified that fitness is not necessarily healthy, associating it with other bodily regimes of femininity.[55]

Many other students noted how constraining fitness regimes are in general, stating that she must do "100 situps a day," or "clearly works out every single day." Students were critical of her body practices, either balking that she "lives in the gym," or stating that she was "not eating enough," "was not healthy."[56] All groups of students commented on her "six-pack" abs, which were either seen as unusual for a woman, as indicated by "Woah!" "Talk about a washboard stomach!" Still another chunk of students viewed her chiseled abs as "sexy," as evidenced by one high-school boy who felt the message was "Screw that six-pack, I've got the hottest 24." Thinking back historically at how Marilyn Monroe or Sophia Loren (or Jack LaLanne) would certainly not be viewed as having to have cut abs (or to show a belly at all?), one is quickly reminded of shifting standards of beauty. Corporations profit tremendously from marketing a variety of products and services to the public so as to rectify "bodily lack." Individual bodily lack is implied when signifiers of success are sold according to the ever-shifting bodily trends.[57]

Students embraced the postmodern nature of the image to some extent, either tagging it as a devalued feminine Barbie, an overly muscular woman, or both—a classic Barbie Doll who was too muscular. For instance, many read the musculature as overpowering and "ruining" the otherwise "attractive," more feminine features of the image, maintaining that the fitness icon was "pretty but the muscles ruin that." Others emphasized the more "masculine" signifiers, claiming that she was a "steroid freak," "too muscular," had "abs" that were "too worked out," "not right" or "weird." Some students commented on her "more natural" look as compared to the female bodybuilder, who was deemed more "unnatural." Similar to the female bodybuilder whose functional use of muscles was limited to "fighting," some students felt that the fitness buff could "beat men up," "wouldn't get messed with," or "could take care of herself." While numerous students read muscles as "ruining" the model's "good looks," a small number of students read the image with a postmodern twist. Here, the image came with some of the associations that icons of emphasized femininity (without athletic status?) might elicit, such as "stupid," "the weight is probably too heavy for her," or devalued her pose as feminine passivity which was conflated with incompetence, for instance, some students commented that she "doesn't look like she is doing anything."[58] A few judged the icon, unlike the hockey player who was seen as "innocent," as sexually immoral for "looking like she wasn't wearing a bra and that that wasn't right."[59] One student wrapped numerous signifiers together with, "Not her body, steroids, I'm a doll. This weight is heavy, am I done yet?" A fascinating third wave moment indeed.

The image appeared to elicit a good deal of consumer-savvy critique in students, with both boys and girls interpreting the model as part of an infomercial or as representative for a corporation who is trying to sell products. This was evident through comments such as "I have my own TV show," "If you want to look like me, eat Subway every day and use a quick-fix workout," or "Looks like an advertisement lady who is trying to sell fitness equipment." Still others seemed to either eat up the tendency for corporations to successfully sell celebrity feminism as shown through statements such as "I feel like she can be anything and she is inspiring other women to have muscles like her and is trying to have other people use fitness equipment."[60] At the same time that the fitness icon was judged harshly for having big muscles, boys very frequently voted the image to be one of two that they deemed to be most attractive (the other was Jeanette Lee), terming the image "cute and sexy," "strong and glamorous," "buff and beautiful." Not unlike P. Markula's 1996 article entitled, "Firm but Shapely, Fit but Sexy, Strong but Thin: The Postmodern Aerobicizing Female Bodies," it indeed seemed to be boys from more elite backgrounds who found this image one of the most attractive.[61] The two contemporary icons of emphasized femininity: Jeanette Lee and the more muscular (but not too much) fitness icon captured the boys' attention the most. Simultaneously, not many boys or girls across focus groups stated that the image inspired them to do sport. Indeed, "cuteness," which has a specific racialized, classed history that emerged in nineteenth-century America, appears to mediate the acceptance of musculature.[62] At the same time, when signifiers of emphasized femininity are perceived as dominating the image, most students reported less inspiration to do sport.

## Elegance, Grace, and Race: Moral Marion Jones in Post–Civil Rights Postfeminist America?

Marion Jones, draped in a black evening gown, hands on hips, peering away from the viewer, is posed staring into the horizon, standing tall in beach sand, chin up, with muscular arms and shoulders revealed. The text that accompanies the image says, "She represents the total package. She can talk easily with Nelson Mandela, then ten seconds later chat with a little girl about a doll." Combining ideologies of race, gender, nation, beauty, and athleticism, the image relies upon a strategic juxtaposition of image and text to produce the meaning of the "total package."

Indeed, images of black female athletes cannot simply be cheered for their "equal opportunity" appeal to beauty and athleticism. The ways in which images of people of color have been packaged in America have long aided white consumers in thinking that they are embracing diversity without the "messy problems of actually distributing resources," "living the affects of affirmative action,"[63] or helping girls and women get access to education, health care, and sport. The appearance of black bodies has tended to be erroneously conflated with a lack of morality, a signal of threat and chaos, and as blameworthy, particularly under the Reagan and both Bush administrations, for the "deterioration" of American society through proliferating images of welfare mothers, crime, drugs, "promiscuity," and "immorality."[64] As such, perhaps the public more easily embraces people of color who are constituted within media as having "morality," distinguishing them from those who are poor or are seen as having less "appropriate" backgrounds.[65] At the same time, race intersects with gender in unique ways in American culture, and African-American women have long been constructed as standing outside of the norms of white, middle-class ideals. Instead, black women's physical fortitude and strength has been linked not to elegance or beauty, but to a "different" womanhood frequently presented as a desexualized Mammy image, a welfare queen, a matriarch responsible for pushing away black men, a strong woman doing arduous labor or as somehow more athletically inclined.[66] Inherent in this particular image of black womanhood, then, lie a number of tensions around assimilation, difference, eroticization, athleticism, independence, morality, winning, femininity, and race.

Upon viewing the image of Jones, nearly half of students embraced the image as "elegant," "beautiful," "strong and pretty," "glamorous," and "powerful." Several girls touted the famous Helen Reddy line, "I am woman, hear me roar," while some reminded the class that "black is beautiful," linking it to the significance of 1960s civil rights marches that challenged conflations of whiteness with beauty. At the same time, however, just as many students referred to Jones with powerfully negative sentiments that were infused with intersections of gender and race in American society, with language such as "ugly," "frightening," "big feet," "too tall," "doesn't look right in a dress," "having a bad hair day," or "doesn't look good in a dress because of her big muscles." Although wholly consistent with past research that highlights how easily women in sport can be seen as undesirable and how othering can occur when viewing images of women and/or African-Americans, it was shocking to hear how many students centered on critiques of Jones's powerful body.[67] No students challenged these comments with mention that height and feet might provide a function when attempting to produce Olympic gold medals in track.

Again indicative of the fact that gender and race intersect in American culture, many students offered that Marion Jones was "too serious," was "threatening," "scary," "shadowy," "angry," "mafia," "frightening," "had attitude," or "needed to lighten up." Further moral judgments about Black America were powerfully reinforced, for instance, one ten-year-old girl offered that "she looked respectful of America," while another stated that "she holds her head high and is a good role model for her family," and a third noted that "she is a good influence on others." No other athlete was given these designations, again indicating that Jones was seen as linked—even if through her "superior" morals—to immorality, threat, and chaos. Seen as a "good role model," she represents achievement in a land of supposed equal opportunity, standing in as an icon for the classic liberal story that obscures how sport is by no means an equal playing field, and that society offers widely different levels of access to health care, work, wages, sport, and more. Silently juxtapositioned against other black women, who will be judged to see if they are the "moral sisters" of whites, she not only represents powerful athleticism but also is lauded for her feminine efforts to carry out the tasks of world peace, chat about dolls, and stand beautifully posed in an elegant dress under a cloud-filled sky.[68] Indeed, the need to reinforce her femininity was critically read into the image, even by fifth-graders. For instance, a few students discussed how they "felt badly" for Marion Jones, stating that "maybe boys made fun of her for not being more feminine, and so she is trying to show a more feminine side." Among Hispanic girls, there were a sprinkling of themes that revealed that Jones represented "pride" and "equality to men," although it was rare for students to vote for the image of Marion Jones as their favorite image, as the most attractive image, or as making them most want to do sport. Those who did were typically girls who stated, "The picture is so powerful. It brings a lot of strength and passion out. She's beautiful and in her power as a woman! I like!" or boys, who commented that Jones was "independent and glamorous," has "gone where no other woman has gone" or "should feel proud to be a woman." Perhaps the dual nature of the responses about Jones reflect wider public structural realities and sentiments about how things have never been so good—and so bad—at the same time within "black America."[69] At the time this book went to press, it was not coverage of Marion Jones but print-media discourse on tennis champions Venus and Serena Williams that captivated the public. Print media was dominated by concerns with winning records, but also credit-card debt, hair beads, fashion, beauty, and the effect of sibling rivalry on play. As representations and discourse surrounding high-profile African-American female athletes continue to flourish, researchers can and should continue to consider critically what it means to champion athletes of color as inspirational representatives for women's sport. This is particularly the case given the broader track record that media has concerning representations of African-American women more generally, and the burden that women of color in sport carry given the contentiousness of cumulative, sociopolitical, racialized, and gendered power relations.

## Winning Builds, Built to Win, and Ensuring Athletic Alpha Female Futures

As students laughed, talked, and shouted out charged interpretations surrounding images of female athletes, the sweat gathered from soccer games earlier that day cooled. As sessions ended, when we asked if there were any questions that students had on their mind, we were again made aware of the disjuncture between their daily sports prowess and the lack of a sea of images of female athletes in which they were immersed. Students helped us to remember the potentially politicizing effects of the focus-group work and reminded us of the tenuous and complicated relationship between cultural iconography and experiential reality. One ten-year-old boy, sounding sad and curious at the end of a session asked, "Why is there no professional women's baseball team?" while an eleven-year-old girl asked, "Why are women's sports so much less popular than men's?" Another ten-year-old girl linked the subject matter at hand to gender inequality in general when she asked, "Why are women paid so much less than men?" Girls rushed up for privacy after focus groups and asked, "What did you think of the boys who criticized all those girls' muscles? I was mad. . . . I wanted to know what you think." Indeed, raising the subject of media imagery of female athletes may be rather new for students and had clear links to topics of gendered social inequality and empowerment. Whether or not we could capture the depth of how focus-group dynamics impacted the content of our discussions does remain (more of the methodological concerns brought to bear are examined in depth in the appendix). The very fact that some resistances were not consistently raised during the classroom discussion but rather were only written down for us highlights how power relations within the classroom may, in fact, be linked to social locations such as race, class, gender, and sexuality.

However, as the bubbling of resistances during focus-group discussions indicated, we rejected an analysis of popular culture as an uncomplicated reinforcement of dominant ideologies and attempted to offer an analysis of groups that takes creative resistance and a "multiplicity of discourses" into account.[70] We thought of focus groups as a way to initiate an urgency for or promote social change, particularly after we learned of the very real institutional concerns students had. This urgency was reinforced when we listened to the hope that the imagery infused into girls coupled with a dearth of recognition of even the most popular female athletes.[71] Right at an age when girls might just be beginning to get societal messages that make them feel like they "can't," sport—and its imagery—can intersect with youth culture in ways that produce powerful, alternative, subcultural, and someday mainstream possibilities for more.[72] This, coupled with the unique importance that sporting imagery and practice can play for youth, cannot and should not be underestimated.

While our convenience sample of fifth- and tenth-graders was by no means random or representative, and we caution the reader from making generalizations, several important themes deserve attention here. Echoing in the memory of classroom discussions was the profound way in which girls glanced at images and declared that they thought they could be taught a sport or wanted to be taught more sports skills. Perhaps reflective of a lack of opportunities, such statements may reveal not only a need for athletic female role models but how a desire to do sport cannot be reduced to the realm of the natural. Peers, family, media, and other social institutions shape sporting desires and demands, both in terms of attendance and participation. Larger cultural valuations of behaviors, perceived support and discouragement, institutional opportunities, and the availability of circulating imagery play an immense role in whether or not such desires take hold, stick, grow, or halt. Powerfully athletic images of women in sport were said to "represent confidence," and action shots in particular elicited discussions of respect, talent, and admiration that were unparalleled when compared with images

described as "passive" modeling poses. Athletic icons in hockey and soccer were voted by both boys and girls as those that most elicited a desire
to do sport, while those that were perceived as unmuscular, as being a
model on display for one's looks, or as "too muscular" were consistently
voted as those least likely to make students want to do sport. Researchers
can and should continue to work with youth and might consider working with producers of media images concerning how imagery shapes
sports desires (and purchases?). Such (brave) coalitions might help to
close the disjuncture between girls "liking the aggressive feelings" they
get from watching and playing sport, the respect and admiration that
boys have for such athleticism, and the quantity and quality of available
images.

It's the twenty-first century, and we'd like to think it's time. Women's
sports could go any which way, and we are sure it will in fact go every
which way. It could prove to be a blip of a trend, or a corporate pill
that's successfully sold false hopes to us all, directing attention away
from "real" social and institutional change. Or, alternatively, it could
build on the hopes and dreams of little girls and women, newfound
surges of respect and appreciation from boys and men, encouragement
from parents, coworkers, friends. Sport could prove to aid collaboration
across women's organizations, international groups, schools, media advocacy (even calling on responsible aspects of corporations?), embracing the cause of girls' and women's sports. Building these bridges more
overtly and intentionally can help to form a strong sporting infrastructure that works to make and keep real changes that are possible within
and through sport. And of course, it is time for a more critical and serious examination of how money is spent in schools on sport, to examine
how to move away from popular discourse that pits men against women,
negating empirical realities and sidestepping the dire need for Title IX.[73]
Research has already shown that we need better quality and quantity of
women's sports coverage. Our focus groups highlight the need for a
wholehearted embracing of an array of iconography of female athleticism that more profoundly circulate throughout kids', adolescents', and
adults' popular cultural forums.

After all, boys are actually impressing their male peers now by slap-
ping down the latest stats on their favorite WUSA team on their desk.
Girls and women are increasingly etched into the minds of the public
for the way their bodies achieve. How might it become time for adult

men and women to slap it into one another's backs on a Monday morning at work after watching the big game? For girls to not just be allowed to play, but to know it is their bodily right? While sports can be a positive source of strength and self-development for girls, they can accomplish this only if society embraces and respects girls, and takes them seriously as workers, people, athletes. We ask the reader what have we missed, what might have to take place to allow for these possibilities to exist more widely, as everyday parts of our culture? Let's join forces to make and keep safe the spaces that the world has begun to make (again) for the Lesters, Animals, and other girls and women striding across soccer fields, weight rooms, from San Francisco to Portland, Maine, and back. Access to sport. Access to a better world of sport. Institutional support. A wider range of powerful, not just pretty imagery. The health and well-being of our girls and women depends on us all. It is more than a yearning, and sport is its name.

# EPILOGUE

## It's an Image

Slide 1: it's an image, so you can change it—wash in the colors from gray to red, elongate a little of the hind part, add depth to breast and chin. You can spin from gamine lines of straightness with all hairs a wisp, blue ruffles, long arms like bones caved in. Thin torso, narrow hip bones, lips parted as though for a kiss. The Princess, light easy locks in a tousle. Head thrown back against a tree, all gamine dreams, light, lightness, airy space: lips and breasts and caved-in waist, belted hips to hold her firm in place.

Slide 2 blinks in, a shape walks out of the waves. From model to model athlete—not much of a change? Look again. Arm still thin but more than bones, stretching a muscled, not insubstantial thigh. Dressed to move, smooth lycra lines. Eyes straight ahead, lips fixed in a determined line. Hair pulled back in preparation for her run, to make the waves roll clean.

Slide 1, slide 2—two ideal images in *Vogue,* spring 2002. What does it mean that the second slide, a Nike ad, has made it there? That the female athlete is mainstream enough to flip by as one option among the Gisele gazelle-like dolls, set as if on her own path? As we mentioned in the prologue, one of the pressing questions we raised here is "the splits between consciousness and desire and self-awareness and self-image that so many of us live with today."[1] Maybe the second image hasn't changed enough for some of us. But its existence tells us that some things have changed. The rise of the female athlete as cultural icon marks a complicated trajectory that occurs in a larger context of frenzied image-selling, includes this context gender shift characterized by the sexualized,

Idealized femininity, two views: Nike and Polo Ralph Lauren in *Vogue* (February 2002).

objectified male body, the closure of the entry-level wage gap in younger demographics of women and men, and the disappearance of permanent jobs with benefits for both sexes. Given this context, the importance of personal appearance and image, as well as how particular images are dictated and sold, is something by which American culture seems painfully captivated.

In the absence of other sources for identity, the pressure to live up to bodily ideals has spread to both sexes, and our focus groups, kids both self-conscious and naive, showed a sophisticated awareness of what they were sold. The voices in our focus groups showed that gender relations have shifted in important ways from traditional models while still being haunted by old stereotypes. Both questioning and reinforcing old ideas, their reactions weren't wholly positive or wholly reactionary—they were most often *both*. Their largely positive reaction to images of female athletes showed a shift in thinking about gender, but their inability to identify the athletes by name pointed to media coverage of women's games, which still lags far behind men's. But the old associations of girls and women with incompetence and weakness, and the stigmatization of female athletes as "unnatural" and "masculine," have clearly broken down, although some stereotypes remain. Action shots of Brandi Chastain elicited comments such as "healthy," "powerful," "talented," "really in the game," showing that the old associations between white women and a passive role have clearly changed. The fact that responses to a shot of Marion Jones in an evening gown were mixed, with half of students categorizing the image as "elegant," "beautiful," "strong and pretty," "glamorous," and "powerful," and the other half using language like "ugly," "frightening," "doesn't look right in a dress," "having a bad hair day," suggest that racial stereotypes that equate whiteness with beauty still have a powerful hold, and that muscles are acceptable as beauty ideals more on white women than black. But that *half* the students reacted in a positive way does indicate change. Overall, the students' responses to the images revealed a new social context in which there is a provocative and confusing mix of same old/same old with real change.

But change to what end? No one, particularly younger generations, seem entirely immune to the pressure to match up to an ideal, despite the fact that we know the images we see are often digitalized composites. Though we are conscious of how the marketplace manipulates us, our desires to construct ourselves according to those images, to continually "improve" in their terms, still remain. There is no easy way out. Self-awareness and self-image have perhaps never seemed so important nor so fundamentally divided. In this cultural context, the rise of the female athlete as an alternative ideal for women seems a progressive development despite its many limitations. It encourages participation in an activity that has multiple health benefits and suggests that strength and achievement are as much expected from women as from men. It broadens the range of gender roles to make activity and achievement beyond looks an ideal for women. Though not proceeding far enough, it gestures toward something else. Instead of advertising, like Gisele in the Polo Jeans shot, extraneous beauty, a body that is clearly of value only for what smooth surfaces it has managed to attain, the runner in the Nike ad suggests movement, going somewhere, the preparation to do. In an ideal world, of course, no one would strive to live up to either ideal, or any ideal at all. Each person would be valued intrinsically, and would be loved—as is said of Bridget in the movie *Bridget Jones's Diary*—"just as they are." But we are a long way from living in that particular place. In the world of media culture, the female athlete can stand as a positive alternative, and her emergence as an icon, a cultural hero, is a tangible sign that some social justice struggles have, in some limited and contradictory ways, been achieved. To attempt to live up to an ideal is to be marked by stereotypes and cultural dreams. But it matters which dreams.

The physicality of the female athlete icon suggests a presence absent from other ideals, shows resolution. These athletes are resolute in the double sense of this word: *resolution* can mean "a loosening, an untying, a relaxation," while *resolute* means "having or showing a fixed, firm purpose, determined, bold, firm, steady, unwavering" *(Webster's)*. Images of female athletes can loosen and untie traditional gender stereotypes by showing a fixed, determined purpose most often absent from the models that only reproduce old feminine codes. Track star Marion Jones or powerlifter Cheryl Haworth in dresses are much more than a traditional model in a dress, and—contrary to some established feminist readings—such images show much more than athletes made over into old stereotypes, an imposed femininity that mitigates their strength.

For the athletes themselves, and for younger generations like those in our focus groups, people who've grown up with an easier relationship to difference, more at ease with multiple forms of sexuality, a multiracial

"No matter how much I've won, or how much outside praise has come my way, or where it goes from here, there's one clear fact that has never, ever been lost on me. PowerBar I didn't do this alone."

Iconic possibilities in an unstable place: Brandi Chastain for Power Bar, *Sports Illustrated for Women* (May/June 2001).

world where masculinity and femininity no longer mean what they once did, their perceptions, voices, ways of making meaning take place outside of this feminist frame that was of great value historically, but which does not apply in the same ways to the present moment. As Carol Siegel so persuasively shows, "In the last two decades of the millennium, the emergence of a still unnamed new wave of feminism gave rise to new gender styles, such as parodic butch/femme, lipstick lesbian, riot grrl...which complicated the gendering of sexuality in interesting ways."[2] Old oppositions, between white culture and black culture, lesbianism and femininity, female masculinity and heterosexuality, have broken down in multiple, fascinating ways, like some suburban white boys walking, talking, dressing like their hip-hop heroes, girls playing hockey and football, lesbians more glamorous and traditionally feminine than any heterosexual girl, boys who are valued for their beauty and put on display as much as any female model. Indeed, violent reactionary trends like the rise of white supremacists, violent, homophobic hate crimes like the killing of Matthew Sheppard, or groups like the Promise Keepers who want to reinforce traditional gender roles, are all reacting to this breakdown, to a mainstream cultural context that has become more inclusive and more fluid. Both/and, not either/or, as figures of identification, of possibility, in this decentralized, fluctuating social context, female athletes become the stuff of heroic legend, the symbol of imagination, dreams of more.

While the female athlete image surely does not address the widening gap between "haves" and "have-nots" (have-nots who are increasingly men as well as women), and though it is part of a global corporate culture that is the cause of the problem as well as one of its solutions, it can work in positive ways. Like the dragons in Celtic and Chinese mythology who offered a fantasy of power and possibility, the image of the female athlete who is built to win provides at least a temporary sense of solidity, possibility, and relief for younger generations who have seen a close in the gender wage gap, but a downsizing and decline of real wages for everyone, the disruption of dreams. The female athlete's positive imagery needs to take its place alongside broader struggles for social justice that can help make illusions of possibilities real. We'll take what we can get, while continuing to work for more. This is our horizon, the air we breathe: a mad whirl of images, negative and positive, enabling some and not others, shifting, changing, morphing fast, existing in the frenzy of global markets, immeasurably powerful things.

# APPENDIX

## Focus-Group Research on Youth Attitudes about Female Athletes

### Focus Groups as Postmodern Method

The frequency with which focus-group methodology has been used has waxed and waned over the years. Such groups were used during World War I to get inside the heads of army troops so as to examine the impact of media propaganda and training efforts.[1] At approximately the same time, focus groups were infused into market research to investigate the impact of radio broadcasts on target audiences.[2] It might be somewhat surprising, then, to witness a profound retreat from focus groups in the decades following World War I within the social sciences. Indeed, the method made a comeback in postindustrial society when corporations sought to understand consumer needs and satisfaction. Medical sociology and public health also make wide use of the method, where there is the imperative to better understand human behaviors so as to inform prevention and education programs. Why were focus groups less popular within the social sciences and cultural studies until much more recently? Within cultural studies this may be due to critiques of empiricism more generally, while within sociology this may be due to the fact that positivistic or quantitative methods have dominated the field. Still, among qualitative researchers, interview methods have been primary within the social sciences, even among feminist researchers, though focus groups are now said to be "rediscovered."[3]

There are numerous advantages and disadvantages to using focus groups for our purposes, and the method is seen as fairly distinct from either qualitative interviewing or ethnographic fieldwork, though there is indeed overlap among all three.[4] Focus-group interviews, like in-depth interviews, are seen as potentially less constraining than survey methods, which are often less open-ended in their style. Yet, like interviews, focus groups might collect data that is more outside the realm of day-to-day interaction when compared with participant observation. Many researchers raise concerns about the power of researchers to influence, direct, or have control over interview subjects during qualitative interviews, and focus groups have been viewed by some as a partial solution to this problem.[5] Focus groups are seen as less directed by the interviewer, allowing for horizontal interaction (between participants), not just vertical interaction (between researcher and researched), and hence allow for a looser structure that provides a wider range of responses perhaps more reflective of the views of the person(s) speaking.[6] We are cautious to make this claim given that students might simultaneously experience power differentials vis-à-vis teachers, peers, and in front of researchers.

At the same time that focus groups offered unique insight into cultural ideals as these unfolded in a group dynamic, the method was less beneficial in terms of offering more in-depth information when compared to either qualitative interviews or fieldwork. This may be due to the fact that the mode of a one-on-one interview provides a more detailed examination of information without the impact of a dynamic presence of other individuals. And, when compared to the time-consuming and expensive period of data collection that comes with fieldwork, focus groups might be seen more in line with interviews, both of which offer a less-expensive and a one-time (or two) snapshot into reality. Given our tendency to embrace the stance that there is a shifting field of power relations within groups and within society at large, it would be beneficial to follow up with students over time.

Clearly, one powerful reason for our choice of focus-group methods is the ability for researchers to see collective human interaction unfold before one's eyes.[7] Currently, focus groups are considered by some to be the most efficacious manner to find out about a previously unexplored subject when it is otherwise difficult to do so.[8] This was particularly important to us given that it has been rare for those who study sport and culture to use focus groups. It is also only a very recent move within these disciplines to increasingly study youth. Audience analysis specifically on the subject of youth, media, and female athletes is rare. We chose focus groups as a way to give voice to those who are marginalized, silenced, subjugated, or previously underresearched.

There might be some question as to what precisely constitutes a focus group. To maximize the frequency and depth of comments, it is typical to limit the number of participants from eight to ten people. In this way, some might contest our use of the term *focus group*, since we carried out interviews with some groups that had eight or ten students while others had twenty or thirty. It was more difficult to hear from all students in the larger groups, so we also asked for written responses to the questions so as to maximize the range of views. We also tried to minimize the tendency for discussions to end up focusing on love/hate or accept/reject extremes, particularly in larger groups, by mediating with questions such as "any other points of view?" or "do you agree or disagree with that?"[9] It is also considered typical for focus-group participants to not know one another and to attend the group outside of a typical daily setting. We carried out groups by attending classrooms during a regularly scheduled school period, and students knew one another in their peer-laden setting. We therefore use a very broad definition of focus groups to define our method: "a research technique that collects data through group interaction on a topic determined by the researcher."[10] Indeed, there was a degree of formal structure to our groups, but there was also the opportunity for students to allow ideas to spark off of one another.

There is a tendency in this type of research to compose groups out of similar race, class, or gender categories, making it easier for members to speak.[11] Homogeneous groups are useful given that these enable making comparisons across groups possible. We did have relatively homogenous groups across socioeconomic status measures, given that students tend to be (as a general rule, but not always) of a similar background in a classroom.[12] However, we did carry out groups that were somewhat mixed by race and made up of approximately equal numbers of boys and girls. Consistent with the current goals of relational studies of gender that seek to simultaneously understand gender within the dynamics of shared space,[13] and consistent with the goals of postmodern and poststructuralist thought that view identity as fractured and multiplicitous, we did not carry out same-sex groups or a girl-centered study. This technique might be seen as problematic by some given researcher findings that highlight that boys tend to dominate girls in the classroom and on the playground.[14] There are cogent rationales for separating out girls and boys; for instance, it has been noted that both girls and boys "do gender" and "do difference"[15] as early as fifth grade, when boys are actively constituting masculine identity. At this time, girls are frequently feeling somewhat silenced, or squeezed by the pressures of emphasized femininity and/or gaining heterosexual approval.[16] We did not find an overwhelming tendency for boys to overtly dominate the discussion, which may be due not only to the subject matter, but also to the fact that both researchers and research assistants were women. We may have received very different results if we had male moderators for the groups, or if we separated groups out by gender.

## Speakin' and Writin': The Benefits of Triangulating Methods

We more accurately fleshed out how much boys and girls are "doing gender" and other axes of difference given that we asked students to not just participate in focus-group discussions but to write down their responses to questions. When cross-checking written responses with oral ones, we found that girls tended to state responses during interviews that pleased boys. For instance, in one fifth-grade classroom, the discussion led (as it often did) to a scathing critique of the "ugliness" of female bodybuilders that linked muscularity with masculinity. In this particular classroom, when we examined the written responses, only two girls wrote that they felt the image was "ugly," while numerous girls made positive written remarks, such as "this inspires me to work out," "I think I can be as strong as her," "I am proud of being a girl," "She is really tough and I bet boys don't mess around with her," and "it's good, because she's working out like men and a lot of people think we can't work out." We found some of the reverse tendency among boys, with their public declarations at times being more supportive of female athletes, and their written responses focused more on their fears and disapproval of the images. We plan on further fleshing out these findings in the near future. We ask future research teams to also consider the power of triangulating different methods so as to embrace an ecletic methodology that can capture the complexity of social reality.[17]

## Bring on the Classrooms, Kids Come on Down

We carried out seven focus groups in cities in the southwestern and western United States. Overall, there were 152 students from three high schools and four grade schools, ranging in age from ten to seventeen.

We had nearly the same number of boys/men and girls/women in each group and overall (51.7 percent girls, 48.7 percent boys). In terms of race, 38.1 percent of the sample identified as Hispanic, Latino, or Mexican-American, 5.9 percent was black, 8.5 percent were Asian, 11 percent of students identified as biracial/multiracial, and 29.7 percent of the sample was white. Although whites appeared to constitute nearly one-third of the sample interviewed, this is somewhat misleading, as three-quarters of the white students came from two upper-middle-class schools. When race data were recalculated by removing the two wealthiest schools, we found that the remaining schools in the sample were 60 percent Latino/Chicana and only 10 percent white. Within the more elite schools, our sample was 60 percent white, 16 percent Asian, 14 percent multiracial, and 10 percent Latino. Indeed, our sample is somewhat representative of the shifting demographics in Southern California, which indicate increases in the Asian-American and Latino population over the last decade; however, the proportion of African-Americans in our sample certainly falls short of the percentage of African-Americans relative to the population in the area. Given the above data, and the local income data that we acquired from the census, it is clear that race and class still intersect in American culture in profoundly important ways.[18] For instance, classrooms with higher percentages of minorities and a smaller percentage of whites had students who lived in areas with a lower median family income, a greater percentage of students on free lunch programs, and higher rates of unemployment. At the same time, students from classrooms with a higher percentage of whites lived in areas with higher median family income, a significantly smaller percentage of students on food vouchers, and lower rates of unemployment.

Not unlike Kozol's 1991 work, *Savage Inequalities*, which chronicles disparate worlds in inner-city and suburban schools, differences in re sources across our classrooms were clear. In one predominantly white classroom, there was air conditioning, the newest computers, televisions, and video camcorders, and inspirational banners that defined "honesty" and "integrity" hung on the walls. In a predominantly Hispanic classroom, makeshift classrooms, older computers, more crowded spaces, and less artwork hung on the walls. The ways in which students were treated by teachers and the rules within school culture were strikingly different across classrooms. Students from lower socioeconomic classrooms were seemingly overtly controlled with strict rules and guidelines for behavior.

Upon entering one predominantly Hispanic classroom, teachers clapped in a rhythmic fashion, signaling to stop all activity and talking. Another group of students from a lower socioeconomic setting were practically rounded up like cattle outside during recess through a similar clapping routine. Kids stopped jumping rope, playing soccer, four square, and tree climbing as if the social landscape suddenly froze midstep. In the ensuing stillness, as we glanced at one another, students' faces looked simultaneously excited, afraid, cautious. We were not simply divided by student/researcher status or student/adult age gaps, but also by race and class: schools filled with students of color may have reacted quite differently to researchers of color than to two white researchers.

Given how race and class status intersect in our nation, students from poorer schools generally experience a lower likelihood that they will graduate and go onto high school and college, and generally experience lower levels of access to workplaces, health care, and organized sport. Similar to the institution of sport, then, the American educational system has a profound degree of stratification. We would be remiss if we did not highlight how many of the students we spoke to might have much less access to health care, microscopes, books, and/or the opportunity to play team sport than did students from predominantly white, middle-class schools.[19] It may be particularly important, then, to hear the hopes and dreams that are elicited from students in particularly disadvantaged schools as they gaze over "empowering" images of powerful female athletes. It may also be particularly important to be cautious toward the patterned content of individual narratives given that social structural realities may diverge from readings of media imagery.

Consistent with the American Sociological Association's Code of Ethics and given that the students were all under the age of eighteen, we provided students with a written consent form in advance of the study. The form briefly explained the study, noted its voluntary nature, and asked for formal parental consent. In three of the six classrooms, it was necessary to translate the forms into both Spanish and English, as a large percentage of these classrooms contained students who self-identified as either Mexican-American, Chicano/a, or Latino/a. Access to classrooms was attained through initial teacher contacts, which we acquired through a combination of personal contacts, cold calls, and university ties. Given time and access constraints, the sample is not randomly selected or representative of youth in the United States or southwestern United States. Making generalizations to all "youth in the United States" or youth in the southwest based on our convenience sample would be unwise. We ensured that we had formal permission from school principals before setting up classroom meetings. We audiotaped the sessions, transcribed afterwards, and all names of schools and towns have been changed so as to protect confidentiality.[20]

## "Where'd You Learn Those Big Words?" and "Come on! Say It!"

The general feel of groups differed widely from a wicked silence that felt difficult to break in a grade school in Arizona, to students who were barely able to contain themselves in a high school in the same area. Overall, we found that students were extremely well behaved, had an incredible number of questions for us (though not always related to sport), and seemed to experience our visit as an enjoyable respite from their regular schoolwork. The level of enjoyment on their part is somewhat difficult to ascertain, but there were two instances that led us to think we were seen more as nonauthoritative visitors. One was when we left one grade-school classroom. Here, three kids who didn't take part in the study (since they forgot to return their consent forms) were waiting outside. "What'd you do?" asked one boy aloud, to which his female peer replied, "it was totally cool—on women in sport, really fun!!" After three of the six groups, little girls ran up to ask us more questions, asked if they could contact us in the future.

The world of classrooms was by no means uniformly peaceful, however. Adolescents were much more likely to yell at and chastise one another ("That's stupid!" or "Where did you learn *those* big words?" "Why did you just say that?") than preadolescents. Preadolescents extended a surprising aura of respect and consideration to one another; for instance, students would call out, "Come on, say it, it's okay," or "You're shy, but try" so as to encourage quiet voices and alternate points of view. Simultaneously, students were not passive recipients of a researcher-researched power differential and seemed interested at times in flipping the power relation by asking, "What was *your* favorite picture and *why*?" At other times, students found a way to let us know that they were more preoccupied with issues of popular culture outside of sport, for instance,

"Who is your favorite band?" and "What is your favorite color?" We answered honestly, but only when questions were asked after the group, and otherwise refrained from answering.

## Limitations, Areas for Future Research

While we had a unique opportunity to access previously marginalized voices on a topic that is widely underanalyzed, there were certainly not just methodological imperfections with the study but also substantive ones. One is how our line of inquiry made it far too easy to conflate interpretations of images with classic evaluative beauty contests. This may be due to the fact that students, when engaging in the event (looking and writing), trained in a culture that frequently evaluates the aesthetics of women's bodies (and is frequently misogynist), began to participate in a scathing critique of women's bodies. We hope that we provided a challenge to this even as it was difficult not to reinforce this to some extent. Furthermore, we did not couple our discussions and written responses with more formal survey work, which could have helped us to more rigorously examine other social variables that may affect interpretations of images such as family structure, occupation of parents, and so on. Other limitations included the fact that we provided some closed-ended questions that may have facilitated the tendency for focus group respondents to respond with extremes. For instance, we asked, "Which picture did you like the most? Why? The least? Why? Which pictures make you most want to do sport? Least?" In this way, our questions could have been developed to emphasize more subtle gradations in responses. Last, as highlighted by many media-studies researchers, it can be useful, when analyzing media imagery and texts, to not only examine preferred meanings and the meanings that audience members make and create, but to carry out ethnographies of the values that producers hold dear when creating imagery of female athletes.[21] We agree that combining all of these tactics simultaneously would offer the most well-rounded picture of the social landscape at hand. We are hopeful that future researchers and activists join forces in critically analyzing the production process with the hope of influencing shifts in such production. This is especially the case given our preliminary findings covered in chapter 6 on which images made students most and least like to do sport. We are, of course, aware that corporate cultures may value profits over putting forth a wide array of powerful female athletes, and that the sports/media complex offers some formidable obstacles. However, we find the struggle not only worthwhile but vital, necessary for girls and women—boys and men—inside and outside of sport.

## Focus Group Question Guide

1. What is your first name?
2. What is your age?
3. What is your race?
4. What grade are you in?
5. What sports do you play now? What sports have you participated in in the past? What sports do you plan to participate in in the future?
6. Close your eyes and think of a popular female athlete. Who first comes to mind? Write down her name. [probe on no name but can describe] [probe on male athletes for those who cannot think of a female athlete]
7. [showing imagery] If this picture could talk, what would it say to you? How do you feel about the picture? Why? [probes: What is the first thing that comes to mind when viewing this picture? How do you feel about that?] [probe: if she came walking into the room, what do you think she would say to you?]
8. Which picture did you like the best? Why?
9. Which picture did you like the least? Why?
10. Which pictures did you find the most attractive? Why?
11. Which pictures did you find the least attractive? Why?
12. Which pictures make you most want to do sport? Why?
13. Which pictures make you least want to do sport? Why?
14. Is there anything that we did not discuss that you wanted to talk about or ask? What is it?

# Notes

## Prologue

1. Karen Karbo, "The Ubergirl Cometh," *Outside,* October 1995, 60–66.

2. This is a complex development: while white women were the primary beneficiaries of corporate affirmative action, women of color are increasingly relied up on more than ever to fill the growing needs of a service economy.

3. Again, some ambiguities: The history of Title IX has been much more contentious than might be imagined. Although it passed in 1972, it was not up and running anywhere near 1972; it took approximately fourteen years for Title IX to get rolling. Title IX still elicits a great deal of controversy, there is much backlash, and only time will tell how this legislation will be handled. For details, see Mary A. Boutilier and Lucinda F. SanGiovanni, "Politics, Public Policy, and Title IX: Some Limitations of Liberal Feminism," in *Women, Sport, and Culture,* ed. Susan Birrell and Cheryl Cole (Champaign, Ill.: Human Kinetics, 1994). Unfortunately, there is no formal institutional enforcement mechanism which aids whether or not—and to what extent—schools will comply with Title IX. So as to increase public awareness of this problem, and to pressure schools to comply, the Women's Sports Foundation recently published the "Gender Equity Report Card: A Survey of Athletic Opportunity in American Higher Education" (2000), which revealed the failure of most schools to make adequate attempts to meet Title IX.

4. As this manuscript goes to press, the U.S. Department of Education has convened a task force to reevaluate Title IX and whether it is unfair to male athletes. One of the goals seems to be a revision of the proportionality requirement, based on a claim that girls don't have as much "interest" in sport as do boys.

5. See Susan K. Cahn, *Coming on Strong: Gender and Sexuality in Twentieth-Century Women's Sport* (Cambridge: Harvard University Press, 1994).

6. Karbo, "The Ubergirl Cometh," 60; "Shortchanging Girls, Shortchanging America," American Association of University Women study, 1991; Carol Gilligan, *In a Different Voice: Psychological Theory and Women's Development* (Cambridge: Harvard University Press, 1982), and *Making Connections: The Relational Worlds of Adolescent Girl at Emma Willard School* (Cambridge: Harvard University Press, 1990).

7. Karbo, "The Ubergirl Cometh," 60. Perhaps there is so much emphasis on girls' agency and ability to "take control," as well as the findings about low self-esteem, because there are still so many gender inequalities. For example, though to a lesser extent than previously, girls are still sometimes socialized to follow the script of men's pleasure in sex, denying their own wants and needs, even if muscular power is encouraged. Second, perhaps advocating a strong body that speaks "don't mess with me" through sport will reduce the number of women who get raped in their lifetime (now approximately one in four), and reduce their chances for becoming victims of violence, most of which is domestic and at the hands of a family member. In fact, Leslie Heywood, in *Bodymakers: A Cultural Anatomy of Women's Bodybuilding* (New Brunswick, N.J.: Rutgers University Press, 1998), argues that sports like powerlifting can serve as a positive response to this kind of trauma. It might be accurately said that agency and inequality are intricately intertwined.

8. Holly Brubach, "The Athletic Esthetic," *New York Times Magazine,* June 23, 1996, 48–51.

9. It is a commonplace that some ask, however, as did a few of the respondents in our study (see chapter 6), why her popularity can't be based on strength rather than sex appeal. What Brubach doesn't note is that these are constructed images—the "contentment" the athletes show is constructed—it would be helpful to ask the athletes how they feel about it to know. But again, sexual desirability as constructed through mass-media conventions isn't as easily separable from the construction of the body as a signifier for female independence as Brubach might think.

10. Gabrielle Reece and Karen Karbo, *Big Girl in the Middle* (New York: Crown, 1997), 175. There are limitations to these changes. Media only endorses a certain kind of femininity, now stretched to include some musculature, but often still endowed with long hair, nails, or other signifiers that are (perhaps erroneously) assumed to be heterosexual. Media is known to reject many lesbians and not endorse them. Martina and Billie Jean openly discussed how they lost all of their endorsements when they came out. Marketing executives within the WNBA now clearly state that they choose the more "model-like" (meaning "heterosexually feminine") women on the team, despite the fact that it is fairly well known that many women on the team are lesbian. Most recently, though, there has been some larger but limited degree of acceptance: Martina was featured in a long-running ad for Subaru, cyclist Missy Giove was featured by Reebok, and Nike featured Amelie Mauresemo.

11. These leagues are struggling financially. Though it could be said that numerous sports—both men's and women's (with the possible exceptions of golf and tennis)—are struggling with declining ticket sales and television ratings, the women's leagues are often given more superficial, feel-good kinds of rhetorical support than actual financial backing.

12. See Michael Messner, *Taking the Field: Women, Men, and Sports* (Minneapolis: University of Minnesota Press, 2002).

13. Anne Janette Johnson's *Great Women in Sports* (Detroit: Visible Ink Press, 1996), and Robert Markell, Susan Waggoner, and Marcella Smith, eds., *The Women's Sports Encyclopedia* (New York: Henry Holt, 1998). More nuanced and analytical is the Berkshire Reference Works' *The International Encyclopedia of Women and Sports,* ed. Gertrude Pfister and Allen Guttman (New York: Macmillan, 2001), which is an invaluable resource for exploring not just the biographies of athletes from around

the world, but also for the key philosophies and concepts that have informed debates about women's sports.

14. Reece and Karbo, *Big Girl in the Middle;* Jackie Joyner-Kersee, *A Kind of Grace: The Autobiography of the World's Greatest Female Athlete* (New York: Warner Books, 1997); Madeleine Blais, *In These Girls, Hope Is a Muscle: A True Story of Hoop Dreams and One Very Special Team* (New York: Warner Books, 1996); Alexandra Powe-Allred and Michelle Powe, *The Quiet Storm: A Celebration of Women in Sports* (Indianapolis: Masters Press, 1998).

15. Joan Ryan, *Little Girls in Pretty Boxes: The Making and Breaking of Elite Gymnasts and Figure Skaters,* rev. ed. (New York: Warner Books, 2000); Mariah Burton Nelson, *The Stronger Women Get, The More Men Love Football: Sexism and the American Culture of Sport* (New York: Avon Books, 1994).

16. See C. L. Cole and A. Hribar, "Celebrity Feminism: Nike Style Post-Fordism, Transcendence, and Consumer Power," *Sociology of Sport Journal* 12, no. 4 (1995): 347–69; and Melissa R. Lafrance, "Colonizing the Feminine: Nike's Intersections of Postfeminism and Hyperconsumption," in *Sport and Postmodern Times,* ed. Genevieve Rail (Albany: SUNY Press 1998).

17. Ellen Samuels, "Mixed Messages," a review of *Women and Dieting Culture: Inside a Commercial Weight Loss Group, The Women's Review of Books* 19, no. 3 (December 2001): 16.


# 1. Powered Up or Dreaming?

1. See S. L. Dworkin and Michael A. Messner, "Just Do . . . What?: Sport, Bodies, Gender," in *Revisioning Gender,* ed. Judith Lorber, Beth Hess, and Myra Max Ferree (Thousand Oaks, Calif.: Sage, 1999), 341–64.

2. While corporations helped make female athletes much more visible, numerous forces came together to make a slice of the public to be hungry, ready for this. A white, middle-class, female demographic with increased purchasing power is only possible through decades of cumulative federal policy that claims to be race-neutral but in fact has greatly aided the upward mobility of many middle-class whites through housing, education, and mortgage policies. See George Lipsitz, *The Possessive Investment in Whiteness: How White People Profit from Identity Politics* (Philadelphia: Temple University Press, 1998). Strategically then, Nike drew on this privilege by pitching American individualism and "you can do anything" to largely white, middle-class women who had experienced the benefits of Title IX and increased upward mobility. In effect, Nike brilliantly capitalized on the sensibilities of the women who benefited the most from the above policies and who thought they had done it themselves.

3. Even as late as 1999, when comparing women's and men's print and visual media, it is clear that media specifically covering sport, that is, the sports pages of newspapers, and sports channels like ESPN, lags in catching up to real world trends. In these specific sites (as opposed to mass culture and advertising more generally), representation of female athletes remains abysmal. In 1999 men's print news stories in the *Los Angeles Times* outnumber women's by a ratio of 6 to 1, and the percentage of time given to women's sports on three Los Angeles television networks was only

8.7 percent, a remarkably similar percentage to 1989 and 1993, even though stark shifts have occurred in women's professional sport since both time periods. See M. C. Duncan and M. Messner, "Gender in Televised Sports: 1989, 1993, and 1999," report by the Amateur Athletic Foundation of Los Angeles, 2000.

4. Incomes of adult U.S. women have increased 30 percent since 1980 but this figure is for the most part only white women. For examples, see Cynthia Lont, "The Influence of Media on Gender Images," in *Gender Mosaics,* ed. Danna Vannoy (Los Angeles: Roxbury, 2001), 114–22.

5. Lafrance, "Colonizing the Feminine," 121. See also Cole and Hribar, "Celebrity Feminism," 347–69; Dworkin and Messner, "Just Do ... What?," 341–64; M. J. Kane, "Resistance/Transformation of the Oppositional Binary: Exposing Sport as a Continuum," *Journal of Sport and Social Issues* 19, no. 2 (1995): 191–218; M. J. Kane, "Media Coverage of the Post Title IX Female Athlete: A Feminist Analysis of Sport, Gender, and Power," *Duke Journal of Gender Law and Public Policy* 2 (1995): 21–48; Toby Miller, *Sportsex* (Philadelphia: Temple University Press, 2001), 10; and M. C. Duncan and C. A. Hasbrook, "Denial of Power in Televised Women's Sports," *Sociology of Sport Journal* 5 (1989): 1–21.

6. It is Lafrance's contention, for instance, that "Nike feminism" falsely empowers a few privileged women whose illusions are dependent on the exploitation of third world women: "No matter the benefits that some white, North American, bourgeois women might extract from Nike products, no matter how much more they like themselves after they work out, or how much self-esteem they muster up because someone has 'let them play sports,' they acquire these benefits inevitably at the expense of women workers in the Third World. No matter how empowering or disempowering Nike manages to be toward these North American women, they are doing so on the backs of Third World women" (Lafrance, "Colonizing the Feminine," 133).

7. David Andrews, "Excavating Michael Jordan: Notes on a Critical Pedagogy of Sporting Representation," in *Sport and Postmodern Times,* ed. Rail, 186, 185. Andrews is writing about the image of Michael Jordan rather than that of the female athlete, but the theoretical frame of his analysis is applicable to both.

8. These results may be due to the mediating variable of class (socioeconomic status) and not sports participation per se. The same can be true of the research on self-esteem and future success in the workplace.

9. Please see M. Ann Hall's discussion of "Liberal and Radical Feminist Agendas in Sport," in her *Feminism and Sporting Bodies: Essays on Theory and Practice* (Champaign, Ill.: Human Kinetics Press, 1996), 90–92. Hall argues that "feminist activism around sport has been almost exclusively liberal in philosophy and strategy. Attempts to push the agenda to a more 'radical' feminist approach have not met with much success. However, the scholarship about gender and sport is becoming increasingly more radical in its critique; yet little of this research is actually used by those working towards sex equality and gender equity in sport" (90). Hall points to one of the fundamental limitations for the critical poststructuralist approach to sport—the disjunction between researchers who produce work based on this model, and the accessibility of that model to sport practitioners.

10. Participation is not even guaranteed by the positive cultural image, as evidenced by the current lack of Title IX compliance, even in a boom of women's professional sports, and certainly a boom of imagery. And, equality within institutions,

once they are accessed, is not guaranteed as evidenced by facilities, uniforms, and sports team funding discrepancies.

11. President's Council on Physical Fitness and Sports Report, "Physical Activity and Sport in the Life of Young Girls: Physical and Mental Health Dimensions from an Interdisciplinary Approach," U.S. Department of Health and Human Services, Washington, D.C., spring 1997. Correlations, however, need to be interpreted cautiously, as correlational analysis does not point to causality among variables. Several researchers, including Lafrance, above, note that this finding is lost when race and class status are controlled, so it is not sport participation but class status that matters most on the above measures.

12. Jennifer Hargreaves, *Heroines of Sport: The Politics of Difference and Identity* (New York: Routledge, 2000), 3.

13. The core of radical feminist stances argues that men categorically oppress women through bodily oppression, control of women's reproduction, sexual exploitation, and compulsory heterosexuality. Male characteristics such as aggressiveness and competitiveness are rejected, and "female qualities" are embraced. For example, see Mary Daly, *Gyn/Ecology: The Meta-Ethics of Radical Feminism* (Boston: Beacon Press, 1978); Kate Millet, *Sexual Politics* (London: Sphere, 1972); and Adrienne Rich, "Compulsory Heterosexuality and Lesbian Existence," *Signs: Journal of Women in Culture and Society* 5, no. 4 (1982): 631–90.

14. Caroline Ramazanoglu, *Feminism and the Contradictions of Oppression* (London: Routledge, 1989), 10; Hall, *Feminism and Sporting Bodies*, 90, 91.

15. For instance, see Boutilier and SanGiovanni, "Politics, Public Policy, and Title IX," 97–110.

16. Cahn, *Coming on Strong*, 4, 64.

17. For a more specific formulation of third wave feminism, please see Leslie Heywood and Jennifer Drake, "Introduction," in *Third Wave Agenda: Being Feminist, Doing Feminism*, ed. Heywood and Drake (Minneapolis: University of Minnesota Press, 1997), 1–20.

18. Alice Echols, *Daring to Be Bad: Radical Feminism in America, 1967–1975* (Minneapolis: University of Minnesota Press, 1989), 4.

19. Contemporary concerns of radical feminism include an analysis of violence off the field, and the potential link between participating in certain sports and rape. For example, cite Lisa Disch and Mary Jo Kane, "When the Looker Is Really a Bitch," in *Reading Sport: Critical Essays on Power and Representation*, ed. Susan Birrell and Mary G. McDonald (Boston: Northeastern University Press, 2000); Mary Jo Kane and Lisa Disch, "Sexual Violence and the Reproduction of Male Power in the Locker Room: The 'Lisa Olsen' Incident," *Sociology of Sport Journal* 10 (1993): 331–52; Jeff Benedict, *Public Heroes, Private Felons: Athletes and Crimes Against Women* (Boston: Northeastern University Press, 1997). Our analysis is not centered beyond the image, but we recognize important links with this work.

20. Echols, *Daring to Be Bad*, 5, 13. The turn to cultural feminism that became known as "radical feminism" that Echols describes is exemplified in work like Daly (*Gyn-Ecology*), which argued that men were more violent—that's part of why this form of radical feminism thinks about rape as male violence against women. Earlier forms of radical feminism, such as Shulamith Firestone's *The Dialectic of Sex: The Case for Feminist Revolution* (New York: Quill, 1970), are more in line with the poststructuralist gender construction arguments that inform the third wave.

21. Radical feminism in the '60s was also about lesbian separatism, and a third wave perspective differs here. Because third wave feminism aligns itself with what Susan Birrell calls "queer theory and the transgender challenge," which is "that there may be more than two mutually exclusive sexes [and this] challenge[s] the notion of difference itself" (Birrell, "Feminist Theories for Sport," in *Handbook of Sport Studies*, ed. Jay Coakley and Eric Dunning [Thousand Oaks, Calif.: Sage, 2000], 69), for third wave feminism, influenced by this idea, categories of identity based on difference have fallen into question. At the same time, gay and lesbian liberationist work might disagree—for instance, some claim that "queer" claims to deconstruct difference but tends to erase lesbians and privilege white gay men. See, for instance S. D. Walters, "From Here to Queer: Radical Feminism, Postmodernism, and the Lesbian Menace (or: Why Can't a Woman Be More Like a Fag?)," *Signs* 21 (1996).

22. See Kane, "Resistance/Transformation of the Oppositional Binary," 192–218.

23. We acknowledge that the link between institutions and imagery is not easy to make, and that this is not the grounds for claiming that men and women are now facing institutional equality, given obvious institutional inequities that persist, some of which include wage gaps, access to sport, glass escalators for men in promotions, ghettoization into certain occupations, glass ceilings in jobs, and so on. See Barbara Reskin, "Bringing the Men Back In: Sex Differentiation and the Devaluation of Women's Work," *Gender and Society* 2, no. 1 (1988): 58–81; J. Lorber, *Paradoxes of Gender* (New Haven: Yale University Press, 1994).

24. Miller, *Sportsex*, 14.

25. Heywood and Drake, "Introduction," 3, 7.

26. Sarah Gamble, *The Critical Dictionary of Feminism and Postfeminism* (New York: Routledge, 2000), 52; Heywood and Drake, "Introduction," 3, 4, 7, 8. "Postfeminism," as Ann L. Brooks defines it in *Postfeminisms*, is in some ways similar to what we are calling "third wave feminism" in *Third Wave Agenda*, though because of the popular media use of the term at the time (postfeminist = antifeminist) we distanced ourselves from it. "Postfeminism," in the words of Ann L. Brooks, "does not assume that either patriarchal or modernist discourses and frames of reference have been replaced or superseded," but it does assume that they have taken different forms. It also questions universalizing designations like "patriarchy" or "male" because within this volatile, fluid consumer economy, there can be no centralized, top-down, oppressive authority and there are many differences between men (and women) that affect their status—only some men are always "on top." "Postmodernism and poststructuralism," Brooks writes, "with their emphasis on deconstruction and difference, reinforced critiques that had already been directed at the essentialism, ethnocentrism, and ahistoricism of branches of feminist theory. The problematic nature of terms such as 'patriarchy,' 'women,' and 'oppression' was for those at the margins of feminism further highlighted in the debates within the feminist movement instituted initially by women of color." Ann L. Brooks, *Postfeminisms: Feminism, Cultural Theory, and Cultural Forms* (London: Routledge, 1997), 16.

27. Miller, *Sportsex*, 10.

28. Thomas Snyder and Linda Shafer, *Youth Indicators, 1996*, NCES 96–027 (Washington, D.C.: U.S. Department of Education, National Center for Education Statistics, 1996), 4, 53.

29. Jennifer Hargreaves and Ian McDonald, "Cultural Studies and the Sociology of Sport," in *Handbook of Sport Studies*, ed. Coakley and Dunning, 49.

30. Lawrence Grossberg, Cary Nelson, and Paula Treichler, "Introduction," in *Cultural Studies*, ed. Grossberg, Nelson, and Treichler (New York: Routledge, 1992), 1–2.

31. Brooks, *Postfeminisms*, 142.

32. Jim Denison and Robert Rinehart, "Imagining Sociological Narratives," *Sociology of Sport Journal* 17, no. 1 (2000): 1–4.

33. Henry A. Giroux, *Fugitive Cultures: Race, Violence, and Youth* (New York: Routledge, 1996), 133.

34. While sociology is increasingly accepting of media studies, it tends to fall on the critical side when analyzing media studies of female athletes. There is also critique when images are the sole realm of analysis given sociology's emphasis on social change and material social structures. A sociology of gender has been quite progressive in terms of deconstruction. J. Lorber, in "Beyond the Binaries: Depolarizing the Categories of Sex, Sexuality, and Gender," *Sociological Inquiry* 66, no. 2 (1996): 143–59, for instance, calls for deconstruction of sex-gender-sexuality within research. Few empirical studies, particularly within sociology and a sociology of sport, have moved to do this (though more do now, and some may even be in process). In addition, it is rare to examine subjects relationally to hear from boys and girls together, for example, as we have done here.

35. Giroux, *Fugitive Cultures*, 15.

36. Paula M. L. Moya, "Introduction," in *Reclaiming Identity: Realist Theory and the Predicament of Poststructualism*, ed. Moya and Michael R. Hames-Garcia (Berkeley: University of California Press, 2000), 5.

37. This tension is evident in each of our academic experiences. While Leslie's dissertation committee warned her not to "be too empirical" in her analysis of anorexia and literary modernism, Shari's warned her not to be "too postmodern" and to focus on "real institutional structures of domination." Leslie turned to sport as a way to mediate between her theoretical training and her activist impulses, while due to her sociological focus Shari, who came out of a more institutionally laiden analysis, was warned to not fall into rampant individualism, or to overemphasize arguments about individual agency when examining narratives. Rather she was to focus on "group-based agencies and constraints" based in both Marxian terms and postmodern conceptions of agency. The turn to a sport focus was for each of us a way to explore our lifelong athletic experiences as well as the assumptions of our intellectual training.

38. Susan Birrell and Mary McDonald, "Reading Sport Critically: A Methodology for Interrogating Power," *Sociology of Sport Journal* 16, no. 4 (1999): 285.

39. Marjorie Garber, Beatrice Hanssen, and Rebecca L. Walkowitz, eds., *The Turn to Ethics* (New York: Routledge, 2000), 2–3.

40. Laurel Richardson, "New Writing Practices in Qualitative Research," *Sociology of Sport Journal* 17, no. 1 (2000): 7.

41. Leslie Heywood had this experience recently reading a book review of her memoir, *Pretty Good for a Girl: An Athlete's Story* (Minneapolis: University of Minnesota Press, 2000). She wrote that book as a form of what Richardson calls "autoethnography." Richardson defines the genre as follows: "these are highly personalized, revealing texts in which authors tell stories about their own lived experiences, relating the personal to the cultural. The power of these narratives depends on their rhetorical staging as 'true stories,' stories about events that really happened to the writer. In telling the story, the writer calls upon such fiction-writing techniques as

dramatic recall, strong imagery, fleshed out characters, unusual phrasings, puns, subtexts, allusions, the flashback, the flashforward, tone shifts, synecdoche, dialogue, and interior monologue. Through these techniques, the writer constructs a sequence of events, a 'plot,' holding back on interpretation, asking the reader to emotionally 'relive' the events with the writer" (Richardson, "New Writing Practices in Qualitative Research," 11). Because autoethnography is a very new form in sports sociology and is still struggling for acceptance, readers may not be familiar with the rules of the genre such as "holding back on interpretation." For writing in a literary mode, one of the cardinal rules is that the writer does not interpret events to the reader but rather orchestrates the story in a particular way to show the larger themes rather than telling them, letting readers experience the insights themselves through the feeling the narrative creates. But readers unfamiliar with this form may have other expectations. In a recent review of *Pretty Good for a Girl* in the *International Review for the Sociology of Sport* 36, no. 2 (2001), Sandra Kirby writes that "*Pretty Good for a Girl* is more than a good read it is a visceral experience. . . . Heywood does not link the abuse she experienced to other types of violence against women or violence in sport. . . . I kept waiting for some comments about resistance, but discovered none, so found the book wanting in this respect" (225). Because the book was a memoir, the aim was to show the theme of violence in sport and resistance to it rather than presenting analytical arguments about it as one would do in a scholarly article or monograph or journalistic piece. Kirby's desire for this kind of contextualization that retains the power of the literary techniques could be addressed in a form that combines both narrative and analytics. The paperback edition of the book (University of Minnesota Press, 2000) contains a critical introduction that does what Kirby calls for, but it has been an even greater challenge to combine the generic conventions of creative writing, theory, and qualitative method as we have done here.

42.  Hall, *Feminism and Sporting Bodies*, 11; Jane Gottesman, ed., *Game Face: What Does a Female Athlete Look Like?* (New York: Random House, 2001).

43.  For a thorough and illuminating history of the cultural studies tradition in sports sociology that comes out of the British tradition in cultural studies associated with the Centre for Contemporary Cultural Studies at the University of Birmingham, see Hargreaves and McDonald, "Cultural Studies and the Sociology of Sport," 48–60.

44.  Denison and Rinehart, "Imagining Sociological Narratives," 1–20.

45.  Henry Giroux, "Resisting Difference: Cultural Studies and the Discourse of Critical Pedagogy," in *Cultural Studies*, 211.

46.  President's Council Study on Physical Fitness and Sports Report, "Physical Activity and Sport in the Life of Young Girls," 17.

47.  Laurel R. Davis, *The Swimsuit Issue and Sport: Hegemonic Masculinity in Sports Illustrated* (Albany: SUNY Press, 1997), 3. Davis's book is a good example of an empirical analysis of a range of audience responses.

48.  Hargreaves, *Heroines of Sport*, 5.

## 2. Sport as the Stealth Feminism of the Third Wave

1.  Though there has been some improvement in the representation of female athletes as purveyors of products in mainstream women's magazines like *Jump, Teen People*, and *Vogue*, and the movement of the athletic female body onto primetime TV and the mainstream movie screen, there has been much less improvement in

traditional sport venues geared toward men. In a recent 2000 study (Duncan and Messner, "Gender in Televised Sports"), researchers reported that coverage of women's sport among three network affiliates revealed a striking lack of change in the quantity and quality of coverage over the last ten years. In this study, it was found that network affiliates in Los Angeles devoted 8.2 percent and SportsCenter 2.2 percent of their air time to women's sports. This is only a very slight increase in the proportion of sports news that covers women's sports. As noted in Messner (*Taking the Field*), this lack of change must be coupled with an analysis of *how* women's events are covered. In the 2000 AAF study, it was found that women's sporting events received very brief coverage, were frequently covered as pseudo sports and sexual gags, including long features on naked bungee jumping. Messner argues that despite the fact that there may have been increases in the type and quantity of images of female athletes, these are still largely relegated to small, marginal cable channels, websites, or specialized magazines.

2. Michael Bamberger, "Rowing," *Sports Illustrated*, Olympic Preview Issue, July 22, 1996, 124–26.

3. Feminist Majority Women in the Olympics website, "Celebrating 96 Years of Women in the Olympics," http://www.feminist.org/other/olympic/news1/html.

4. Feminist Majority Women in the Olympics website, "Women Shine in 1996 Olympics: A Look Back at Atlanta," http://www.feminist.org/other/olympic/news1/ html; Margaret Carlisle Duncan, "Sports Photographs and Sexual Difference: Images of Women and Men in the 1984 and 1988 Olympic Games," *Sociology of Sport Journal* 7, no. 1 (1990): 22–43; Val Ackerman, comments in "The State of Women's Professional Sports," panel at the Women's Sports Foundation Annual Summit 2001, May 5, 2001.

5. Feminist Majority Women in the Olympics website, "Celebrating 96 Years of Women in the Olympics."

6. Future research needs to analyze the intersections of race and gender in sports coverage of athletes, so as to further flesh out ideologies of fatherhood and motherhood. For instance, we would speculate that different coverage or emphasis is afforded to white male fatherhood versus black male fatherhood given America's preoccupation with the "morality" of Black America. See chapter 5 and analysis of responses to Marion Jones imagery for more on this subject.

7. Jere Longman, "How the Women Won," *New York Times Magazine*, June 23, 1996, 24.

8. We ask this question to highlight that simply objectifying both male and female bodies does not mean that men and women are treated as equals in society. Joe McNally, "Naked Power, Amazing Grace," *Life*, July 1996, 50–64.

9. This point can be debated, for instance, see Messner, *Taking the Field*. When one analyzes, for instance, some of the most profoundly successful endorsements over the past five years, such as Anna Kournikova (who, as Messner notes, has never won a tournament to date), Lisa Leslie, and Mia Hamm, there indeed appears to be a reassurance of heterosexual attractiveness operating. Messner argues that, indeed, some women are pulled to the "cultural center" of sport, while others are pushed to the margins. He concedes that new images exist but offers that we should perhaps temper our celebration of gender fluidity. He concludes that female athletes are mostly in peripheral market niches, and, as such, help to keep the center of sport as a male-subject, female-object realm even as these are challenged in other forums.

10. Longman, "How the Women Won," 25. These types of arguments have been employed historically by cultural feminists who, for instance, claim that women play a "purer" version of basketball than men; see Cahn, *Coming on Strong*. The dangers of such arguments are that they can become consistent with cultural feminist difference arguments, and then these can be used all too easily to justify differential access to resources or to ghettoize women's sport as being secondary to the men's "real" version. To applaud women for "not being greedy" masks the fact that women's sports are very difficult to keep alive without more money.

11. For a detailed presentation and analysis of these politics, please see Hargreaves, *Heroines of Sport,* esp. chaps. 2, 3, and 4.

12. Simultaneously, news stories circulated about Slaney's possible steroid use. Such accusations are frequently launched at powerfully successful female athletes given the historical disbelief that athleticism was compatible with femininity. For more on the history of steroid accusations and IOC "femininity checks," see Laurel R. Davis and L. C. Delano, "Fixing the Boundaries of Physical Gender: Side Effects of Anti-Drug Campaigns in Athletics," *Sociology of Sport Journal* 9 (1992): 1–19. Also see Cahn, *Coming on Strong.*

13. On this alternative tradition see Mary Jo Festle, *Playing Nice: Politics and Apologies in Women's Sports* (New York: Columbia University Press, 1996), especially chaps. 1 and 5; Cahn, *Coming on Strong,* chap. 3; and Mariah Burton Nelson, *Embracing Victory: Life Lessons in Competition and Compassion* (New York: William Morrow), 1998.

14. While these results appear to be self-evident, researchers should be extremely cautious about such statements given that race and class factors frequently intersect with issues of mental and physical health. Race and socioeconomic status can often explain just as much or more about health and esteem for women than can sports participation as a distinct variable.

15. David Wallechinsky, "Vaults, Leaps, and Dashes: Women's Sports Go the Distance," *New York Times Magazine,* June 23, 1996, 47.

16. Longman, "How the Women Won," 26. Longman assumes white, middle-class status, given that numerous working-class women and women of color have always worked outside the home. See Teresa Amott and Julie A. Matthei, *Race, Gender, and Work: A Multicultural Economic History of Women in the United States* (Boston: South End Press, 1991).

17. This is unlike the labor force that Nike employed to catapult the image of the female athlete in the United States—third world women of color who stitch Nike swooshes for approximately two dollars a day.

18. Donna Lopiano, "Don't Touch That Dial," *Women's Sports and Fitness* (July/August 1996): 42.

19. Donna Lopiano, "Women in the Olympics," *USA Today,* August 4, 1996.

20. While it might be argued that gay and lesbian iconography is taken into account given the "postmodern multiplicity of signs" (see Griggers, "Lesbian Bodies in the Age of [Post]mechanical Reproduction," 178–92), one needs to be cautious to interpret a lessening hesitancy of media to endorse openly gay and lesbian athletes as a sign that the margins have faced "equal opportunity" representation. For a more in-depth discussion of how race, gender, and sexuality operate within representations of female athletes, see chapter 6.

21. This might be somewhat ironic given that some argue that black and white America have never been more separate and unequal. See Andrew Hacker, *Two Nations: Black and White, Separate, Hostile, Unequal* (New York: Ballantine Books, 1995). Other researchers argue that women of color are both better off than ever before (see Bart Landry, *The New Black Middle Class* [Berkeley: University of California Press, 1987] and *Black Working Wives: Pioneers of the American Family Revolution* [Berkeley: University of California Press, 2000]), and far worse off. See Ruth Sidel, *Women and Children Last: America's War on the Poor* (New York: Penguin Books, 1996).

22. This did not just involve classic assumptions that female athletes are lesbians, as is discussed in depth below, but also included racialized and classed constructs of femininity. For instance, in the 1940s, white middle-class women began to flee track and field due to its classification within media that it was "masculinizing." This allowed for women of color and working-class women to enter the sport in new numbers. For more on the racialized and classed aspects of women in sport, see Cahn, *Coming on Strong*. Indeed, this example serves to inform the current historical moment whereby certain women receive more endorsements when "appropriately" feminine. This helps to explain why we see more acceptance among the more model-like stances from Lisa Leslie, Flo-Jo, and Marion Jones, which serve to reinforce them as feminine "enough."

"Lesbian baiting"—the disparagement of a female athlete because she is athletic and therefore by some traditional definition "too masculine" and therefore lesbian—is still a common homophobic practice that negatively affects homosexuals and heterosexuals alike (see chapter 3 for a more detailed explication of this problem). We do not mean to suggest here that the problem is solved, only that it was previously a more explicit, normative practice. Now it functions in more covert ways. See Eric Anderson, an openly gay track coach at the University of California–Irvine, who found in his 2000 study "Homophobia in Sport: Is It As Bad As They Say?" based on interviews and surveys with forty-two gay male high school and collegiate athletes that "organized high school and collegiate sports in North America are not as uniformly homophobic as previously assumed." See also Pat Griffin's groundbreaking book *Strong Women, Deep Closets: Lesbians and Homophobia in Sport* (Champaign, Ill.: Human Kinetics, 1998). Griffin's work is responsible for many of the major activist initiatives on homophobia in sport.

23. Part of our shared jubilation is linked to our shared class status. People who share socioeconomic status may be more homogeneous in their views. And those who watched women playing soccer on that day may have also shared middle- or upper-middle-class status. Social locations certainly impact what sports programs students watch, read about, and play. As will be discussed in chapter 6, students from more wealthy schools recalled Chastain and Hamm as the first female athlete who came to mind, while students from poorer districts tended to first think of female wrestlers and WNBA players.

24. See chapter 1 for a discussion of claims that women in sport are better than or somehow different and inferior to men.

25. Who is allowed to be popular and when within representation depends on which versions of femininity are included in widely proliferating representations of women in sport. See Kane, "Media Coverage of the Post Title IX Female Athlete,"

21–48. The Love quote is from Katherine Dunn, "Courtney Love," *Rolling Stone* (November 13, 1997), 166.

26. Whether or not this equation would work equally for white, middle-class women when compared to black, lesbian, working-class, or other women of color is an empirical question that needs to be explored. On the men's side of the equation, it is disproportionately men of color who gain the very short-term benefits of sport. After a sports career, there is often a great deal of difficulty faced when transitioning into other aspects of the occupational structure. It is the more rare case when these skills translate "off the field," despite perception that such transitions are common.

27. Gabrielle Reece, "Grace in Your Face," *Condé Nast Sports for Women*, December 1997, 78.

28. Indeed, one must ask "Just Do What?" and "For Whom?" See Dworkin and Messner, "Just Do . . . What?," 341–64.

29. Heywood, *Bodymakers.*

30. For coverage of gross inequities in the American educational system given the fact that schools are funded through property taxes, see J. Kozol, *Savage Inequalities: Children in America's Schools* (New York: HarperCollins, 1991). For coverage of the harsh realities of American inner cities, see William Julius Wilson, *When Work Disappears: The World of the New Urban Poor* (New York: Vintage Books, 1996).

31. For an excellent empirical examination of the realities of the contemporary American occupational structure as it relates to race, class, and gender intersections, see Irene Browne, "Latinas and African-American Women in the U.S. Labor Market," in *Latinas and African American Women at Work: Race, Gender, and Economic Inequality,* ed. Browne (New York: Russell Sage, 1999), 1–31.

32. Joan Morgan, *When the Chickenheads Come Home to Roost: My Life as a Hip-Hop Feminist* (New York: Simon and Schuster, 1999).

33. Joanna Cagan, *Nerve,* http://www.nerve.com/ Cagan/hotMamas.html.

34. Jeanette Lee, personal interview with Heywood, February 14, 2001.

35. Susan Faludi, *Backlash: The Undeclared War Against American Women* (New York: Crown, 1991).

36. Morgan, *When the Chickenheads Come Home to Roost,* 59. Subsequent page numbers appear in the text.

37. Some women appear to have fewer opportunities than ever. See Sidel, *Women and Children Last.*

38. Morgan, *When the Chickenheads Come Home to Roost,* 57–58. Her narrative reveals her more privileged class position. People who live in unsafe working conditions or among conditions of inequality that include domestic or sexual violence cannot worry about whether power is sexy or not. Indeed, those who have the most control over their health, well-being, wages, and mobility can be concerned with how to "play with" the "sexiness" of power. There also needs to be more reflection on sexuality and patriarchy, for some lesbian women clearly seek egalitarianism in their relationships with women but also eroticize difference through butch and femme displays. Is this patriarchal?

39. Some biologists have caught on, are increasingly catching on, and swing toward constructionist arguments. See, for instance, B. Beale, "The Sexes: New Insights in the X and Y Chromosomes," *The Scientist* 15, no. 15 (July 23, 2001): 18. Also see Anne Fausto-Sterling's *Myths of Gender: Biological Theories about Women and*

*Men* (New York: Basic Books, 1985). Also see Fausto-Sterling, *Sexing the Body: Gender Politics and the Construction of Sexuality* (New York: Basic Books, 2000).

40. Wendy Shalit, *A Return to Modesty* (New York: Free Press, 1998), 14.

41. F. Carolyn Graglia, *Domestic Tranquility: A Brief Against Feminism* (Dallas: Spence Publishing, 1998), 5. This analysis is invariably flawed in more than a few ways. Graglia forgets that the reality of declining real wages and huge increases in the cost of living over the last several decades (not feminism) requires that more women work outside the home to increase wages. This is particularly the case for those women who are not married, or are married to working-class men of color who have, due to deindustrialization, faced the worst occupational structure in decades. And her comments negate the fact that men were the primary childrearers in preindustrial America, and that the "propensities" of motherhood and fatherhood have long been contested and debated. Such "propensities" are clearly not natural but are the result of bolstering specific family forms within certain economic, social, and political contexts. Indeed, it has now been well established, though very slow to enter the public discourse (and Graglia's mind), that the rise of the white, middle-class, heterosexual family with "traditional" male breadwinner and stay-at-home mom norms was a historical aberration, not a norm.

42. Nancy Etcoff, *Survival of the Prettiest: The Science of Beauty* (New York: Doubleday, 1999), 6; Kim France, review of *Survival of the Prettiest*, in *Spin*, February 1999, 64.

43. At the same time, some new classes include "cardio striptease," emphasizing how powerful workouts can end up being sexualized experiences that may not in fact aid ideologies of athletic female incompetence.

44. Danielle is not her real name; her name was changed per her request. Personal interview, May 1999.

45. We recognize that the analysts needs to take race, class, and sexuality into account. For instance, self-esteem can be hurt in very different ways if one does not have access to basic nutrition or educational needs when compared to those who do have these basics for survival. In this case, girls from relatively underprivileged backgrounds might turn to sport the most—and have access to it the least—and still face the problems mentioned in this chapter. For a discussion of how this esteem is "conditional worth" within a system where most will eventually fail, see Michael Messner, *Power at Play: Sports and the Problem of Masculinity* (Boston: Beacon Press, 1991). Very little has been written on athletic identity and women of color.

46. Personal interviews, May 1998.

47. For a discussion on how sport and athleticism can undo the socialization of girls into a bodily "inhibited intentionality," see Iris Young, "Throwing Like a Girl: A Phenomenology of Feminine Body Comportment," *Human Studies* 3 (1980): 137–56.

48. Leslie has found in interviews with former or current athletes that roughly the same percentage protest, "I'm not a feminist!" compared to the number of the general student population that does so (one-half to two-thirds). Like many other researchers have found, however, once you define *feminism* as a commitment to equality between men and women, most would then agree to call themselves feminists.

49. Festle, *Playing Nice*, 113.

50. Hall, *Feminism and Sporting Bodies*, 8.

51. Diana Baroni, "Feminist: What Is It about That Word?" *Cosmopolitan,* May 1994, 196.

52. "Reads," *Teen People,* October 1998, 40.

53. Though some would criticize the Women's Sports Foundation for having a "liberal" edge because of its collaboration with corporations, or because liberal feminism tends to overvalue white, middle-class, heterosexual experience (for instance, see Messner, *Taking the Field*), as a trustee Leslie has seen first-hand the wide variety of projects the foundation is committed to. The foundation is involved with projects ranging from grassroots through the elite levels, and there is no one branch of feminism that can fully account for and encompass the foundation's agenda. It works for the advancement of women in sport on all levels, and in its use of liberal, radical, and market strategies, it might fall more under the "postmodern," montage rubric than any of the older branches of feminism.

## 3. A New Look at Female Athletes and Masculinity

1. Varda Burstyn, *The Rites of Men: Manhood, Politics, and the Culture of Sport* (Toronto: University of Toronto Press, 1999), 267.

2. Ibid., 267, xii. In fact, one thing Burstyn doesn't consider in her injunctions against female athletes who "sell out" to masculinity is that, by her own logic, the masculine sport model offers the very definition of "success" in American culture, and to ask women to renounce success and the privileges that go with it is asking a great deal of most people (if they can gain access to enjoy these at all).

3. Jennifer Lawler, *Punch: Why Women Participate in Violent Sports* (Terre Haute, Ind.: Wish Publishing, 2002), x.

4. Burstyn, *The Rites of Men,* 3.

5. Heywood, *Pretty Good for a Girl.*

6. Burstyn, *The Rites of Men,* 266, 267, emphasis added.

7. Teresa de Lauretis, *Technologies of Gender* (Bloomington: Indiana University Press, 1987), 2, 1.

8. Judith Butler, *Gender Trouble: Feminism and the Subversion of Identity* (New York: Routledge, 1990), vii.

9. Sherrie A. Inness, *Tough Girls: Women Warriors and Wonder Women in Popular Culture* (Philadelphia: University of Pennsylvania Press, 1999), 89–90.

10. "Begun to surface" in a mainstream way, in mass-media representations, and therefore in white femininity, that is, and surfacing as a new kind of ideal rather than as an object of derision.

11. Cahn, *Coming on Strong,* 4, 64.

12. Nelson, *Embracing Victory,* 8.

13. Jere Longman, *The Girls of Summer: The U.S. Women's Soccer Team and How It Changed the World* (New York: HarperCollins, 2000), 173.

14. Annalee Newitz, Ana Marie Cox, Freya Johnson, and Jillian Sandell, "Masculinity Without Men: Women Reconciling Feminism and Male Identification," in *Third Wave Agenda,* ed. Heywood and Drake, 178.

15. Kaja Silverman, *Male Subjectivity at the Margins* (New York: Routledge, 1992), 4.

16. Burstyn, *The Rites of Men,* 44.

17. Gottesman, *Game Face*, 11.

18. See Barrie Thorne, *Gender Play: Girls and Boys in School* (New Brunswick, N.J.: Rutgers University Press, 1993). Also see C. Shawn McGuffy and B. Lindsey Rich, "Playing in the Gender Transgression Zone: Race, Class, and Hegemonic Masculinity in Middle Childhood," *Gender and Society* 13, no. 5 (1999): 608–27.

19. See Minnie Bruce Pratt, *S/he* (New York: Firebrand, 1995).

20. Kane, "Resistance/Transformation of the Oppositional Binary," 191–218.

21. I am grateful to Mariah Burton Nelson for her personal communication with me which helped me to understand this action as a strategic one linked to the spirit of competition and increased chances for winning.

22. See Fausto-Sterling, *Myths of Gender* and *Sexing the Body*.

23. Of course, many women predate Lester and Animal with their courage to act "like men." See, for instance, Paula Gunn Allen, "Lesbians in American Indian Cultures," in *Hidden from History: Reclaiming the Gay and Lesbian Past*, ed. Martin Duberman, Martha Vicinus, and George Chauncey Jr. (New York: Penguin, 1989), 106–17; Judith C. Brown, *Immodest Acts* (New York: Oxford University Press, 1986); Lillian Faderman, *Surpassing the Love of Men: Romantic Friendship and Love Between Women from the Renaissance to the Present* (Tallahassee, Fla.: Naiad Press, 1981); Elizabeth Kennedy and Madeline Davis, *Boots of Leather, Slippers of Gold: The History of a Lesbian Community* (New York: Penguin Books, 1993); Margaret Cruikshank, *Lesbian Studies: Present and Future* (New York: Feminist Press, 1982); Kristin Esterberg, *Lesbian and Bisexual Identities: Constructing Communities, Constructing Selves* (Philadelphia: Temple University Press, 1997); Celia Kitzinger, *The Social Construction of Lesbianism* (London: Sage, 1987); Shane Phelan, *Getting Specific: Postmodern Lesbian Politics* (Minneapolis: University of Minnesota Press, 1994); Siobhan Somerville, *Queering the Color Line: Race and the Invention of Homosexuality in American Culture* (Durham, N.C.: Duke University Press, 2000); Walter Williams, "Amazons of America: Female Gender Variance," in his *The Spirit and the Flesh: Sexual Diversity in American Indian Culture* (Boston: Beacon Press, 1986).

24. Nellie Wong, "Resolution," *Long Shot* 24 (2001): 89.

25. Peggy Orenstein, *Flux: Women on Sex, Work, Love, Kids, and Life in a Half-Changed World* (New York: Doubleday, 2000).

## 4. Bodies, Babes, and the WNBA

1. See Jean Baudrillard, *Simulacra and Simulation*, trans. Shelia Faria Glaser (Ann Arbor: University of Michigan Press, 1994); Chris Rojek, "Baudrillard and Politics," in *Forget Baudrillard?*, ed. Rojek (New York: Routledge, 1993), 107–23.

2. Sally Jenkins, *Washington Post*, September 2000; Melissa Isaacson, *Chicago Tribune*, September 2000.

3. Please see Heywood and Drake, ed., *Third Wave Agenda*.

4. Linda Steiner, quoted in Mark O'Keefe, "Sexploitation or Pride? Female Olympians' Revealing Poses Stir Debate," Newhouse News Service, 2000 (internet).

5. Michael Messner, Margaret Carlisle Duncan, et al., "Gender and Televised Sports: 1989, 1993, and 1999," Amateur Athletic Foundation of Los Angeles, Los Angeles, 2001.

6. Women's Sports Foundation website, www.womenssportsfoundation.org.

7. See Heywood, *Bodymakers.*

8. *Condé Nast Sports and Fitness for Women* (January/February 1999).

9. *Vogue,* January 2001.

10. Judith Butler, "Athletic Genders: Hyperbolic Instance and/or the Overcoming of Sexual Binarism," *Stanford Humanities Review* 6, no. 2 (1998).

11. Miller, *Sportsex,* 52.

12. Ibid., 11.

13. Susan Bordo, *Twilight Zones: The Hidden Life of Cultural Images from Plato to OJ* (Berkeley: University of California Press, 1997), 124–25.

14. Jeanette Lee, phone interview with author, February 14, 2001.

15. Richard J. Lane, *Jean Baudrillard* (London and New York: Routledge, 2000), 98.

16. Miller, *Sportsex,* 64.

17. The current challenge to Title IX, in which one of the arguments is that women don't need as many opportunities as men to play because women "naturally" aren't as interested in sports, may change this experience of rights and entitlement for women.

18. Philip Dixon, "Gabrielle Reece: She's Beautiful, She's Buff, and She's Bold," *Playboy* 48, no. 1 (January 2001): 92.

19. Associated Press, "Harrison Considers Posing for Playboy," http://espn.go.com/wnba/news/2001/0711/1224770.html.

20. *Sports Illustrated for Women,* November/December 2000, 121. For anyone just entering these debates, a good basic introduction can be found in Andrew Edgar and Peter Sedgwick, eds., *Key Concepts in Cultural Theory* (New York: Routledge, 1999).

21. On the modern model of sport, and how it would have to change to fit the contemporary postmodern context, see Deborah Shogan, *The Making of High Performance Athletes* (Toronto: University of Toronto Press, 1999).

22. David L. Andrews, "Posting Up: French Poststructuralism and the Critical Analysis of Contemporary Sporting Culture," in *Handbook of Sport Studies,* ed. Coakley and Dunning, 106.

23. For a good introduction to postmodernism and its application to a reading of sport culture and practice, see Cheryl L. Cole, "Addiction, Exercise, and Cyborgs: Technologies of Deviant Bodies," in *Sport and Postmodern Times,* ed. Rail, 261–75, and Andrews, "Posting Up," 106–37.

24. Butler, "Athletic Genders."

25. Ibid.

26. *Muscle and Fitness Hers,* 1, no. 4 (winter 2000): 19, 11, 39, 105.

27. Glenn W. Most, "The Athlete's Body in Ancient Greece," *Stanford Humanities Review* 6, no. 2 (1998).

28. This is linked to the irony of the modern/postmodern debate we have raised throughout: sport is a form of modernist masculinity reasserted and in fact partially formed in reaction to what was seen as the feminization of the male body due to industrialization and an expanded commodity culture in the 1880s–1920s. Gender-segregated sport was also partly a reaction to women's rising social power that followed suffrage and the increasing presence of women in public sphere as teachers and social service workers. Made "soft" by desk jobs and contact with women, the fear was that boys would be feminized by women, and people like Teddy Roosevelt and his Rough Riders called for men to get out into the wild and

become physically active as a way to combat feminization. Sport was seen as one place to bolster physical and psychological manliness. See Todd Crosset, "Masculinity, Sexuality, and the Development of Early Modern Sport," in *Sport, Men, and the Gender Order: Critical Feminist Perspectives*, ed. Michael Messner and Don Sabo (Champaign, Ill.: Human Kinetics, 1990), 45–54. See also Michael Kimmel, "Baseball and the Reconstitution of American Masculinity, 1880–1920," in same book, 55–67.

29. Leslie Heywood, "The Women's Sports Foundation Report: Addressing the Needs of Female Professional and Amateur Athletes," The Women's Sports Foundation, East Meadow, N.Y., 1999, 4, 6.

30. Gottesman, *Game Face*, 187, 189, 192, 128, 149.

31. Cole, "Addiction, Exercise, and Cyborgs," 273.

32. Miller, *Sportsex*, 1, 2.

33. Joli Sandoz, post to the Frances Willard Society Listserv, FWS@listbot.com, September 1, 2000.


## 5. Body Panic Parity

1. Susan Bordo, *The Male Body: A New Look at Men in Public and Private* (New York: Farrar, Strauss, Giroux, 1999), 220.

2. The term *body project* was coined by Joan Jacobs Brumberg in her book *The Body Project: An Intimate History of American Girls* (New York: Vintage Books, 1997).

3. Harrison G. Pope, Katherine A. Phillips, and Roberto Olivardia, *The Adonis Complex: The Secret Crisis of Male Body Obsession* (New York: Free Press, 2000), xv; Miller, *Sportsex*, 9.

4. I deliberately use the diminutive "boy" here to invoke contemporary usage, as in "Oh, that's a boy thing," a phrase used to indicate a behavior seen as traditionally male. That "boy," like "girl," has come to represent the universal category of males rather than just young males is culturally significant, for it reflects some lack of status that has long been part of girls' and women's experiences. A similar reaction occurred in early twentieth-century America when Teddy Roosevelt and his Rough Riders proposed vigorous physical activity for men as the antidote to a "feminizing" consumer culture.

5. See Michael Kimmel, *Manhood in America: A Cultural History* (New York: Free Press, 1996), for how sport as an institution formed in part as a white, middle-class response to fears of social feminization at the turn of the nineteenth century, given the separation of work from family life. This "left" boys in the feminizing clutches of mothers.

6. P. David Marshall, *Celebrity and Power* (Minneapolis: University of Minnesota Press, 1997), ix.

7. Perhaps structural changes such as women's gains into sport and male-dominated occupations is part of the "feminization" that makes them angry. These structural shifts include consumption being offered as a way of life to both sexes, and the correspondent movement of women into the workplace. Furthermore, the restructuring of the economy into less prestigious service jobs create the threats to traditional masculinity the characters use their "fight-club" to redeem. Though the characters in the club are not exclusively white, most of them are, making it arguable

that it is not just gender that makes them angry, but white male response to race and class shifts, for example, rise of the black middle class, which is also threatening to their masculine status. It is notable that in popular movies it is usually black men who culturally are fetishized for violent acts, acts that construct them as different than the norm, but now that it is primarily white boys acting out, the movie presents it as laudable to be so violent.

8.  Historically, Kimmel highlights how social fears of feminization often lead to "masculinist" (masculine bolstering) responses, among other responses. Building a large body would certainly qualify as a masculinist response to such fears. See Kimmel, "Baseball and the Reconstitution of American Masculinity," 55–67. Also see Kimmel, "Men's Responses to Feminism at the Turn of the Century," *Gender and Society* 1, no. 3 (1987): 261–83, and Kimmel, *Manhood in America*. In *Male Fantasies*, vols. 1–2 (Minneapolis: University of Minnesota Press, 1987, 1989), Klaus Theweleit documents the same trend in the novels and memoirs of the German Freikorps after World War I, arguing that a repudiation of one's body (and therefore of femininity, which is associated with the body) became a psychological compulsion that associated masculinity with hardness, self-denial, and violence.

9.  Pope, Phillips, and Olivardia, xiii.

10.  The tough guy's not going down without a fight, however. The almost-caricatured masculinity evident in the short-lived XFL is a good example of how recent culture has tried to bolster the scarecrow of traditional masculinity discussed in chapter 3.

11.  Bordo, *The Male Body*, 219.

12.  Naomi Wolf, *The Beauty Myth* (New York: William Morrow, 1991); Pope, Phillips, and Olivardia, 7, 9, 10.

13.  Chris Godsey, "How Does It Feel?" http://adiosbarbie.com/features/features godsey2.html, accessed September 16, 2000.

14.  Quoted in Alicia Potter, "Mirror Image," *Boston Phoenix*, posted on http://wwwinfoplease.com:80/spot/mbi1.html, accessed September 16, 2000.

15.  Pope, Phillips, and Olivardia, *Adonis Complex*, 15.

16.  See Shari Dworkin and Faye Wachs, *Size Matters: Body Parity and Consumer Culture* (New York: NYU Press, forthcoming), who find that when men and women "successfully" internalize their respective ideals from mainstream health and fitness discourse within magazines (and they are often "sold separately") men enjoy greater size and power (and low bodyfat). Women often are sold more compact ideals still, with limited size prescribed so as to not be too muscular (and low bodyfat). Both are being sold ideals, and though these have stretched, the masculine ideal is still certainly larger.

17.  John Berger, *Ways of Seeing* (London: Penguin, 1973), 47. Berger's formulation has long been a dominant paradigm in critical analysis of gender. It is precisely this "way of seeing" ("men act, women appear") that must be questioned today, for the "equity of image" has to do with the way appearance (though those appearances differ) has become a dominant paradigm for both genders. Of course, "appearing" also differs between ideal images and actual people.

18.  Bordo, *Twilight Zones*.

19.  Henry A. Giroux, *Impure Acts: The Practical Politics of Cultural Studies* (New York: Routledge, 2000), 6.

20. As Peggy Orenstein argues in *Flux*. However, the supports that are in place favor men, not women in terms of juggling work and family. Even though there's been a shift in image, current data do show that women do much more often take time off from work to take care of families, or are using flextime and other scheduling programs to take care of kids, or are trying to be "super woman" while getting second-class citizenship to men in the workplace since if they take time off for their families they are not seen as serious workers. Men are not expected to do the juggle, and do not do it nearly as often.

21. Benjamin DeMott, *Killer Woman Blues: Why Americans Can't Think Straight about Gender and Power* (Boston: Houghton Mifflin, 2000), ix, 72.

22. This is a variation on a nearly equally conservative theme that was offered by George Gilder, an aide to Reagan during his presidency. Gilder argued that feminism is an affront to nature, that it is women's responsibility to control men's sexual "nature," and that men will continue to relentlessly pursue sex unless women say "no" and force men to settle down. See George Gilder, *Sexual Suicide* (New York: Bantam, 1973); and George Gilder, *Men and Marriage* (Gretna: Pelican Publishing Company, 1986). Gilder also reinforced that it is men's nature to get ahead in the corporate world when he argues that it is the fault of government welfare programs (and black women) for feminizing black men. See George Gilder, *Wealth and Poverty* (New York: Basic Books, 1981).

23. DeMott, *Killer Woman Blues*, 24.

24. Colette Dowling, *The Frailty Myth: Women Approaching Physical Equality* (New York: Random House, 2000), 31.

25. Her cockiness was also likely named as such due to intersections with race and class, which often emphasize black "misbehaving" as different from supposedly more moral or "civilized" white middle-class stances. To examine this debate for masculinity, see M. A. Messner, *The Politics of Masculinity: Men in Movements* (Thousand Oaks, Calif.: Sage, 1997).

26. Dowling, *The Frailty Myth*, xxiii.

27. Black women, working-class women, and lesbians have often long refused the secondary, supportive role with the result that they have still been erased or are not seen as real women anyhow.

28. While the movie focuses on gender reversal, it is in line with class norms— Diana is a working-class woman, and boxing is associated with the working class, where boxing (as in Adrian's narrative) is seen as a "way out."

29. In *Punch*, Jennifer Lawler argues that "as women continue to make strides in all areas of their lives—in their careers, in their relationships—they learn that there are no predetermined limits to what they can do. They challenge previously held opinions about what's good for them, about what goals they can pursue, and what it means to be successful. For all these reasons, and more, women who want to push themselves, to learn what they can do, are taking up contact sports" (21). Lawler postulates, as does *Girlfight*, that a woman (here a half-black, half-Hispanic woman) gains respect and cultural valuation when she proves her toughness through sports.

30. Inness, *Tough Girls*, 181.

31. For further discussion of how physical strength is a feminist response to a violent world, see M. McCaughey, *Real Knockouts: The Physical Feminism of Women's Self-Defense* (New York: New York University Press, 1997).

32. M. Ann Hall, "Boxers and Bodymakers: Third Wave Feminism and the Re-making of Women's Sport," presentation for the Dimensionen und Visionen des Sports conference, Heidelberg, Germany, September 27–29, 1999.

33. Inness, *Tough Girls,* 65, 180.

34. Ibid., 70.

35. Here Lara might be framed as heterosexual, perhaps given her strength. See Lynn Segal, *Straight Sex: Rethinking the Politics of Pleasure* (Berkeley: University of California Press, 1994), for her discussion that the formulation of heterosexuality as active sexuality being a good move for heterosexual women, but it is still clearly heterosexual women who generally get represented in the first place.

36. Inness, *Tough Girls,* 180.

37. Helen Lenskyj, "Running Risks: Compulsive Exercise and Eating Disorders," in *Consuming Passions: Feminist Approaches to Weight Preoccupation and Eating Disorders,* ed. Catrina Brown and Karin Jasper (Toronto: Second Story Press, 1993), 98.

38. Bill Reynolds, *Glory Days: A Basketball Memoir* (New York: St. Martin's, 1998), 42.

39. Godsey, "How Does It Feel."

## 6. She Will Beat You Up, and Your Papa, Too

1. Kids were told by teachers that visitors were going to talk with them about women and sport.

2. In addition to the Bay Area CyberRays and Washington Freedom, other teams included the Atlanta Beat, Boston Breakers, Carolina Courage, New York Power, Philadelphia Charge, and San Diego Spirit. Comparative analysis of the names of these teams versus the names of men's teams has not yet been carried out, but it is indeed intriguing to see so many of the women's teams named after terms that imply emotional and spiritual "power."

3. See E. Metheny, *Connotations of Movement in Sport and Dance* (Dubuque, Iowa: Wm. C. Brown, 1965). Also see M. J. Kane and E. Snyder, "Sport Typing: The Social 'Containment' of Women in Sport," *Arena Review* 13 (1989): 77–96. To read about the role that sex typing plays in masking a continuum of overlapping performance by gender, see Kane, "Resistance/Transformation of the Oppositional Binary," 191–218.

4. Dr. Sohaila Shakib, "Female Basketball Participation and Attrition: Negotiating the Conflation of Peer Status and Gender Status from Childhood through Puberty," *American Behavorial Scientist* (in press).

5. Some researchers argue that fitness in fact emerged in response to the perceived masculinizing influences of sport and provided a separate realm more consistent with emphasized femininity. See J. Hargreaves, *Sporting Females: Critical Issues in the History and Sociology of Sport* (London: Routledge, 1994).

6. See R. Vivian Acosta and Linda Jean Carpenter, "Women in Intercollegiate Sport: A Longitudinal Study—Nineteen-Year Update, 1977–1996," Department of Physical Education, Brooklyn College, Brooklyn, 1996; and Dworkin and Messner, "Just Do . . . What?," 341–64. Also see the Women's Sports Foundation, "Gender Equity Report Card."

7. While it might be expected that age or class status might impact this task, it was 100 percent of the students from one upper-middle-class high school and 100 percent of the students from one poor grade school that were able to think of a female athlete.

8. For an excellent discussion of the historically changing relationship between sport and media, see Suh Jhally, "Cultural Studies and the Sports/Media Complex," in *Media, Sports, and Society,* ed. Lawrence A. Wenner (London: Sage, 1989). For an analysis of new iconography and trends, and how these both reinforce and challenge the center of sport, see Messner, *Taking the Field.* Also see M. A. Messner, M. Dunbar, and D. Hunt, "The Televised Sports Manhood Formula," *Journal of Sport and Social Issues* 24, no. 4 (2000): 380–94.

9. For an excellent compilation on media studies that covers numerous axes of difference, see G. Dines and J. McMahon-Humez, *Gender, Race, and Class in Media: A Rext-Reader* (New York: Sage, 1995).

10. See M. Messner, Margaret Carlisle Duncan, and Faye Linda Wachs, "The Gender of Audience-Building: Televised Coverage of Men's and Women's NCAA Basketball," *Sociological Inquiry* 66 (1996): 422–39.

11. One excellent resource for developing focus group questions was Richard Krueger, *Developing Questions for Focus Groups* (Thousand Oaks, Calif.: Sage, 1998).

12. While numerous researchers have made this argument, Sarah Banet-Wieser, in *The Most Beautiful Girl in the World: Beauty Pageants and National Identity* (Berkeley: University of California Press, 1999), makes it particularly well.

13. See Nancy Spencer, "Reading Between the Lines: A Discursive Analysis of the Billie Jean King vs. Bobby Riggs 'Battle of the Sexes,'" *Sociology of Sport Journal* 17 (2000): 386–402.

14. For outstanding coverage on ideologies and representations that effectively "other" African-Americans, Asian Americans, and other people of color up against a European white norm, please see Patricia Hill Collins, *Black Feminist Thought: Knowledge, Consciousness, and the Politics of Empowerment* (Boston: Unwin Hyman, 1990); Yen Li Espiritu, *Asian American Women and Men* (Thousand Oaks, Calif.: Sage, 1997); Sander Gilman, *Difference and Pathology: Stereotypes of Sexuality, Race, and Madness* (Ithaca, N.Y.: Cornell University Press, 1985); Stuart Hall, "The Spectacle of the Other," in *Representation: Cultural Representations and Signifying Practices,* ed. Hall (London: Sage, 1997), 223–90.

15. For arguments on the messiness of lived reality, see Leslie Heywood and Jennifer Drake, "Introduction" (1–20), and "We Learn America Like a Script: Activism in the Third Wave; or, Enough Phantoms of Nothing" (40–54), in *Third Wave Agenda,* ed. Heywood and Drake.

16. For instance, see Banet-Wieser, *The Most Beautiful Girl In the World;* Cole and Hribar, "Celebrity Feminism," 347–69; C. Cooky, "'If You Let Me Play': Liberal Discourse and Young Girls Sporting Experiences," master's thesis, Miami University, Oxford, Ohio, 1997; and Dworkin and Messner, "Just Do . . . What?," 341–64.

17. This is not to say that those at the "bottom" of the socioeconomic ladder do not internalize dominant values; for instance, see Wilson, *When Work Disappears.*

18. See Cole and Hribar, "Celebrity Feminism"; Cooky, "'If You Let Me Play'"; Messner, *Taking the Field.* Also see the special issue of *SSJ* titled *Deconstructing Michael Jordan: Reconstructing Postindustrial America* for a discussion of the meanings

innercity urban youth offer to Nike TV commercials. (*Sociology of Sport Journal* 13, no. 4 [1996]). Of course, there is some irony to the fact that boys of color were reading the image of white, middle-class Chastain in this way. Highlighting these paradoxical results suggest the need for future researchers to carry out audience reception studies to attempt not just single-sex focus groups (as noted in the appendix), but also separate focus groups by race.

19. For excellent critical analysis on the Nike ad campaign, see Cooky, "'If You Let Me Play'"; see also C. L. Cole, "American Jordan: P.L.A.Y., Consensus, and Punishment," *Sociology of Sport Journal* 13 (1996): 366–97.

20. For instance, such images might work to counter the classic way in which females are socialized to inhibit their own movements and bodies. See Young, "Throwing Like a Girl: A Phenomenology of Feminine Body Comportment, Motility, and Spatiality," In *Throwing Like a Girl and Other Essays in Feminist Philosophy and Social Theory*, ed. Young (Bloomington: Indiana University Press, 1990).

21. Messner, Dunbar, and Hunt, "Televised Sports Manhood Formula," 380–94.

22. A very large number of grade school girls across the classrooms provided that they played soccer, and several of the classrooms we visited had co-ed games on a regular basis. What actually happens during the games was not directly viewed or discussed. When examining written responses from high school girls, however, a much smaller percentage played soccer when compared to grade school girls.

23. A love of sport could be interpreted as a more functionalist approach to sport and society, as argued by S. Eitzen, *Sport in Contemporary Society* (New York: Worth, 2001). No critiques of a "love" of sport were offered by students, who could have interpreted the sport as part of nationalism, commercialism, or race, class, gender, or sexuality inequality.

24. Though we would have liked to, we were not able to further probe whether this response was indicative of the fact that girls were valuing male definitions of sport, activity, or were responding to inequality or stereotypes by rejecting passively posed images but also did not probe why boys stated these themes.

25. For more on this subject, see Espiritu, *Asian American Women and Men*.

26. For work on the constructedness of heterosexual identity, see S. Jackson, *Heterosexuality in Question* (London: Sage, 1999), and J. N. Katz, *The Invention of Heterosexuality* (New York: Penguin Books, 1995). For how this might operate specifically in sport, see M. A. Messner, "Studying Up on Sex Sociology," *Sociology of Sport Journal* 13 (1996): 221–37. For theorizing on the subject of sexuality, parody, and whether or not there is an "original" to parody to begin with, see Butler, *Gender Trouble*.

27. See Thorne, *Gender Play*. For excellent discussions surrounding adolescents and desire, and how girls learn, through compulsory heterosexuality, to know themselves from the perspectives of men, see M. Fine, "Sexuality, Schooling, and Adolescent Females: The Missing Discourse of Desire," *Harvard Educational Review* 58 (1988): 29–53; Deborah Tolman, "Doing Desire: Adolescent Girls Struggles for/with Sexuality," in *Gender Through the Prism of Difference*, 2nd ed., ed. Maxine Baca Zinn, Pierrette Hondagneu-Sotelo, and Michael A. Messner (Boston: Allyn and Bacon, 2000), 155–67; Deborah Tolman and Elizabeth DeBold, "Conflicts of Body and Image: Female Adolescents, Desire, and the No-body," in *Feminist Treatment and Therapy of Eating Disorders*, ed. M. Katzman, P. Fallon, and S. Wooley (New York: Guilford, 1993). Alternatively, perhaps where there are increasing tendencies for girls to ex-

plore the complexities of their sexuality, there is less willingness to publicly proclaim possible contradictions in sexual identity.

28. The media studies literature that emphasizes how race, class, gender, and sexuality impact audience reads of media texts is massive and far too long to list here. For excellent overviews, see John Fiske, *Media Matters: Everyday Culture and Political Change* (Minneapolis: University of Minnesota Press, 1994); and John Fiske, *Media Matters: Race and Gender in U.S. Politics* (Minneapolis: University of Minnesota Press, 1996).

29. Butler and others highlight how sexuality is not a natural, fixed essence, but rather a social construct and cumulative public performance with fluidity. See Butler, *Gender Trouble,* and Judith Butler, *Bodies That Matter* (London: Routledge, 1993). For work that discusses "doing difference," (race, class, and gender), see Candace West and Sarah Fenstermaker, "Doing Difference," *Gender and Society* 9, no. 1 (1995): 8–37. See Rich, "Compulsory Heterosexuality and Lesbian Existence," 631–60, for her groundbreaking theorizing on heterosexuality as compulsory. For more historical work on how heterosexuality, homosexuality, and bisexuality are not fixed natural essences, but rather social constructs infused with historically specific power relations, see S. L. Dworkin and Faye Linda Wachs, "'Disciplining the Body': HIV Positive Athletes, Media Surveillance, and the Policing of Sexuality," *Sociology of Sport Journal* 15, no. 1 (1998): 1–20. J. Weeks, *Sexuality and Its Discontents: Meanings, Myths, and Modern Sexualities* (New York: Routledge, 1985); and M. Foucault, *The History of Sexuality* (New York: Vintage, 1978).

30. The actual likelihood of boys and girls making it into professional sport is extremely thin. See Wilbert Leonard, "The Odds of Transitioning from One Level of Sports Participation to Another," *Sociology of Sport Journal* 13 (1996): 288–99.

31. See Dworkin and Messner. "Just Do . . . What?"

32. See Cahn, *Coming on Strong,* and Dowling, *The Frailty Myth.* Dowling highlights how, when a woman first beat a man in fencing in the Olympics, the title was revoked on the grounds that men could "not go all out" when competing with women. She argues that assumptions of needing protection all too easily elide into grounds for exclusion. The underlying reality may be recognition of a continuum of ability by gender.

33. Superior work on preferred meanings in media texts is offered by Darnell Hunt, *O. J. Simpson Facts and Fictions: News Rituals in the Construction of Reality* (Cambridge: University Press, 1999), and Hall, "The Spectacle of the Other," 223–90. Whether or not audiences receive preferred meanings as intended is a different matter. For discussions on multiple meanings within media images and texts, see Fiske, *Media Matters: Everyday Culture and Political Change.*

34. A. McRobbie, *Feminism and Youth Culture: From Jackie to Just Seventeen* (Boston: Unwin Hyman, 1991), 139.

35. Signifiers of femininity that are carefully negotiated with signs of masculinity are analyzed in work by A. Balsamo, "Feminist Bodybuilding," in *Women, Sport, and Culture,* ed. Birrell and Cole; J. Felshin, "The Triple Option . . . for Women in Sport," in *Sport in the Sociocultural Process,* ed. M. Hart and S. Birrell (Dubuque, Iowa: Wm. C. Brown, 1981); L. A. Fisher, "Building One's Self Up: Bodybuilding and the Construction of Identity among Professional Female Bodybuilders," in *Building Bodies,* ed. P. Moore (New Brunswick, N.J.: Rutgers University Press, 1997); Kane, "Resistance/Transformation of the Oppositional Binary," 191–218; P. Markula, "Firm

but Shapely, Fit but Sexy, Strong but Thin: The Postmodern Aerobicizing Female Bodies," *Sociology of Sport Journal* 12, no. 4 (1996): 424–53.

36. For an analysis of how individuals tend to say "but" in reference to female athletes and frequently do so to negate the positive words that come before the "but" (e.g., "She's a really good athlete but she's still feminine"), see Nelson, *The Stronger Women Get, The More Men Love Football.*

37. See Ann Chisolm, "Defending the Nation: National Bodies, U.S. Borders, and the 1996 U.S. Olympics Womens Gymnastics Team," *Journal of Sport and Social Issues* 23, no. 2 (1999): 126–39.

38. For discussions of what constitutes "natural" and "unnatural" markings within public discourse, see Davis and Delano, "Fixing the Boundaries of Physical Gender," 1–19, and J. K. Wesley, "Negotiating Gender: Bodybuilding and the Natural/Unnatural Continuum," *Sociology of Sport Journal* 18, no. 2 (2001): 162–180. For discussions of how muscularity operates/ed in tender conjunction with constructs of femininity, see Balsamo, "Feminist Bodybuilding"; Cahn, *Coming on Strong;* D. B. Daniels, "Gender (Body) Verification (Building)," *Play and Culture* 5 (1992): 378–400. Hargreaves, *Sporting Females;* M. A. Messner, "Sports and Male Domination: The Female Athlete as Contested Ideological Terrain," *Sociology of Sport Journal* 5 (1988): 197–211; L. Schulze, "On the Muscle," in *Building Bodies,* ed. Moore, 135–64.

39. See Betty Farrell, *Family: The Making of an Idea, An Institution, and a Controversy in American Culture* (Boulder, Colo.: Westview Press, 1999).

40. See Nancy Theberge, *Higher Goals: Women's Ice Hockey and the Politics of Gender* (New York: SUNY Press, 2000).

41. There was an interesting pattern across focus groups where ideologies of equality easily elided into comments reminiscent of cultural feminism's valorization of "superior" feminine qualities. It is also noteworthy that when women were posed in a sport that was previously all-male or male-dominated, girls made comments about women "being better than" boys.

42. See McRobbie, *Feminism and Youth Culture,* for an excellent discussion on power, youth, feminism, and consumption. This student's comment may also be indicative of how sport, often seen as a realm of bodily performance, is now also rife with fashion and style. This may be part and parcel of a reinforcement of the aesthetics of women in sport, as opposed to their powerful performances, or it may indicate a broader trend of the pursuit of personal style within commodity culture as a limited form of "power."

43. See Kane, "Media Coverage of the Post Title IX Female Athlete," 21–48, and Messner, "Sports and Male Domination," 197–211. For more discussion of methodological nuances, such as the need for researchers to triangulate methods so as to flesh out public versus private behavior, please see the appendix.

44. See Balsamo, "Feminist Bodybuilding"; A. Bolin, "Vandalized Vanity: Feminine Physique Betrayed and Portrayed," in *Tattoo, Torture, Mutilation, and Adornment: The Denaturalization of the Body in Culture and Text,* ed. F. E. Mascia-Lees and P. Sharpe (Albany: SUNY Press, 1992); A. Bolin, "Flex Appeal, Food, and Fat: Competitive Bodybuilding, Gender, and Diet," *Play and Culture* 5 (1992): 378–400; Daniels, "Gender (Body) Verification (Building)," 378–400. S. Dworkin, "Holding Back: Negotiating a Glass Ceiling on Women's Muscular Strength," *Sociological Perspectives* 44, no. 3 (2001); Fisher, "Building One's Self Up,"; S. R. Guthrie and

S. Castelnuovo, *Feminism and the Female Body: Liberating the Amazon Within* (Boulder, Colo.: Lynne Rienner Publishers, 1998); and Heywood, *Bodymakers.*

45.  See A. Hochschild, *The Second Shift* (New York: Avon Books, 1989); Also see Scott Coltrane and Michele Adams, "Men, Women, and Housework," in *Gender Mosaics*, ed. Vannoy, 145–54.

46.  For similar discussions of bodies and practice, see R. W. Connell, *Masculinities* (Berkeley: University of California Press, 1995), and J. Hargreaves, "Where's the Virtue, Where's the Grace? A Discussion of the Social Production of Gender Relations in and Through Sport," *Theory, Culture, and Society* 3, no. 1 (1986): 109–21.

47.  See Davis and Delano, "Fixing the Boundaries of Physical Gender." Also see Wesley, "Negotiating Gender."

48.  See Judith Halberstam, *Female Masculinity* (Durham, N.C.: Duke University Press, 1998).

49.  Sex ("biology"), gender (social definitions of masculinity and femininity), and sexuality (sexual identity) need not be linked, as in the case of "butch" gay male bodybuilders, "butch" straight female athletes, "femme" heterosexual male ice skaters, lipstick lesbians, and so on. Also see cross cultural differences for alternatives to a sex-gender-sexuality triad, such as Williams, *The Spirit and the Flesh.* E. Blackwood and S. E. Wieringa, eds., *Same Sex-Relations and Female Desires: Transgender Practices across Cultures* (New York: Columbia University Press, 1999), and T. Almaguer, "Chicano Men: A Cartography of Homosexual Identity and Behavior," *Differences* 3, no. 2 (1991): 75–100.

50.  Indeed, Maria Lowe's work highlights how male bodybuilders who are much larger than their female partners frequently partner with female bodybuilders. See Maria Lowe, *Women of Steel: Female Bodybuilders and the Struggle for Self-Definition* (New York: NYU Press, 1999).

51.  See Heywood, *Bodymakers;* and Dworkin, "Holding Back."

52.  See Dworkin and Messner, "Just Do . . . What?"

53.  See Dworkin, "Holding Back," for the argument that there is a historically produced and shifting glass ceiling or upper limit on women's muscular strength that is shifting upwards toward more musculature over time. Such a glass ceiling has both normalizing effects on the female body across social locations and is at times distinctive within categories of race, class, gender, and sexuality.

54.  See Susan Bordo, *Unbearable Weight: Feminism, Western Culture, and the Body* (Berkeley: University of California Press, 1993). Dworkin, "Holding Back." See Hargreaves *Heroines of Sport.*

55.  See S. L. Bartky, "Foucault, Femininity, and the Modernization of Patriarchal Power," in *Feminism and Foucault: Reflections on Resistance*, ed. I. Diamond and L. Quinby (Boston: Northeastern University Press, 1988). See M. C. Duncan, "The Politics of Women's Body Images and Practices: Foucault, the Panopticon, and *Shape* Magazine," *Journal of Sport and Social Issues* 18, no. 1 (1994): 40–65.

56.  Mainstream fitness magazines tend to conflate fitness with healthiness. Some students challenged this with their comments. For more on how health and fitness magazines tend to erroneously conflate health with fitness, see Dworkin and Wachs, "Gender for Sale: Size Matters, Consumption, and Bodies in Mainstream Fitness Magazines," unpublished paper presented at the August 1998 American Sociological Association (ASA) annual meeting held in San Francisco. Also see Duncan, "The

Politics of Women's Body Images and Practices," 40–65, and Moya Lloyd, "Feminism, Aerobics, and the Politics of the Body," *Body and Society* 2, no. 2 (1996): 79–98.

57. See Dworkin and Wachs, *Size Matters*.

58. This may work in the opposite direction from men, who are assumed to be "dumb jocks" merely through their participation in sport.

59. This is part of a larger frame of gender inequality where women are sexually constructed as either being madonnas or whores. See A. Snitow, C. Stansell, and S. Thompson, "Introduction," in *Powers of Desire: The Politics of Sexuality,* ed. Snitow, Stansell, and Thompson (New York: Monthly Review Press, 1983), 9–47.

60. See Cole and Hribar, "Celebrity Feminism."

61. Markula, "Firm but Shapely, Fit but Sexy, Strong but Thin." Also see Chisolm, "Defending the Nation," 126–39.

62. See L. Merrish, "Cuteness and Commodity Aesthetics: Tom Thumb and Shirley Temple," in *Freakery,* ed. R. G. Thomson (New York: NYU Press, 1996), as cited in ibid.

63. Banet-Wieser, *The Most Beautiful Girl In the World.*

64. Gray, "Television, Black Americans, and the American Dream."

65. Banet-Wieser, *The Most Beautiful Girl In the World.*

66. See Collins, *Black Feminist Thought;* S. Hall, *Representations: Cultural Representations and Signifying Practices* (London: Sage, 1997).

67. For work on racial othering, also see Frantz Fanon, *Black Skin, White Masks* (New York: Grove Press, 1967), and Hunt, *O. J. Simpson Facts and Fictions.*

68. See Banet-Wieser, *The Most Beautiful Girl In the World.*

69. See Wilson, *When Work Disappears.*

70. For solid analysis surrounding the complexity of the social world as it relates to qualitative methods, see Banet-Wieser, *The Most Beautiful Girl In the World.*

71. Methods as political acts are covered very successfully in M. Fine, "Working the Hyphens: Reinventing Self and Other in Qualitative Research," in *Handbook of Qualitative Research,* ed. N. K. Denzin and Y. S. Lincoln (Thousand Oaks, Calif.: Sage, 1994).

72. For an excellent discussion on the promise and limits of resistance and agency within youth culture, see McRobbie, *Feminism and Youth Culture.*

73. See the Women's Sports Foundation report card which reports bloated football budgets in Division I schools. In many cases, these programs lose money for schools, and spend monies that could be used for other men's and women's sports.

## Epilogue

1. Samuels, "Mixed Messages," 15–16.

2. Carol Siegel, *New Millenial Sexstyles* (Bloomington: Indiana University Press, 2000), 5. Siegel's "unnamed generation" of feminists sometime go by the name "postfeminism" or "third wave."

## Appendix

1. For an excellent overview of the historical uses of focus groups, see Bruce Berg, *Qualitative Research Methods for the Social Sciences* (Boston: Allyn and Bacon,

2001), and David Morgan, *Focus Groups as Qualitative Research* (Thousand Oaks, Calif.: Sage, 1997).

2. See Robert Merton, "The Focused Interview and Focus Groups," *Public Opinion Quarterly* 51 (1987): 550–66.

3. For excellent coverage of focus groups as feminist methodology, see Esther Madriz, "Focus Groups in Feminist Research," in *Handbook of Qualitative Research*, ed. Norman K. Denzin and Yvonna Lincoln (Thousand Oaks, Calif.: Sage, 2000), 835–50.

4. For solid discussion of pros and cons of focus groups in comparison to other methodologies, see Berg, *Qualitative Research Methods for the Social Sciences.*

5. For instance, see A. Oakley, "Interviewing Women: A Contradiction in Terms," in *Doing Feminist Research*, ed. H. Roberts (London: Routledge, 1981). Also see Judith Stacey, "Can There Be a Feminist Ethnography?" *Women's Studies International Forum* 11 (1988): 21–27.

6. For further discussion on horizontal and vertical power in focus groups, see Madriz, "Focus Groups in Feminist Research."

7. For a more indepth examination of this subject, see David Morgan, *The Focus Group Guidebook* (Thousand Oaks, Calif.: Sage, 1998).

8. Excellent coverage of these debates is seen in D. W. Stewart and P. M. Shamdasani, *Focus Groups: Theory and Practice* (Newbury Park: Sage, 1990).

9. For help with moderating focus groups at the novice, intermediate, and expert levels, see Richard A. Krueger, *Moderating Focus Groups* (Thousand Oaks, Calif.: Sage, 1998).

10. See Morgan, *The Focus Group Guidebook*, 6.

11. Researchers should direct their attention to works that consider the composition of focus groups, as discussed extensively by Richard A. Krueger and Mary Anne Casey, *Focus Groups: A Practical Guide for Applied Research* (Thousand Oaks, Calif.: Sage, 2000); Richard A. Krueger, *The Focus Group Guidebook* (Thousand Oaks, Calif.: Sage, 1998); Krueger, *Planning Focus Groups* (Thousand Oaks, Calif.: Sage, 1998).

12. For a discussion of how race and class intersect in grade school classrooms, see Kozol, *Savage Inequalities.*

13. For theoretical and empirical examples of relational analyses of women and men, boys and girls, within work and school environments, see Patricia A. Adler and Peter Adler, *Peer Power: Preadolescent Culture and Identity* (New Brunswick, N.J.: Rutgers University Press, 1998); R. W. Connell, *Gender and Power* (Stanford, Calif.: Stanford University Press, 1987); C. McGuffy and B. Rich, "Playing in the Gender Transgression Zone: Race, Class, and Hegemonic Masculinity in Middle Childhood," *Gender and Society* 13 (1999): 608–27; Jim McKay, *Managing Gender: Affirmative Action and Organizational Power in Australian, Canadian, and New Zealand Sport* (New York: SUNY Press, 1997); and Thorne, *Gender Play.*

14. See previous note. Also see the AAUW report, "How Schools Shortchange Girls: A Study of Major Findings on Girls and Education," AAUW Educational Foundation and National Education Association, Wellesley, 1992.

15. See West and Fenstermaker, "Doing Difference," 8–37; and Candace West and Don H. Zimmerman, "Doing Gender," *Gender and Society* 1 (1987): 125–51.

16. See Adler and Adler, *Peer Power;* Thorne, *Gender Play;* Shakib, "Female Basketball Participation and Attrition."

17. For more on the pros of triangulating methods, see W. L. Neuman, *Social Research Methods: Qualitative and Quantitative Approaches* (Boston: Allyn and Bacon, 1997).

18. Intersections of race and class in America are very well examined within H. E. Ransford, *Race and Class in American Society Black and Latino* (Rochester, Vt.: Schenkman, 1994).

19. For an outstanding discussion of how the subject of sport ranks vis-à-vis health and other variables within the realm of women's well-being, see Hargreaves, *Heroines of Sport.*

20. We would like to offer our warm gratitude to Lindsey Dawson, who acted as research assistant during the summer of 2001 for this study. Lindsey attended focus-group meetings and was able to keep track of each student's thoughts, which aided a great deal given the size of some of the groups. She also logged data into spreadsheets and aided in calculating initial percentages for our coding scheme.

21. See Hunt, *O. J. Simpson Facts and Fictions;* McRobbie, *Feminism and Youth Culture;* and Davis, *The Swimsuit Issue and Sport: Hegemonic Masculinity in Sports Illustrated* (Albany: SUNY Press, 1997), for discussions on producers' intentions when creating texts and imagery.

# Index

Abercrombie & Fitch catalog (spring 2000), 101
abusive behaviorL power of mirror effect to cure, 121. *See also* violence
academic critique: of evolution of women's sports, 46; of image of female athlete, mass-media advocacy vs., 4–6
Ackerman, Val, 26
action movie genre: ascendance of female athlete icon in, 123–27; double-sidedness to female action hero, 126–27
Acuff, Amy, 77, 84, 96
ad campaigns, 1–4, 179n.2. *See also specific companies*
Adios Barbie website, 129
adolescence: AAUW study of girls in, xix; sports played in, 132. *See also* youth attitudes about female athletes
Adonis complex, 103–4, 111–12
Akers, Michelle, ix
alpha female role model, Chastain as, 137–39. *See also* youth attitudes about female athletes
American Association of University Women (AAUW): 1991 study, xix
American Sociological Association's Code of Ethics, 172
Andrews, David, 4, 90–91

appearance: beauty and beauty culture, xxv, 44–45, 103–4, 111–12, 152; endorsements and, 185n.9; marketing of female athletes according to their, 39. *See also* babe factor in representation of women's sports
Armstrong, Duncan, 86
Arnell, Peter, 111
Asian-American perspective, 74–75
Asian-American women, images of: Jeanette Lee, 139–43; students' responses to, 139–43, 151–53
athletic aesthetic: risks and benefits of mainstreaming, 127–29
"Athletic Esthetic, The" (Brubach), xx
athleticism as activist tool, 45
autoethnography, 183n.41

babe factor in representation of women's sports, 39–40, 76–99; context of image, 80; controversial images, 84–85; "creaking old school" vs. "new age feminists" on, 77–85; disappearance of subject/object dichotomy in hyperreal and, 85–86; economics of gender inequity in sports and, 95–99; nonsexual images, 96–98; "pornographic" images, 76, 77–96; post–Title IX empowerment narrative and, 86–95

*Basic Instinct* (movie), 124
basketball, women's, 45
Bassett, Angela, xviii, 61
Batten, Kim, 25
Baudrillard, Jean, 76, 105, 113
Bauer, Sybil, xx
beauty: Adonis complex and, 103–4, 111–12; male beauty culture, xxv; preference for, 44–45; shifting standards of, 152
*Beauty Myth, The* (Wolf), 110
Bennett, Brook, 97
Berger, John, 112, 194n.17
Bertram, Russ, 27
*Big Girl in the Middle* (Reece), xxvii
binary gender order: overreliance on, 149
biological determinism, 43
Birrell, Susan, 6, 15, 182n.21
black female athletes: student responses to images of, 153–56. *See also specific athletes*
black feminist perspective, 41–43
black womanhood: images of, 154
Blais, Madeleine, xxvii
bodybuilders, female, 80–81, 136; fitness model compared to, 152; student responses to images of, 147–51
body image, 44; Adonis complex and, 103–4, 111–12; athletic body as ideal for both sexes, 81–82; commodification of male body, xxii, xxiv, 100–105; as great equalizer, 112; ideals, xvii–xix, xx, 38–39, 81–82, 160–63; male obsession with, 110–11; size, ideal male and female, 194n.16
body panic parity: Adonis complex and, 103–4, 111–12; commodification of male body and, xxii, xxiv, 100–105; *Fight Club* and, 105–13
body projects, 100–101, 129, 193n.2
Bordo, Susan, 83–84, 100, 110, 112
boy-toys, xxii, 103, 105. *See also* commodification of bodies
Brant, Monica, 92
Brooks, Ann L., 182n.26
Brooks, Louise, xviii
Brubach, Holly, xx, 178n.9

Burstyn, Varda, 57–60, 63, 67, 116, 190n.2
Bustos, Crystyl, 60–61, 97
Butler, Judith, 11, 61, 70, 81–82, 84, 91, 129, 199n.29

Cagan, Joanna, 39, 40
Cahn, Susan K., 6, 8, 63
Calvin Klein ad, 103
Carter, Helena Bonham, 105
categoric research, 16
celebrity, power of, 107
"Champion's way, the," 64
*Charlie's Angels* (movie), 123, 125
Chastain, Brandi, 24, 29, 32, 39, 52, 77, 84, 103, 105, 133, 135; Power Bar ad, 164; sports-bra controversy, x, 34, 103, 134; student responses to image of, 137–39, 162
Cheerleader model of self-effacement, 64–65
Chisolm, Ann, 146
Chyna, 133
Citizen watch ad, xxv
Clark, Mary Ellen, 27, 29, 80
class: intersection with race in American culture, 171–72; name recognition of female athletes and, 133–34; sports played by students and, 132; student responses to female athlete images and, 146–47, 150, 153
coaches: pressures to train and compete from, 47, 49; psychological manipulation by, 47–48, 49
Cole, C. L., 6, 90–91, 98
Columbia University, Partnership for Women's Health at, 44
commercial culture: homogenization of, 12–13. *See also* consumer culture; corporations
commodification of bodies: female body, 103; male body, xxii, xxiv, 39, 100–105; normalization of, 88; of sports stars, positive but unintended consequence of, 82
competitive, individualist model of sport, 8

competitiveness, 64, 74

competitive sport: criticism of, 59–60; women as part of talented minority associated with, 63

compulsive training, 128–29

*Condé Nast Sports and Fitness for Women:* Citizen watch ad in, xxvi; "Got Milk?" ad with female basketball players in, 30; G-Shock ad, 61, 62; Nike ads in, 20, 83; PHYS.com ad in, xxviii, 93

confidence: sports and, viii

consumer culture: consumption as power, 146–47; *Fight Club* and male reaction to emasculating, 102, 105, 106–9; male bodies as objects in, 10; negative and positive aspects of contemporary, xxvi–xxix; postmodern erasure of self in, 90; preservation of self-sovereignty ideal though sport in, 90–95; students' understanding of, 136

consumer market, cultivation of girls/women as, xix, xxiv, 29–35; ad campaigns for, 1–4, 179n.2

control: illusory sense of, 48

corporations: bottom-line mentality, killer woman as scapegoat and figurehead for, 114; capitalization on public health arguments, 1–4, 179n.2; capitalization on women's consumer market, xix, xxiv, 29–35. *See also* consumer culture

Cox, Ana Marie, 65–66

*Crouching Tiger, Hidden Dragon* (movie), 123–24, 125

cultural context, 160 65

cultural feminism, 8–9, 181n.20, 186n.10; masculinity in female athlete and, 57–60, 63, 64, 65

cultural iconography and experiential reality: relationship between, 156

cultural shift, viii, xvii–xviii; female hockey player images and, 145; new hurdles of growing cultural conservatism, xxii–xxiii

cultural studies methodology, 13–14

Davidon, Ruth, 25

Davis, Laurel R., 19

decentered subject and ethical struggles for social justice: tension between theories of, 15–16

Declaration of Sentiments, 37

degendering of society, 9, 11

de Lauretis, Teresa, 61, 63

demographic characteristics: structural discrepancies in, 12

DeMott, Benjamin, 114–17, 119, 121, 124, 126

Denison, Jim, 18

desire: powerful structuring mechanisms of, 123–27

desire to do sport: Chastain image, 138; female bodybuilder image, 150–51; fitness model image, 153; images of female athletes and, 157–58; Jeanette Lee image, 142. *See also* sports participation

devaluation: vulnerability of athletes suffering from forms of, 48–50

Devers, Gail, 27, 80

Didrikson, Babe, xviii

Diet Coke ad, 103

distributive research, 16

*Domestic Tranquility: A Brief against Feminism* (Graglia), 44

Dowling, Colette, 116, 199n.32

Draglia, Stacy, 97

Drake, Jennifer, 10–11

Duncan, Margaret Carlisle, 6, 26

eating: monitoring by coaches, 48, 49

eating disorders, 48, 128

Echols, Alice, 8, 9, 181n.20

economics: as basis of need for new interpretive paradigms, 11–14; of gender inequity in sport, 95–99; structural equality for young men and women, 88–89

economy: changing unstable status of men in workplace and, 110; ideal female body shape and state of, xviii; restructuring of, into service jobs, 193n.7

Ederle, Gertrude, xx

Education Act of 1972. *See* Title IX of Education Act of 1972
educational system: stratification in, 172
elitist model of sport, 58, 63
"Empathy Campaign," 1
emphasized femininity, 76; icons of, 139–43, 151–53; intersection with racialized code, 139–43. *See also* babe factor in representation of women's sports
empirical and linguistic research: tensions between, 14–15
empowerment of women: marketing through sports of, 3–4
endorsements, 178n.10, 185n.9, 187n.22
Enlightenment ideals of individuality: sport and preservation of, 91
"equal access under the law": liberal feminist overreliance on principles of, 7–8
equality of image, 80, 81
equality of valuation: from demonstrable erosion of gender difference, 116–17; *Girlfight* and, 117–23
Espiritu, 139
ESPN coverage of male vs. female athletes, 78
ESPN Magazine website poll, 88
*Esquire*'s "Girls of Summer," 77
essentialism, 62, 63, 64; gender, 115
Etcoff, Nancy, 44–45
ethical struggles for social justice: tension between theories of decentered subject and, 15–16
ethnographic fieldwork, 168
experiential reality and cultural iconography: relationship between, 156

Faludi, Susan, 41, 51
family and work, juggling, 195n.20
fantasy: powerful structuring mechanisms of, 123–27
Fasting, Kari, 6
*Fatal Attraction* (movie), 124
female athlete icon. *See* iconic female athlete

female athlete image. *See* images of female athlete
female athlete triad, 52
female body: commodification of, 103
femininity: arbitrary nature of, 146; boundaries of "natural," 146; defined as "being a babe" (sex appeal), 88; defined as (hetero)sexual access, 78–80, 82, 83; emphasized, 76, 139–43, 151–53 (*see also* babe factor in representation of women's sports); images of, ix; new heterosexual, 123
feminism: athletes considering selves as feminist, 50, 189n.48; black perspective, 41–43; "creaking old school" vs. "new age" (post-), 77–85; cultural, 8–9, 57–60, 63, 64, 65, 181n.20, 186n.10; liberal, 3, 7–8, 179n.2, 180n.9; Nike, 180n.6; in 1990s, bad public relations and media representation of, 51; radical, 7, 8, 9, 180n.9, 181n.13, 181n.19; revaluation of the masculine within, 65; second wave, 10–11, 12, 40–41, 42, 65; stealth, 29, 50–54; third wave (*see* third wave feminism)
feminization of male: formation of sport as, 192n.28; "masculinist" responses, 194n.8; reactions to, *Fight Club,* 102, 105–9
fencing in Olympics: female victory in, 199n.32
Festle, Mary Jo, 50
*Fever Pitch* (Hornby), 34
fieldwork, ethnographic, 168
*Fight Club* (movie), xxiv, 102, 117, 118; occupatio as first rule of, 105–9; reaction to emasculating consumer culture, 102, 105, 106–9; social contexts for, 110–13; source of bad faith of, 108–9
"Firm but Shapely, Fit but Sexy, Strong but Thin: The Postmodern Aerobicizing Female Bodies" (Markula), 153
first wave feminism, 40–41
fitness: conflating healthiness with, 201n.56; participation in fitness activities, 132, 196n.5

fitness model: student responses to image of, 151–53

flapper era of Roaring Twenties, xviii, xx

*Flex* magazine, 80–81

fluidity, gender, xxv, 70, 97, 185n.9

*Flux* (Orenstein), 195n.20

focus-group research on youth attitudes about female athletes, 131–59, 167–75; advantages/disadvantages to using focus groups, 167–68; areas for future research, 174–75; broad definition of focus group, 169; composition of groups, 170–73; focus-group dynamics and content of discussions, 156–57; homogeneity of groups, 169–70; limitations of, 174–75; name recognition of male/female sports figures, 132–35, 197n.7; postmodern method of, 167–70; question guide, 175; responses to female athlete images, 136–56; response to researchers, 173–74; triangulating methods in, 170

Ford, Harrison, 124

Foster, Jodie, 61

Foudy, Julie, 52

*Frailty Myth, The* (Dowling), 116

France, Kim, 45

fund-raising for women's teams, 96

Gamble, Sarah, 10

*Game Face: What Does a Female Athlete Look Like?* (Gottesman), 16–17, 97–98

Garber, Marjorie, 14

gay and lesbian athletes, 178n.10, 186n.20; homophobia and, 122, 123, 187n.22

*Gear:* Chastain photos in, 84

gender: dichotomization in thinking about, 61; intersection with race in American culture, 154–55; student response to images of female athletes by (*see* youth attitudes about female athletes)

gender as sexual difference model, 61–64

gender continuum model of sport, 9–10, 45; overlapping physical performance, 71–72

gender difference: contested in *Girlfight,* 117–23; culture of, impact on girls, 121; erosion of, equality of valuation resulting from demonstrable, 116–17

"Gender Equity Report Card: A Survey of Athletic Opportunity in American Higher Education" (Women's Sports Foundation), 177n.3

gender essentialism, 115

gender fluidity, xxv, 70, 97, 185n.9

gender inequalities, 178n.7

gender inequity in sport: economics of, 95–99

gender performativity, 11, 84, 129

gender roles, 44

gender-specific issues, 52

gender stereotypes, xxv

gender studies, 61, 65

*Gender Trouble* (Butler), 61

generation X and Y: feminism of, 41. *See also* third wave feminism

Gilder, George, 195n.22

Giove, Missy, 178n.10

*Girlfight* (movie), 117–23

girl next door: female athletes as, xxv

Giroux, Henry, 13–14, 18, 100, 113

glamorization of pain and sacrifice, xxiii

*Glory Days* (Reynolds), 128

Godsey, Chris, 111, 129

"Golden Era of Women's Sports" in 1920s, xx

"Got Milk?" ads, 21, 22, 30

Gottesman, Jane, 16–17, 68, 97

Graglia, F. Carolyn, 44, 189n.41

*Great Women in Sports* (Johnson), xxvi

Griffith-Joyner, Florence (Flo-Jo), 19, 133, 134, 187n.22

Grossberg, Lawrence, 13

G-Shock ad, 61, 62

gym, the, 73; sense of bravery from, 53–54. *See also* masculinity, female athletes and

Hall, M. Ann, 6, 7–8, 16, 50, 121, 180n.9
Hamilton, Linda, 61
Hamm, Mia, 24, 34, 52, 116, 133, 141, 185n.9
Hanssen, Beatrice, 14
Hargreaves, Jennifer, 6, 7, 21–22
Harrison, Lisa, 88
Haworth, Cheryl, 97, 163
healthiness: conflating fitness with, 201n.56
health issues, women's: dangers of overtraining and, 47–48, 49; female athlete triad, 52
Hegel, G. W. F., 91
"Helping Girls Become Strong Women" (social initiative), 44
Henry, Mark, 27
heroic tradition, 24
*Heroines of Sport* (Hargreaves), 22
heterosexual identity: constructedness of, 139–41, 198n.26
heterosexual order: female bodybuilders and, 147–51
Heywood, Leslie, 10–11, 150, 183n.41
Hingis, Martina, 21
Hispanic "masculine" woman: idealization of, 60–61
hockey players, female, 143–47
Hoggart, Richard, 12
Holly, Molly, 133, 151
homogenization of commercial culture, 12–13
homophobia, 122, 123, 187n.22
Hornby, Nick, 34
humanist view of essential self, 89–90
hypermasculinity of contemporary "sport nexus," 57, 59–60
hyperreal, the, 113; disappearance of subject/object dichotomy in, 85–86

iconic female athlete, 21–24: action movie genre and ascendance of, 123–27; as alternative ideal for women, benefits of, 163; *Girlfight* and, 117–23; individualist orientation of, criticism based on, 21; "killer woman" critique of, 114–17; problematic paradox of, 122; resolution shown in physicality

of, 163; as resource in ongoing struggles for social justice, 24
images of female athlete: academic vs. mass-media advocacy of, 4–6; cultural context of rise of, 160–65; mass-media images, xxvi–xxix, 1–2, 179n.3 (*see also* babe factor in representation of women's sports); new mainstream status of, xv–xvi; sports desires shaped by imagery, 138, 142, 150–51, 153, 157–58; wide range of, 21. *See also* youth attitudes about female athletes
immunity, sense of: to degradation, 89; to exploitation, 87, 89; to sexual objectification, 95
incorporating destructive practices, 49–50
Independent Women's Forum, 51
individualism: competitive, individualist model of sport, 8; fight against devaluation of women linked to concept of, 116–17; mixture of liberal feminist ideals and American, 3, 179n.2; Nike ads capitalizing on American, 179n.2; sport and preservation of Enlightenment ideals of, 91
inequalities: gender, 178n.7; in generations born after 1960, 11–12
inequity: economics of gender inequity in sport, 95–99; institutional, 182n.23
Inness, Sherrie A., 120, 126
innocence of white female hockey player, reading of, 146
inspiration to do sport. *See* desire to do sport: images of female athletes and
institutional inequities, 182n.23
*International Encyclopedia of Women and Sports* (Pfister and Guttman), 178n.13
International Olympic Committee: women on, 25
interviews, focus-group, 168
*In These Girls, Hope Is a Muscle* (Blais), xxvii
invincibility: sense of, 89
Isaacson, Melissa, 77

*Jane* magazine: Nike ad in (2001), 78, 79
Jenkins, Sally, 77
Jockey ad, 104
Johnson, Anne Janette, xxvi
Johnson, Freya, 65–66
Johnson, Michael, 25, 27, 80, 81
Jolie, Angelina, 124, 125
Jones, Marion, 28, 92, 99, 133, 134, 135, 136, 163, 187n.22; on cover of *Vogue*, xv, xvii, 81; "Got Milk?" ad, 21, 22; student responses to image of, 19, 20, 153–56, 162
Jordan, Michael, 34, 141
Joyner-Kersee, Jackie, xxvii, 27, 29

Kane, Mary Jo, 6, 9, 71, 80
Kerrigan, Nancy, 133
*Killer Woman Blues* (DeMott), 114–17
killer women: paradigm shift away from, 124
Kimmel, Michael, 194n.8
*Kind of Grace, A* (Joyner-Kersee), xxvii
Kirby, Sandra, 184n.41
Kournikova, Anna, 77, 80, 84, 133, 185n.9
Kozol, J., 171
Krone, Julie, 97
Kwan, Michelle, 133

Lafrance, Melisse R., 3, 180n.6
LaLanne, Jack, 152
Lane, Richard, 86
*Lara Croft: Tomb Raider* (movie), 124–27
*Late Show with David Letterman:* World Cup team on, ix
Lawler, Jennifer, 58, 59, 195n.29
Lee, Jeanette, 28, 39–40, 85, 86, 134, 135, 136, 146; students' attitudes toward image of, 19–20, 139–43, 151–53
Leibovitz, Annie, ix, 84
Lenskyj, Helen, 128
lesbian athletes, 186n.20; homophobia and, 122, 123, 187n.22; media treatment of, 178n.10
"lesbian baiting," 187n.22
Leslie, Lisa, 30, 133, 185n.9, 187n.22
Leto, Jared, 108
Letterman, David, ix

Lewis, Carl, 27, 80
liberal feminism, 7–8; activism around sport, 180n.9; American individualist ideals mixed with, 3, 179n.2; critiques of, 7–8; defined, 7
*Life* magazine: 1996 images of male and female athletes in, 27–28, 80
limitation: fight against traditional female role of, 119
linguistic conception of reality, 14
linguistic (textual) and empirical research: tensions between, 14–15
*Little Girls in Pretty Boxes* (Ryan), xxviii
Liu, Lucy, 134
Lobo, Rebecca, xxvii
Longman, Jere, 26, 28, 31, 64
Lopiano, Donna, 26, 31
Loren, Sophia, 152
Love, Courtney, 34
love of sport, 198n.23
Lowe, Maria, 201n.50

machine: disassociating from body and treating it as, 49, 50, 86–87, 122
machismo, 66–67. *See also* masculinity
Madonna (rock star), 61
male beauty culture, xxv
male body(ies): Adonis complex and, 103–4, 111–12; commodification of, xxii, xxiv, 39, 100–105; objectification of, 10, 82, 111–12
*Male Body: A New Look at Men in Public and Private, The* (Bordo), 100
Mark, Marky, 103
Markell, Robert, xxvi
market conditions, 11; economic basis of need for new interpretive paradigms and, 11–14
marketing of women's empowerment through sports, 3–4. *See also* corporations
Markula, P., 153
Marshall, P. David, 107
Martino, Angel, 77, 84
masculinity: arbitrary nature of, 146; defined, xxiv; women's role to critique, 115–16

masculinity, female athletes and, xxiv, 55–75; acceptance of female masculinity through female athletes, 74–75; defined as "being a tomboy" (achievement), 88; ectomorphic "Animal" version of, 68–75; in *Game Face* photos of, 97–98; hyper-masculine sports nexus, criticism of, 57, 59–60; idealization of masculine female athlete, 60–61, 82; masculinity as resource, 67; mesomorphic "Lester" version of, 55–68

"Masculinity Without Men" (Newitz, Cox, Sandell, and Johnson), 65–66

mass media: classification of track and field as "masculinizing" in 1940s, 187n.22; comparing coverage of men's vs. women's sports, 179n.3; coverage of Women's World Cup soccer match, 32–34; cycles of media attention, xxi; images of women in sports in, xxvi–xxix, 1–2, 179n.3 (*see also* babe factor in representation of women's sports); power to construct audience recognition of athletes, 133–34; preferred meanings of media images, 145, 146, 199n.33; representation of feminism in 1990s by, 51; sports portrayed as great equalizer by, 35–40. *See also specific magazines*

Matildas (Australian national women's soccer team), 96

Mauresemo, Amelie, 178n.10

*Maxim* magazine: retro poses of swimmers in, 95

Max Lean ad, 92

McDonald, Mary, 15

McKay, Jim, 6

McKray, Nikki, 30

McNally, Joe, 27

McPeak, Holly, 27, 80

media. *See* mass media

media studies, 183n.34

Meiyuan, Ding, 97

*Men Are from Mars, Women Are from Venus*, 62

Messner, Michael, 6, 78, 185n.1, 185n.9

middle-class white women: upward mobility of, 179n.2; women's consumer market and, xix, xxiv, 1–4, 29–35, 179n.2

Milbrett, Tiffeny, ix

Miller, Toby, 10, 11, 82, 86, 99, 103–4

mirror effect: power of, 121

Moceanu, Dominique, xxvii

money spent in schools on sport, 158, 202n.73

Monplaisir, Sharon, 27

Monroe, Marilyn, 152

moral judgments about Black America, 155

Morgan, Joan, 38, 41–43, 45

Moses, Ed, 97

Most, Glenn W., 95

Moya, Paula M.L., 14

muscle: equating muscularity with violence, 150; of female bodybuilder, student response to, 147–51; on fitness model, 151; as positive signifier of sports performance, 142; public acceptance of muscular ideal for women, xviii; role of muscularity in signaling/disrupting gender and sexuality, 149, 150–51; shifting glass ceiling on women's muscular strength, 201n.53

*Muscle and Fitness Hers*, 92

name recognition of male/female sports figures by youth, 132–35, 197n.7

National Girls and Women in Sports Day, xix

nature: women's role in changing men's, 115, 195n.22

Navratilova, Martina, xx, 81, 178n.10

Nelson, Cary, 13

Nelson, Mariah Burton, xxviii, 64

network affiliates: coverage of women's sport among, 185n.1

Newitz, Analee, 65–66

*Newsweek:* coverage of women Olympians, 27; cover featuring Chastain, 34

*New York Times Magazine*, xix–xx; coverage of women Olympians, 27

Nike ads, 1, 2–3, 44, 137, 179n.2; campaign about sports and body ideal (1999), 38–39; with Hamm and Jordan, 141; of hockey player, 143–47; ideal female image in, 160, 161; "if you let me play" campaign, 29–30; in *Jane* (2001), 78, 79; with Michael Johnson (1998), 80, 81; with Marion Jones, 20; masculine/feminine athlete for, 83; with Gabrielle Reece (1998), 80, 81; sports as great equalizer in, 35–36
"Nike feminism," 180n.6
Noble, Vanessa, 97
Norton, Edward, 105, 106, 108

objectification: economics of gender inequity in sport and, 95–99; immunity to sexual, sense of, 95; of male bodies, 10, 82, 111–12; post–Title IX empowerment narrative vs., 86–95; revision of, 86; of women's bodies, limitations of critique, 76, 77–85, 100. *See also* babe factor in representation of women's sports
occupatio, 105–9
Oglesby, Carol, 6, 26
Olivardia, Robert, 103, 109, 110–11
Olson, Heather, 95
Olympics: American women's performance in 1996, 29; "genderized" coverage of 1984 and 1988, 26; "Year of the Women" (1996) at, xxi, xxiv, 25–29
Orenstein, Peggy, 75, 195n.20
organized sports: increased women's participation in, xxi
*Outside* magazine, xv, xix
overtraining: dangers of, 47–48, 49

Paglia, Camille, 51
participant observation, 168
"participatory" model of sport, 8; elitist model vs., 58, 63
Partnership for Women's Health at Columbia University, 44
patriarchy: sexuality and, 188n.38

performativity: gender, 11, 84, 129; through sports, postmodern, 94
Phillips, Katherine A., 103, 109, 110–11
PHYS.com ad, xix, xxviii, 92, 93
"Physical Activity and Sport in the Life of Young Girls: Physical and Mental Health Dimensions from the Interdisciplinary Approach," 6, 18
Pierce, Mary, 78, 79
Pitt, Brad, 106, 107, 109
*Playboy*, 88; Gabrielle Reece layout (January 2001), 87–88
pluralistic methodology, 15
polarization between old school and new age feminists, 77–85
political activism: ads about working out as only form of activism needed, 36–39; athleticism as activist tool, 45; female athletes and mainstream argument for women's, 28
Polo Ralph Lauren: idealized femininity in ad for, 161
Pope, Harrison G., 103, 109, 110–11
"pornographic" images of female athletes. *See* babe factor in representation of women's sports
pornography: normalization of, 88
postfeminism, 182n.26. *See also* third wave feminism
postmodernism: female athletes' attitudes toward sexualized poses and, 89–95; self-conception in, 89–90, 98
poststructuralism, 14–24, 62; multitude of approaches to knowing and telling in, 16
power: consumption as, 146–47
Power Bar ad, 164
powerlifting, 56–57
preferred meanings in media texts, 145, 146, 199n.33
pregnancy: masculine identity and, 67–68
President's Council on Physical Fitness and Sports Report, 6, 18
*Pretty Good for a Girl: An Athlete's Story* (Heywood), 59, 183n.41
Procter and Gamble, 44
Promise Keepers, 164

protectionist discourse, 144–45
*Punch: Why Women Participate in Violent Sports* (Lawler), 58, 195n.29

qualitative interviewing, 168
quantitative methods, 14–15
queer theory, 65. *See also* third wave feminism
*Quiet Storm: A Celebration of Women in Sports, The* (Powe-Allred and Powe), xxviii
Quindlen, Anna, 51

race: focus group composition by, 171; intersection with class in American culture, 171–72; intersection with gender in American culture, 154–55; moral judgments about Black America, 155; sports played by students and, 132; stereotypes of, 162; student responses to Marion Jones image, 153–56
racialized code: intersection of emphasized femininity with, 139–43
radical feminism, 7, 8, 180n.9, 181n.13; contemporary concerns of, 181n.19; of 1960s, commonality between contemporary third wave feminism and, 9
Rail, Genevieve, 90–91
Ramazanoglu, Caroline, 7
rape, 181n.19, 181n.20. *See also* violence
reactionism: dealing with antifeminist, 43–45
"Reading Sport Critically" (Birrell and McDonald), 15
reality: linguistic conception of, 14
Reebok ad, xxvii, 1, 4; insert in February 1998 *Condé Nast Sports for Women*, 36–37
Reece, Gabrielle, xv, xvi, xxvii, 35, 39, 80, 81, 87
relational analyses, 16
resignification: male and female bodies in process of, 129
"Resolution" (Wong), 74–75
*Return to Modesty, A* (Shalit), 43–44
Reynolds, Bill, 128

Richardson, Laurel, 16, 183n.41
Rinehart, Robert, 18
*Rites of Men: Manhood, Politics, and the Culture of Sport, The* (Burstyn), 57–60
Roaring Twenties: flapper era of, xviii, xx
Rodriguez, Michelle, 118
Roiphe, Katie, 51
*Rolling Stone:* "Unbearable Bradness of Being" feature, 109
Roosevelt, Teddy, 192n.28, 193n.4
Rosie the Riveter, xviii
Rough Riders, 192n.28, 193n.4
Ryan, Joan, xxviii
Ryan, Kelly, 92

Sabo, Don, 6
Samuels, Ellen, xxix
Sandell, Jillian, 65–66
Sandoz, Joli, 99
*Savage Inequalities* (Kozol), 171
Schneyder, Nathalie, 27
Schwarzenegger, Arnold, 124
Scurry, Briana, 32
second wave feminism, 40–41, 42, 65; economic considerations in, 12; limitations of objectification critique of, 76, 77–85; primary difference between third wave and, 10–11
Seles, Monica, xxvii
self: humanist view of essential, 89–90; modern self-conception, sport to bolster, 90–95; postmodern self-conception, 89–90, 98
self-construction, idea of, 92–95; experience of, 94; female athletes' willingness to pose and, 94–95
self-depriving behaviors, 128
self-effacement: cheerleader model of, 64–65
self-esteem, 189n.45; coaches and, 47, 49; as public health issue, xix, xxi
self-image, xix
self-possession: sense of, 87, 95
self-promotion: female athletes' views about, 40. *See also* babe factor in representation of women's sports

self-sovereignty: American ideal of, sport and preservation of, 90–95; criticism of women's, 115–16; sense of "masculinity" defined as, 98

"separate but equal" model, 62–63

sex appeal based on strength, xx, 178n.9

sex, gender, and sexuality triad: assumptions of natural linkages among, 147, 149, 201n.49

sexism, 41

sex objects, 85; female action heroes and, 125. *See also* objectification

sexual difference: gender as, 61–64

sexuality: constructedness of, 149; excessive monitoring by coaches of, 48, 49; female bodybuilders and heterosexual order, 147–51; Lee's image and, 141, 142; patriarchy and, 188n.38; as social construct and cumulative public performance with fluidity, 199n.29

sexualization: of image, as both-genders proposition, 85; of women's sports, 39–40. *See also* babe factor in representation of women's sports

Shalit, Wendy, 43–44

Sheppard, Matthew, 164

"Shortchanging Girls, Shortchanging America" (1991 AAUW study), xix, xxi

Siegel, Carol, 164

*Silence of the Lambs, The* (film), 61

Silverman, Kaja, 66

Sissi (Brazil's center midfielder), 97

Slaney, Mary Decker, 29, 186n.12

Smith, Marcella, xxvi

social initiatives to value girls, xix–xx, 44

socialization, 178n.7

socioeconomic status: internalization of liberal principles and, 137; shared jubilation over Women's World Cup linked to shared, 187n.23. *See also* class

sociological narrative, 18

sociological perspective, 13

splintering of markets, 13

sport: benefits of, 5, 48; dangers of, 47–50; formation in reaction to feminization of male body, 192n.28; as institution, core assumptions of, 6–7

sporting infrastructure, forming strong, 158

"sport nexus": hypermasculinity of contemporary, 57, 59–60

sports career: transitioning to new occupation after, 188n.26

*Sports Illustrated,* 25, 80; covers featuring female athletes, 1–2; naked female athlete images in, 77; Jenny Thompson image in, 84

*Sports Illustrated for Women,* 89, 96; ad for Women's World Cup, 33; Chastain for Power Bar in, 164; *Game Face* ad in, 17; Marion Jones "Got Milk?" ad in, 21, 22; K-Swiss ad in, xxiii; Nike ad of hockey player, 143–47; WUSA soccer ad in, 23

sports participation: academic vs. mass-media advocacy of, 5–6; benefits of, 5, 6; images of female athletes and desire to do sport, 138, 142, 150–51, 153, 157–58; increase in women's, xxi; problems of, 5, 47–48, 49; types of sports, by age and gender, 131–32

star persona: criticism of female, 116; equality of valuation through, 116–17

stealth feminism, 29, 50–54

stereotypes: gender, xxv; racial, 162

stereotypic coverage: media sensitivity to, 26

steroid accusations, 186n.12

Street, Picabo, 36

strength: fight against devaluation of women linked to concept of, 116–17; *Girlfight* and new cultural celebration of strong women, 117–23; to reduce victimization, 178n.7; sex appeal based on, xx, 178n.9

*Stronger Women Get, the More Men Love Football, The* (Nelson), xxviii–xxix

Strug, Kerrie, xxiii, 27

students: attitudes about female athletes (*see* youth attitudes about female athletes); sports participation by, 131–32; sports played by, 132; understanding of consumer culture, 136
subject/object dichotomy in hyperreal: disappearance of, 85–86
*Survival of the Prettiest: The Science of Beauty* (Etcoff), 44–45
Swoopes, Sheryl, xxvii, 30

"Take a Girl to the Game" program, xix
"Take Your Daughter to Work Day," xix
*Teen People,* 51, 60, 61, 96, 97
testosterone: continuum of, 73
Theberge, Nancy, 6
*Thelma and Louise* (movie), 124
Theweleit, Klaus, 194n.8
Thien, Margo, 27
third wave feminism, 25–54, 65, 182n.21; contradictions for third wave feminists in sport, 46–50; defined, 10; historical influences on sport perspectives of, 8–11; multiple methodological strategies, 17–18; negotiating feminism in postfeminist context, 40–45; primary difference between second wave and, 10–11; sport as stealth feminism of, 29, 50–54; sport as ultimate equalizer, 35–40; women as consumer market and, 29–35
third world women: "Nike feminism" at expense of, 180n.6
Thompson, Jenny, 77, 84
Thorne, Barrie, 70
*Time* magazine: coverage of women Olympians, 27
Title IX of Education Act of 1972, xxi, xxii, 26, 158; compliance, current lack of, 38, 180n.10; current challenge to, 192n.17; feminism and passage of, 50; history of, 177n.3; passage of, xviii; reevaluation of, 177n.4
*To Die For* (movie), 124
*Tomb Raider* (movie), 124–27
Torrance, Gwen, 17, 27, 80
Torres, Dara, 77, 84, 95

*Tough Girls* (Inness), 126
trade press books: female athletes as subjects for, xxvi–xxix
training, athletic: benefits of, 127–28; compulsive, 128–29; dissociation or alienation of athlete from her body by, 49, 50, 86–87, 122; overtraining, 47–48, 49; pleasure from, 55–57
Treichler, Paula, 13
triangulating methods: benefits of, 170

USA Track and Field calendar, 96
U.S. Department of Education, 177n.4
U.S. Women's Soccer Team, ix, 64; Women's World Cup (1999) and, viii, ix–x, 32–34, 39, 134. *See also specific team members*
Universal Nutrition, 92
upward mobility of middle-class white women, 179n.2; women's consumer market and, xix, xxiv, 1–4, 29–35, 179n.2

Van Derveer, Tara, 25
Van Dyken, Amy, 25, 29, 77, 84
*Vanity Fair:* Avon ad in, xxv
Vannous, Lucky, 103
Vertinsky, Patricia, 6
victimization: fight against traditional female role of, 119
violence: abusive behavior, power of mirror effect to cure, 121; equating muscularity with, 150; rape, 181n.19, 181n.20; as reaction to emasculating consumer culture, 106–9; strength in women to reduce becoming victims of, 178n.7
*Vogue* magazine: boy-toy ads in, xxii; ideal images in (spring 2002), 160, 161; Marion Jones cover (January 2001), xv, xvii, 81; Nike ad (1992) in, 2–3
VW ad (2000), 101–2

Waggoner, Susan, xxvi
Walkowitz, Rebecca, 14
Wheaties boxes: women athletes on, 25, 34

*When the Chickenheads Come Home to Roost: My Life as a Hip-Hop Feminist* (Morgan), 38

*Whole Other Ball Game, A* (Sandoz), 99

Williams, Serena, 133, 156

Williams, Venus, xx, 116, 133, 156

Willis, Helen, xx

WNBA, 45, 88

Wolf, Naomi, 110

women's rights: athletic female participation in political discourse of, 36–39

*Women's Sports and Fitness,* 77, 84; Jockey ad in, 104; Nike ad in, xvi; Reebok ad in, xxvii, 4

*Women's Sports Encyclopedia, The* (Markell, Waggoner, and Smith), xxvi

Women's Sports Foundation, 5, 51, 177n.3, 190n.53; "Addressing the Needs of Female Professional and Amateur Athletes" (1999), 95–96; position on media representation of female athletes, 80; report card, 202n.73

women's teams: names of, 196n.2

Women's World Cup (1999): babe factor in, 39; as historic tournament, viii, ix–x; mass media coverage of, 32–34; sports-bra controversy at, x, 34, 103, 134; support for, 32–34

Wong, Nellie, 74–75

work and family, juggling, 195n.20

workforce: women in, 44, 189n.41, 193n.7

workplace: changing unstable status of men in, 110

World Wrestling Federation, 151

Wylie, Philip, 106

XFL, 194n.10

youth attitudes about female athletes, 131–59, 162; bodybuilders, 147–51; Chastain, 137–39, 162; female ice hockey players, 143–47; fitness models, 151–53; Marion Jones, 153–56, 162; Jeanette Lee, 139–43; name recognition of male/female sports figures, 132–35, 197n.7; range of views, 19–20; responses to images of female athletes, 136–56; as sports heroes to boys, 52